HENLEY REGATTA

'Ah! much loved banks, my infancy's delight'.

Signed S. GRANDISON, 1794.

from a pencilled verse, discovered when the old summer-house
at Phyllis Court was demolished in 1830.

HENLEY REGATTA

A HISTORY

BY

R. D. BURNELL

LONDON
OXFORD UNIVERSITY PRESS
NEW YORK   TORONTO
1957

Oxford University Press, Amen House, London, E.C.4

GLASGOW NEW YORK TORONTO MELBOURNE WELLINGTON
BOMBAY CALCUTTA MADRAS KARACHI
CAPE TOWN IBADAN NAIROBI ACCRA SINGAPORE

PRINTED IN GREAT BRITAIN

CONTENTS

One

HENLEY'S HISTORY

Two

HENLEY'S REGATTA

Three

HENLEY'S PROBLEMS

Four

RECORDS AND APPENDIXES

LIST OF ILLUSTRATIONS

INTRODUCTION

On a spring day in 1951 I was sitting behind Jim Rathschmidt, newly appointed head coach at Yale University, as we proceeded upstream, between the wooded banks of the Housatonic river, Derby, Connecticut. It was an interesting day, for it was my first experience of an American professional coach at work on his home waters. I was there to report the forthcoming race between Yale and Cambridge University, and was aboard the Yale launch to see the opposition, and the course.

As we proceeded upstream, a row of marker buoys was pointed out:

'That', said my guide, 'is the start of the Henley course.'

Here is food for thought. A Henley course on the Housatonic river; Henley on the Yarra; Henley on the Zambesi. Without doubt, too, there is a 'Henley course' in Moscow, and in Buenos Aires.

How has it happened that a regatta, which started as a local fête, in a small Thames-valley market town, has given its name, and the delightfully illogical length of its course—'about a mile and 550 yards'—to rowing courses all over the world?

To attempt a detailed analysis of how such a thing has come about would be to threaten the genius of the place. Henley is— just Henley. But perhaps some glimmerings of the secret may be revealed, as the story of the place, and of the Regatta, is unfolded.

This book tells something of the history of the surrounding countryside, and of the town in which the Regatta takes place, because a function such as this may become more interesting to people, and especially, perhaps, to people who come from far afield, if they know a little of the background which gave birth to the Regatta.

The records of Henley Royal Regatta have been published up to 1938, and in a few years another volume will bring this great work of reference up to date. In the various volumes of

Henley records can be found the official accounts of every race which has taken place. There must have been nearly 6,000 races over the Henley course. The next volume of official records will bring the tally of the Index of Oarsmen into the region of 20,000 names, and individually these men will have rowed some 30,000 races. Clearly it would be impossible to pack all this information, or even a précis thereof, between the covers of a single book, and no attempt is here made to do so.

But if we claim to cover even the highlights, the exciting and historic races, year by year, it is well to remember that Henley can never be reduced to mere statistics and lists of records. It is a vitally human and individual Regatta. History recalls the great races, and the famous oarsmen. But no race at Henley has ever been dull, or unimportant, to those taking part. Every year there is re-enacted the drama of human muscle and heart and skill, pitted against the like. Those whose relatively humble and un-skilled exploits have escaped the pages of Henley history have none the less played their part in making that history.

Sonning, Berks
1956   R. D. B.

ACKNOWLEDGEMENTS

I AM indebted to the authors of all the books mentioned in the Bibliography on pages 287–8. But something more than mere acknowledgement is due to Mr. H. T. Steward, Sir Theodore Cook, and Mr. C. T. Steward, who were the authors, respectively, of *Henley Royal Regatta*, *Henley Races*, and *Henley Records*. These three books constitute the official published records of the Regatta, from 1839 to 1938.

In addition, my thanks are due to the Hon. Sherman Stonor, Captain Eric Noble, Sir Felix Brunner, and Lady David for information concerning their past or present homes, which are among the great houses of the district. For more general information I am indebted to the Rev. George Palmer, Rector of Benson, and to Mr. G. H. J. Tomalin, for many years a trusted assistant in the Regatta office, who, besides imparting invaluable information on the history of the town, loaned to me the unpublished notes of the late Mr. John Cooper, who, for thirty-seven years, was Secretary of the Regatta.

Finally, my sincere thanks are due to the Stewards of Henley Royal Regatta, and especially to the Secretary, Mr. L. D. Williams, acting on their behalf, and to Mr. H. R. N. Rickett, Chairman of the Committee of Management. It is no exaggeration to say that this book could scarcely have been written without his help, and could certainly not have achieved any degree of accuracy which may now recommend it. For Mr. Rickett found time to check and correct all my manuscript from the confidential Regatta records, and to offer invaluable advice on all matters connected with the Regatta. Notwithstanding the fact that I owe many previously unpublished, and even unknown, episodes to Mr. Rickett's encyclopædic knowledge of Henley history, I should, in fairness to him, emphasize the fact that the interpretation, and the opinions expressed in these pages, are my own.

The extract printed on p. 200 is reproduced by kind permission of *The Times*.

The illustrations are reproduced by kind permission of the following, to whom, especially to Messrs. George Bushell & Sons, of Henley, the author expresses his thanks for their cooperation:

Plates I, IV (bottom), VI (bottom), VIII (bottom), IX, X, XI, XII, XIII, XIV, XV, XVI: Messrs. George Bushell & Sons.

Plates II and III (with key): Leander Club.
Plate IV (top): G. O. Nickalls, Esq.
Plate V: New College, Oxford.
Plate VI (top): Picture Post Library, London.
Plate VII (bottom): Kemsley Picture Service, London.
Plate VIII (top): F. A. H. Pitman, Esq.

One

HENLEY'S HISTORY

CHAPTER ONE

The Place and People

I T is a tradition that there is always someone to be seen resting his arms on the parapet of Henley bridge. Regretfully, as one born scarcely a mile away, I must deny the tradition. But those who know Henley only during the Regatta week might well believe it to be true. For it is a pleasant bridge on which to linger, and provides an admirable grandstand from which to watch the boats. For many years it was so used during the Regatta. Coaches and farm carts were drawn up, in two ranks, and packed with spectators. Traffic across the river was almost impossible.

Except for periods of disrepair, there has been a bridge to stand on at Henley for at least eight hundred years. Camden, the historian, would have us believe that it was there in Roman times. But Camden was sometimes too enthusiastic in his history. He it was, too, who enthused over the marriage of the rivers Thame and Isis, at Dorchester, blessing their union with the name 'Tam-isis'. But the river was always one, 'Tamesa' to the Romans, and 'Tamese' to the Saxons.

Not only the name of the Thames, but even its source has been disputed. Seven Springs, near Cheltenham, as the point farthest from the sea, has had its protagonists. But, in fact, Seven Springs is the source of the tributary Churn. The Thames itself rises at Thames Head, near Cirencester. It is not a spectacular birth, the spring being dry as often as not.

It is an interesting speculation that, but for an accident of geography, Henley might never have had her mile and a quarter of glorious river. No doubt some water would always have come this way, for the river Kennet, which rises on the Marlborough Downs, has always flowed eastward to the English Channel. But to the north of the Kennet, and indeed, right across England, from East Anglia to the Mendips and the West Country, there lies the barrier of the Chilterns and the Berkshire Downs. And the Thames, with all her main tributaries, other than Kennet, rises to the north of this barrier.

From Thames Head the Thames flows north-eastward, through the Vale of the White Horse, towards the Wash. Did the Thames waters, in the remote past, flow into the Wash? How easily they might have done so is shown by the example of the Ouse, which rises near Banbury, with some of its tributary sources so near to the river Cherwell, itself a tributary of the Thames, that in some places the difference between one side or the other of a field, or a road, may decide whether the water flows to the Wash, by way of the Ouse, or to the Thames Estuary, by way of the Cherwell and Isis.

It has been suggested that, at some remote time, there was a tilting of the land, or perhaps a silting up of the waterways, which brought the waters of the Thames back into the great cleft of the hills at Goring. If so, a large part of what is now the Upper Thames Valley, between the White Horse Vale and the Vale of Aylesbury, would then have been a swamp.

We can only speculate as to whether the Thames did, indeed, break through the chalk barrier in the Goring gap, to its present course. But there is at least some evidence to suggest a changing of the water-levels at Goring, at a relatively late date.

Lord Wyfold, in his book *The Upper Thames Valley*, points out that between Oxford and Goring, a distance of twenty-seven miles by river, there are no fewer than seven places with 'ford' endings—Oxford, Sandford, Appleford, Shillingford, Wallingford, Crayford, and Moulsford. Below Goring, in the eighty-five miles of river to the sea, there is only one other 'ford'. And that is at Harleyford, opposite Hurley. There is no evidence that there was ever a ford here, in the accepted sense, and both names suggest a derivation from the word 'harl' or 'haul'—the crossing, perhaps, where the ferry boat was 'hauled over' by rope.

Undoubtedly there were other places at which the Thames

could be, and was, forded, in Roman times and later. But this concentration of the 'ford' suffix, just above Goring, does suggest that here things were not as elsewhere, and that a number of new crossing-places came into use at roughly the same time.

Our ancestors lived on the high ground, rather than in the river valley. Their tools were inadequate for tilling the heavy soil, and the river bank was generally marshy, and liable to flood. Had the Upper Thames Valley been a vast area of swamp and lake, it would have been largely impenetrable, except perhaps in dry years, and one would expect to find the settlements of man on the high ground surrounding the valley. And that is exactly where they, together with their trackways, are found. Suppose, then, that the lake began to drain away. There would be left rapidly drying creeks, and rich alluvial soil, which, for a time at least, would require practically no cultivation at all, the nests and eggs of water-fowl—and new crossings of the river, offering short cuts between the settlements on the Chilterns and those on the Berkshire Downs. What more natural than that, in a short period of time, many new fords should be found and named?

So much, of course, is speculation. But it is no speculation that, from the earliest times, the Thames and Kennet provided a vital highway to the west. For until the advent of the metalled road, and the railway, in the nineteenth century, water provided the only practicable medium for the transport of heavy loads.

To this the Thames owed its early importance. Insignificant, perhaps, amongst the great rivers of the world, it was nevertheless the living artery between the heart of England and the sea. The ancient University of Oxford grew up on its banks, and a score of religious foundations, such as Godstow, Dorchester, Medmenham, and Bisham, together with Abingdon and Reading Abbeys—which once ranked with Glastonbury and St. Albans among the four great Abbeys of the south of England. At Windsor there was the royal castle, with the College of Eton across the river. Below Windsor the Thames flowed past Runny-mede, scene of the signing of Magna Charta, and on, past the great palace of Hampton Court, to Westminster, London, and the sea.

Henley stands as the upstream guardian of the first valley which must be negotiated on the way westward from the sea. It is also the pivotal point of the great S-bend, described by the river between Wallingford and Maidenhead, in its efforts to shake itself free of the chalk. As the crow flies—and it would fly very nearly over Henley—the distance from Wallingford bridge to Maidenhead bridge is about eighteen miles. By water the distance is almost exactly forty miles.

Though the river remained, so to speak, the 'Great West Road'[1] from Roman times until the nineteenth century, it was often convenient to cut off the corners. Two remarkable earthworks, one of which left the river bank almost opposite the finish of the modern Regatta course, bear witness to this fact. The one was Grim's Ditch, or Dyke, which runs eleven miles across the Chilterns, from Henley to Wallingford, cutting off a twenty-five-mile loop of the river. Nobody knows its purpose, or origin. Once, it seems, it marked the boundary between the kingdoms of Mercia and Wessex; Dr. Plot, in his *Natural History of Oxfordshire*, suggested that it was part of the Roman road from Gallena (Wallingford) to Pontes, which he equated with the modern Colnbrook. It is easily traced on the one-inch Ordnance Survey map, and in many places as easily found on the ground. Some few miles north of Grim's Ditch, the second, less-well-defined track, or earthwork, runs for nearly fifteen miles, from Medmenham to Benson, cutting off no less then thirty-two miles of the river. It is generally knows as the Medlers' Bank.[2]

Wharf Lane, near the finish of the Regatta course, bears witness to the days when Henley was an important centre of commerce on, and to and from, the river. There were wharves all

---

[1] Perhaps, even earlier, the 'Great West Road' was the Icknield Way, which, two thousand years before the Roman invasion, ran from the eastern counties to the heart of Wessex. This, too, passes close to Henley, following the escarpment of the Chiltern Hills and Berkshire Downs, and crossing the main Henley–Oxford road at Nettlebed. The Icknield Way crossed the Thames at Goring, and led on towards Stonehenge and Avebury, in Wiltshire.

[2] The name Medmenham probably derives from the town (Ham) of the 'middle men' (Medlers), i.e. those who dwelt between the two earthworks.

along the frontage on the town bank. And, long after the origins of Grim's Ditch had been forgotten, it was found more convenient to disembark merchandise at Henley, and forward it overland. Beyond the Town Hall, and branching off the road to Greys, can still be found Pack and Prime Lane, the name of which has intrigued many. In the sixteenth and seventeenth centuries a well-established trade route led thence, by way of Peppard, to Goring, where it rejoined the river, saving some ten miles in distance. Perhaps, as the party left the town, the cry rang out to 'Pack and prime'. Certainly it was a necessary precaution to prime the pistols, for the thickets and beech woods of the Chilterns were notorious for uncomfortable characters.[1]

It was to enforce some sort of law and order in these hills that the office of Steward of the Chiltern Hundreds was established, in 1750. The post still exists, as a sinecure, enjoying a salary of one pound a year. Under English Parliamentary Law a Member of Parliament cannot resign his seat, but neither can he hold 'an office of profit' under the Crown. To be granted the Chiltern Hundreds, therefore, automatically terminates membership of the House of Commons.

Today, when barge traffic on the upper reaches of the Thames has practically disappeared, it is hard to visualize the busy comings and goings on the river, which continued for more than a thousand years, until the era of the railways. The towing-path, along which coaches now bicycle, exhorting their crews, during Regatta week, once echoed to the hooves of horses, towing heavy strings of barges up the river. Even today, there is, technically, in most places, only a 'right of tow' on the bank. Nor has there ever been any obligation, either on the Conservators or on the riparian owners, to keep the banks and footpath under repair. But the owner must provide the statutory width of ground, on which the horses may pass without hindrance. If the bank is washed away,

---

[1] The Florentine, Brunetto Latini (died 1294), tutor to Dante, passed through Henley, en route from London to Oxford, and recorded that, in the Chiltern forest around Henley, were 'hills of hazardous ascent, bad roads, dense woods full of robbers, who for blackmail were connived at by the Barons'.

the 'right of tow' merely moves inland. Today, however, the right of tow is an empty one, for there remain few of the ferries which were maintained for transporting towing teams across the river, wherever the towing-path changes sides.

Towing was a chancy and laborious business, and Dr. Plot recorded, in 1673, that on the reaches near Shiplake, barges were wont to run aground on the shallows, where they might sometimes remain fast for several weeks.

Navigation was made possible by 'flash' locks. The old-style flash lock consisted of a barrage, made up of stakes and 'paddles', which were lowered into the water, against a sill, constructed on the bed of the river. When all the paddles were in position, the barrage was complete. To allow a boat to pass, a section of the paddles had to be removed. Proceeding downstream it was possible to shoot through a comparatively narrow gap, on the flush, or 'flash', of water. But to surmount the barrage against the stream required a much wider opening, and a long, hard haul. This resulted in a heavy loss of water.

Flash locks were built for a variety of purposes—to provide a head of water for a mill, to improve the local fishing, or to facilitate the passage of boats, by increasing the depth of water at shallow places. Often these interests clashed, and there were frequent quarrels over the loss of water occasioned by opening the barrage. Sometimes this was so severe that no further boats could pass for twenty-four hours.

A 'pound' lock is simply a basin in which water can be impounded, with a gate at each end for the passage of boats. Leonardo da Vinci invented the pound lock, about 1488, and the first pound locks in England were built on the Exeter canal, in 1563. They appeared on the Thames in the middle of the seventeenth century, and came into general use with the widespread building of canals in the eighteenth century.[1] However,

---

[1] Some of the first pound locks on the Thames were built by the Rev. Humphrey Gainsborough, brother of the famous artist, and a resident of Henley. A most gifted man in many directions, he built, from masonry from the ruined refectory of Reading Abbey, the Rugged Arch bridge, which oarsmen know from the river above Marsh lock, and visitors to Henley as a death-trap on the

the last flash lock on the Thames, at Eaton, below Lechlade, was still functioning just before the last war.

A hundred years ago most of the locks on the upper reaches of the river were still of the 'flash' variety. W. B. Woodgate, of whose exploits at Henley we shall hear much, recalled that in his schooldays at Radley a veritable fleet of barges used to come down river, carrying coal from Warwickshire to London. Twice a week there were 'flash days', as the barges passed down river. The effect was sometimes spectacular, for ahead of the flotilla there came a flood of high water, as the locks above were opened. The *non nantes*, at one moment splashing happily in shallow water, might find themselves, without warning, floundering in the turgid deep. Conversely, small boys sculling their boats in the shallower parts of the river would find themselves aground, or bumping along the bottom, as the barges passed through the lock below, carrying with them their head of water.

Like many innovations, the improvement of navigation by locks and weirs has not always met with universal approval. In 1715, when an Act of Parliament was passed providing for the improvement of the Kennet navigation between Reading and Newbury, the inhabitants of Reading believed that this would carry their rightful business to their rivals. In fact, of course, they benefited considerably from the general increase in traffic. And they benefited even more when the Kennet-Avon canal was built, making it possible for barge traffic to work right across England, from London to Bristol. But by 1725 they were still not

Wargrave road. It was he, too, who engineered the main London road, up White Hill from Henley bridge, to replace the old road, which can still be traced within the Park Place grounds, and which was so steep that trace-horses had to be constantly in attendance to help travellers. To make the embankment at the bottom of the hill, Gainsborough devised a two-way trolley system, the full trucks pulling up the empties. Gainsborough was also credited with ante-dating Watt as the inventor of the separate condensor for steam engines, a device which made it possible to conserve and re-use the water, and designed and built some fine clocks, including an ingenious affair in which the motive power was supplied by musket balls, descending from a tower in an ivory bucket. He planned to raise the musket balls by a wheel driven by a current of air, which would have made his clock self-winding. However, it seems that even in England he could not find a house in which the draught was sufficient for this purpose.

persuaded of their blessings, as the following letter shows. It was addressed to a bargemaster in Maidenhead.

Mr Darvall wee Bargemen of Redding thought to Acquaint you before 'tis too Late Dam you if y work a bote any more to Newbury wee will Kill you if ever you come any more this way wee was very near shooting you last time wee went with pistolls and was not too Minnets too Late, the first time your Boat lays at Redding Dam you wee will bore hols in her and sink her so Don't come to starve our Fammeleys and our Masters for Dam You if You do we will send you short home for you have no aceation to come to teak the bred out of Oure Childrens Mouths. . . .[1]

The poor bargees were always in trouble, Now, alas, they are a vanished race, and the river, and certainly river idiom, is the poorer for their going. No longer are they met with the taunt:

'Who ate puppy pie under Marlow bridge?'

That was an uncharitable story, which owed its popularity to the urchins who have always loved to hurl stones, and abuse, upon the heads of those who pass under the Thames bridges. Nevertheless, it was widely believed that the landlord of the inn at Medmenham, suspecting thieving hands in his larder, had put an unwanted litter of puppies to this somewhat macabre use.

Some may wonder how it is that the Thames at Henley has come to be the scene of the world's most famed regatta. We shall see later how the Regatta came to be founded; but there is no doubt that environment played an important part. The early development of the river as a highway of commerce, and the fact that it flows, neither so fast as to make rapids and shallows, nor so slowly as to favour the interminable meanderings of some other streams, makes it especially suitable for rowing. And at Henley there is the near-perfect course for racing, whilst the town itself is conveniently situated, between Oxford and London, and is easy of access from all quarters.

The origin of the name of Henley is obscure. It may have

---

[1] *A History of the Town of Reading*, by Michael Hinton (George G. Harrap & Co.).

derived from the British *hen* (old) and *ley* (place). But it has been variously recorded as Henlegh, Hauleganz, and Harneburgh with variations on the spelling of all these names. Above Henley to the west, where Rotherfield Court now stands, there was once a castle or camp. On some ancient maps the name Ancastle appeared in large letters, with Henley, below, in smaller letters. So the town may have grown up as a settlement below the walls of the castle. Again, the *ley* may have described the water meadows beside the river.

At the time of the Roman invasion of Britain, the country round Henley was occupied by the tribe of Dobuni. The Romans reached the district quite early, and it has been suggested that nearby Benson was the scene of the decisive battle between the Britons and the army of Aulus Plautius and Vespasian in A.D. 43.

During the lifetime of Christ, the loop of the Thames, with Henley in its centre, formed the south-western boundary of the kingdom of Cunobelinus.[1] His capital was at Verulamium,[2] and later at Colchester. Cunobelinus was king of the Catuvellauni. Later, his son, Caractacus, was defeated by Claudius, and there followed a period of Roman occupation. As evidence that the Romans settled in the Henley area, the sites of Roman villas have been found at Harpsden and Hambleden. The latter is considered to have been built about A.D. 50, and to have been occupied for some three hundred years.

Under the Romans the country prospered, and Christianity came to the Thames Valley. But the Roman tide ebbed, and the Britons, accustomed to rely on the protection of their conquerors, fell prey to fresh invaders.

In 571 the Saxon Cuthwolf, probably coming from the west, and crossing the river at Wallingford, captured the British fortress of Sinodun. This was on Sinodun Hill, otherwise known as Wittenham Clumps, which dominates the main road between Huntercombe and Oxford. Cuthwulf gave the whole of this area, from Dorchester to Henley, and from Medmenham to Monge-

---

[1] Shakespeare's King Cymbeline.　　　　[2] St. Albans.

well, to one of his followers, by the name of Bensa. Bensa made
his home here, and it was called Bensington.

The Saxons were pagan, and generally stamped out Christianity. But it survived where the Britons were left unsubdued.
And this loop of the Thames, enclosing an area of dense beech
woods and chalk hills, was a natural stronghold for the Christian
Celts.

In 635 St. Birinus came from Lombardy, as a missionary to the
West Saxons. He converted and baptized their king, Cynegils, and
by him was given Dorchester, as the see for the first Saxon
Bishopric. It stretched from the Humber to the Thames. The
see was transferred to Lincoln in 1078. It would indeed be
interesting to know whether Birinus, when he reached the district,
found Christianity surviving from the Roman era.

Although Christianity had returned, Henley remained a
frontier town, at the base of a Wessex 'salient', north of the
Thames. Some believe that Grim's Ditch was then the boundary
between Wessex and Mercia. However that may be, Benson was
soon to be the site of another battle, when Offa, king of Mercia,
defeated Cunewulf, king of the West Saxons, in A.D. 777. Once
again Henley changed hands.

Nearly a hundred years later, in 871, the Danes pushed up the
river as far as Reading, which became their headquarters until they
were defeated by Ethelred and Alfred. Certainly Henley must
have felt their heavy hand, but no doubt the beech thickets hid
many of the refugees. The Danes returned in 1006, once again
pillaging and burning, all along the river. At Medmenham, Danesfield Camp bears witness to their occupation. The great ditch,
with which they surrounded the promontory of chalk, is still
easily traced.

After this invasion, the Saxons turned and massacred the
Danish settlers. Retribution was swift, for in 1013 King Sweyn
came to wreak vengeance. This time, however, he was repulsed,
near London, by Ethelred. Sweyn retreated to Wallingford, passing through Henley, no doubt along the line of Grim's Ditch.
Eventually some sort of peace came, and the Danish Canute

became king of Mercia, marrying Ethelred's widow, Queen Emma of Normandy. Emma, as part of her dower, had a residence at Wargrave.

The Normans were as quick as their predecessors to penetrate to the heart of the Chiltern country. Naturally they were so, for he who held the ridge of the Chilterns and Berkshire Downs held the key both to the West and to the Midlands.

Shortly after the Conquest, William reached Wallingford and seized all the lands which had belonged to Bensa, the Saxon. He gave fifteen hides to Walter Giffard, later Earl of Buckingham; hence we have Crowmarsh Giffard, just across the river from Wallingford. Another five hides he gave as endowment to the great Abbey he was building, at Battle, to commemorate his victory over Harold's Saxons at Hastings. This land became Crowmarsh Battle, and Preston (Priests' town) Crowmarsh. Note how the suffix 'marsh' crops up, and remember the many 'fords' hereabouts. Thus is English history engraved on the map, and in the countryside.

The rest of Bensa's lands became the Royal Manor of Bensington, for it was the era when all land belonged to the king, unless specifically granted to somebody else. Henley was then on the extreme outskirts of the Manor of Bensington.

In 1243 Henry III gave Bensington to his brother Richard, Earl of Cornwall. The Countess of Cornwall held the manor house at Henley in 1301, and its site is marked today by Countess Gardens.

Henley is lacking in mediæval history, a fact for which the townsfolk were no doubt grateful at the time. Even the date of the building of the church is uncertain. The earliest mention of the church is from 1204, and there were restorations in 1272, 1398, and 1420. The last was probably so extensive as to amount to a rebuilding, and 1400 is generally given as the approximate date of the present church.

The tower, which has recently been under repair, has been ascribed to Cardinal Wolsey. But almost certainly it was, in fact, built by Bishop Longland. Longland was Confessor to Henry

VIII, and Bishop of Lincoln from 1521 to 1547, and he and his family lived in Henley. By a stroke of genius he placed his tower at the intersection of all the main approaches to the town. Whether one enters Henley by river, up or down stream, or by road from Oxford, London, or Wargrave, the magnificent Perpendicular tower serves as a guiding and welcoming landmark.

In the Civil War Henley was unhappily placed, being once again, so to speak, on the frontier. For the King held Oxford, and Parliament held London. And although there were no pitched battles in this area, the opposing forces were for ever harassing each other along the river. All too often the townsfolk of Henley were expected to billet the soldiers of both factions, and to pay for the privilege.

In 1602 the old manor house of Fawley, dating at least from the fourteenth century, which stood on much the same site as the present house, was rendered virtually uninhabitable by Royalist troops billeted therein. The offenders were Sir John Byron's troop of Prince Rupert's cavalry. Sir Bulstrode Whitelock, the owner of Fawley, wrote:

> there being about a thousand of the king's horse quartered in and about the house . . . there was no insolence and outrage usually committed by common soldiers on a reputed enemy which was omitted by these brutish fellows at my house. They had their women with them, they littered their horses with sheaves of good wheat. Divers writings and books . . . they burnt to light their tobacco. . . . They broke down my park pales, killed most of my deer . . . and let out all the rest. . . . They ate and drank all that the house could afford, and broke up all trunks, and where they found linen or any household stuff they took it away with them, and cutting the beds let out all the feathers, and took away the ticks. . . .

It is hardly surprising that the house was never fit for habitation again. At the Restoration, Sir Bulstrode Whitelock was forced to sell the property, to pay the fines imposed upon him. The present house, designed by Sir Christopher Wren, was completed in 1684.

Sir Bulstrode Whitelock also owned Phyllis Court. This was a very old house, outside the town boundaries, and a manor in its own rights, though at various times linked by ownership with the manor of Henley. Situate in the Honour of Wallingford, it used to be held of the King, by tenure of a red rose, presented at the feast of Pentecost. In 1347, as the Manor of Fillets, it was granted by Edward III to John de Molyns. In 1385 it belonged to Johanna, Princess of Wales, the mother of Richard III. Sir Bulstrode Whitelock wrote again in his *Memorials*, that:

> In 1643 the 4th of March, by the direction of Major General Skippon [Skipton, one of Cromwell's generals], Phyllis Court house was made a strong and regular fort, and the Thames brought into the grafts [diggings] round about it. Cannon, and a considerable garrison of about three hundred foot and a troop of horse in it; and this was rather done to watch the garrison of Greenlands, which for a little fort was made very strong for the king, and between the garrisons stood Fawley Court, miserably torn and plundered by each of them.

Greenlands then stood rather nearer to Hambleden lock than the present Italian-styled house, which was built by the late W. H. Smith and is now so familiar a landmark to Henley oarsmen. In the King's name, Sir John D'Oyley, who owned Greenlands, and Colonel Hawkins, the governor, held the house during a six months' siege by the Parliamentary troops. When they finally surrendered it was on honourable terms, with a safe passage for the garrison as far as Nettlebed.

I recall being told, as a child, that there was a battle at Aston, below Hambleden, on the Berkshire bank of the river. It is mentioned in no history book. But this much is certainly true. In a corner of a wood, near Culham Court, and just below the crest of the hill which overlooks Aston, there were, and indeed still are, two old iron cannons. Thirty years ago the oak carriage of one of the guns was still largely intact. Today there is not much left of the carriages, apart from a few mouldering baulks of timber. But the two cannons still lie in the grass, virtually indestructible. Both were long ago spiked in their touch-holes.

Until I am proved wrong I shall continue to believe the cannons to be relics of the Civil War, and perhaps of the siege of

Greenlands. With Greenlands 'very strong for the king', it would have been only prudent for Cromwell's troops to have covered the lane which runs up from Aston to the main London road.

During 1642 the old wooden bridge at Henley was breached, and in the following year the Earl of Essex marched from Windsor, with a strong force, to seize Henley, which at that time had no garrison. The bulk of the force was billeted at Phyllis Court and elsewhere, whilst four companies of foot, under a Captain Turner, were detailed to guard the town. Captain Turner placed one company about the bridge, one on the Reading road, one above the town on West Hill, and one on the Oxford road. Each company, except for that on the bridge, had one cannon.

In the meantime Sir Arthur Aston, commanding the King's troops at Reading, received word that Henley had been lost without a blow. Determined on a quick counter-attack, and hoping to take Essex's men by surprise in the darkness, he despatched a troop of horse, with two men to each horse. In the small hours of the morning they charged up the Reading road, driving the Parliamentary infantry before them, and shouting, 'The town is ours!'

For a few minutes confusion in Duke Street made it impossible for the cannon to fire, for fear of killing the defenders. But as they extricated themselves from among the horsemen, the cannon poured its charge of grapeshot down the narrow street. As a matter of fact not many of the King's men were killed in the 'battle of Henley', four cavalrymen, and four horses, and six more Royalist troopers, found later, in a wood outside the town, being the total of their casualties. But the moral effect of the cannon firing between the houses was enough to put Aston's horse to flight. The skirmish was all over in fifteen minutes, and Henley was saved for Parliament, at the cost of three Parliamentary soldiers, and one, Thomas Hyatt, a local fishmonger's man, who was accidentally wounded.

On the following day Essex marched on Caversham, and, after a fierce encounter, King Charles and Prince Rupert withdrew to Nettlebed, and later to Wallingford.

Throughout the winter of 1643, Henley and the surrounding countryside were plundered and despoiled by both factions. An unfortunate Henley woman, for complaining of the taxes levied, was nailed by her tongue to a post in Henley. Another, an aged widow named Elizabeth Cary, was condemned to the gallows. But these excesses resulted in both Henley and Reading being placed under martial law. Elizabeth Cary was reprieved and imprisoned, and survived to see the Restoration and to receive a pension of forty pounds from the Crown.

Once again, at least, Henley was to be the scene of great events. For in 1688, when William of Orange displaced James II in the 'Bloodless Revolution', William came to Henley, after relieving Reading. He lodged at Phyllis Court, and there received a deputation from the House of Lords, and from the City of London, issuing his first orders 'From my court at Henley'.

No account of Henley would be complete without some mention of the great houses of the neighbourhood, for great houses are part of the heritage of England. On them we have lavished the same loving care which our Gallic neighbours have devoted to their cuisine. Both, perhaps, are expressions of national character.

In the neighbourhood of Henley, none can deny pride of place to Stonor Park.

The roots of Stonor are lost, almost in prehistory. The name probably derives from the 'hill of stones', or from the stone circle, a place of pagan worship, part of which can still be traced near the Chapel. Indeed, one of these stones was incorporated as a corner-stone when the Chapel was built, probably in the early seventh century. It was then a common practice to establish the new faith on the old pagan sites. Where we find family names, originating thus in descriptive place-names, it is a sure sign of antiquity.

Stonor lies in that semicircle of the Chilterns, which has the river for its circumference and the Medlers' Bank for its base. Certainly it was a Celtic stronghold, and it is claimed that Christianity reached the valley in Roman times, and survived there throughout the Dark Ages. If this is so, then Stonor can claim an unbroken record of Christianity for nearly two thousand years. Throughout the persecutions and proscriptions of Tudor times, Stonor was a militant stronghold of Roman Catholicism, and it was here, perhaps hidden in the roof, that Father Campion printed and published the *Decem Rationes*, which caused such consternation when distributed in the University of Oxford. Campion paid the price of his faith at Tyburn, and the fortunes of the Stonor family were later crippled by the fines imposed upon them as proscribed Catholics. But, if one takes the long view, one might say that once again the wilds of the Chilterns had proved a sure defence.

The house at Stonor dates from about 1270. In 1416, Thomas Stonor bought 'bryks' from the community of Flemish brick-workers at Crocker End, near Nettlebed, for extensions at Stonor, and notably for building the clock tower. The tower still stands, with its original clock. It is said that these bricks were the first baked south of the Humber since Roman times.

Stonor has a strong tie with Henley Regatta, although it has produced no rowing men. Thomas Stonor, born in 1797, became one of the founder Stewards of the Regatta, and later its first President. In the year of the first Regatta he was created Baron of the newly revived Barony of Camoys, although, of course, there was no connection between the two events, that being before the days of honours for sportsmen. The Barony of Camoys had been in abeyance for four hundred years, having been first granted to Sir John de Camoys, who commanded the left wing of the English army at Agincourt.

At Stonor there rises the Assenden Water, which flows only at intervals of several years, an event which is said to presage war. Below the Assenden Valley the bed of the stream is the ditch which skirts the south side of the Fair Mile. Dr. Burn, the historian of Henley, wrote in 1861 that the Assenden Water had then not flowed since 1853. He also recorded that in 1674 'several mills might have been driven with the current', and that a child, who fell in at Northfield End, was carried underground, beneath New Street, to the river. Fortunately a man saw the accident, and rescued the child unharmed from the Thames. The Assenden Water is still active. The spring was full in 1955, but there was not sufficient force of water to carry the stream down to the Fair Mile.

The original avenue of elms on the Fair Mile was planted in 1752 by Sir Thomas Stapleton, of Grey's Court, who, at that time, was Lord of the Manor of Bensington. In Burn's day the trees were in their prime, and he described the Fair Mile as '... not perhaps, surpassed by any public road in the Kingdom'. He also wrote that 'The trees ... cannot, in the course of nature, last many years longer'. In fact they were destined to last another ninety years, though by the time the last of them was felled, almost exactly two hundred years after their planting, there were many gaps. In 1953 the whole avenue was replanted, with two hundred Turkey oaks, in commemoration of the Coronation of Her Majesty Queen Elizabeth II. The first tree was ceremonially planted by H.R.H. Princess Margaret.

It is possible that Grey's Court may surpass even Stonor in antiquity. For Grim's Ditch passes through the park, and there are signs of earthworks which may mark the site of a prehistoric camp. A feudal castle stood there in the thirteenth century, probably built by Walter de Grey, who was Archbishop of York from 1191 to 1216, for his nephew John de Grey. In 1347 Lord Grey, who fought at Crecy and was one of the original Knights of the Garter, obtained a licence from Edward III to 'fortify' his castle. The ruins of his work are still to be seen today, though apparently the castle fell into disrepair fairly quickly. For Leland, who died in 1552, speaks, in his *Itinerary*, of 'three or four very olde towers of stone, a manifest to men it was some tyme a castle'.

Grey's Court was built in the quadrangle of the old castle, close under the walls of the keep. Probably it was demolished in Elizabethan times, when the present house was built, a little farther to the west. There is still intact an interesting well, more than two hundred feet deep. Above it there is a building known as the Donkey House, which contains a wooden wheel, twenty-five feet in diameter, in which a donkey used to walk, tread-mill fashion, to raise water.

Another rival in antiquity is Harpsden Court, which was built on the site of a Roman camp or villa. Harpsden, as Harpendene, was mentioned in the Domesday Book, 1086. The present house was built in early Tudor times, and was once much larger than it is today. In pulling down three sides of one of the courts, early in the last century, no fewer than thirty-four rooms were destroyed.

Badgemore, too, is of interest, chiefly by virtue of its builder. The farm of Badgemore was purchased in 1710, by Richard Jennings, who was a master carpenter of St. Paul's Cathedral. He enlarged the farm to make the present house; and he did the work with bricks which had been used temporarily in the building of the Cathedral. The municipal records show payments by Jennings for the use of the town wharves, where the bricks were unloaded after the long barge haul from London.

Of Culham Court, which lies below Hambleden lock, but only a short distance overland from Remenham, I know no history—save that of the cannons, already mentioned—but one amusing anecdote. The Hon. R. West there entertained George III to breakfast, and fed him on hot rolls, brought direct by relays of horsemen from Gunters, in London, and wrapped in flannel to keep them warm. Apparently the monarch saw nothing unusual in this solicitude for his taste, for he simply remarked, 'Ah, Gunter, Gunter; I am glad you deal with Gunter, West! Nobody like Gunter'.

Finally, there are two other houses at Henley, both, as they stand, quite modern, yet none the less remarkable in a special way. To describe such houses and, more especially, the embellishment of their gardens, Englishmen have evolved a special usage of the word 'folly'. It implies a mild surprise, bordering on admiration, rather than censure, that large sums of money should be thus spent, with apparently frivolous ingenuity. Facing each other, across the roofs of Henley, and each abounding in 'follies' of different kinds, stand Park Place and Friar Park.

Park Place was built by Lord Archibald Hamilton, son of the third Duke of Hamilton, early in the eighteenth century. It became a royal residence in 1738, when it was purchased by H.R.H. Frederick, Prince of Wales. In 1752 it passed to General, later Field-Marshal, Conway, and it was he who transformed the estate into one of the most remarkable, and in many ways beautiful, in the country. Conway commissioned the Rugged Arch bridge, already mentioned, and also constructed the Dark Arches, which can be seen from the bridge, at the top of the Happy Valley. Faced by a ruined Greek amphitheatre, which, of course, is not Greek, and was ruined from its building, the Dark Arches are massive caves, hollowed out of the chalk rock. The work here was ordered by General Conway to provide employment after the Peninsular War, so it was not without some useful purpose.[1]

The most remarkable of General Conway's acquisitions was the Druids' Temple. Discovered on the Mont de la Ville, at St. Helier, in Jersey, during the levelling of a new parade ground, it was presented to General Conway by the people of Jersey, when he relinquished the Governorship of the island. It must be questionable whether it was ever connected with the Druids, but it may have been a Celtic burial place, and was certainly a genuine antiquity, for a Roman coin of Claudius' reign was discovered in the earth above it. At Park Place, Horace Walpole affectionately christened it 'little Master Stonehenge'. It stands on the hill, not far from the Rugged Arch bridge, beside Temple Combe house.

General Conway's activities did not cease with the importation of a prehistoric temple, and the despoliation of the—let it be admitted—already despoiled Abbey at Reading. At Park Place

---

[1] General Conway's daughter, Mrs. Damer, designed and executed the keystones of the centre arch of Henley bridge. They depict *Father Thames* and *Isis*, thus recording Camden's pleasant conceit (see p. 1). The bridge was completed in 1786, at a cost of £10,000, replacing the old wooden bridge, which was washed away by a flood in the year 1774, 'occasioned by the incessant rain and snow which fell from the evening of the 12th [March] to the 16th'.

he planted the first Lombardy poplar to reach England. It was brought from Paris by Lord Rochford, in his carriage. And he also started a lavender plantation, on the slopes of the hill above the Wargrave road. He built coke ovens and stills, for the distillation of scent, and also, more sensibly some oarsmen may think, 'to draw an ardent spirit from potatoes'. Woodlands House, which stands at the foot of White Hill, was built for the 'chemical professor' in charge of the plant. The ovens and still were dismantled by Lord Malmesbury.

The original house at Park Place, a brick building of late Queen Anne style, was considerably enlarged by General Conway, and again by the Earl of Malmesbury, who bought and extended the estate after Conway's death. After Lord Malmesbury's death the estate was split up, and the house was bought by Mr. Henry Piper Spurling, who later exchanged it, with Mr. William Fuller-Maitland, for Norbury Park, in Surrey. Fuller-Maitland was a founder Steward of Henley Regatta.

In 1837, to commemorate the accession of Queen Victoria, Fuller-Maitland erected, on the highest point of the estate, the top section of the spire of St. Bride's Church, Fleet Street. The original spire, built by Christopher Wren, had been struck by lightning in 1769, and subsequently lowered by eighty-five feet.

Fuller-Maitland was a Roman Catholic, and in 1840 he built the boathouse, at the foot of the Happy Valley, as a chapel. It used to contain some fine Flemish sculpture, and an old seat which was reputed to be the original woolsack from the House of Lords. This boathouse is today the house named Conways, which thus commemorates the builder of the Rugged Arch bridge, below which it stands. Fuller-Maitland had two eccentricities. He collected carriages—it was said that he tried to buy one in every town he visited—and he expressed the ambition to own land in every county in England. He died in 1858, and the house was occupied by his widow until her death in 1865.

By then great changes were impending. The house remained empty for a time, and Queen Victoria inspected it as a possible home for the Prince of Wales, later King Edward VII. But in

1867 it was bought, for £71,400, by a Mr. Charles Easton, who planned to build several houses on the estate, and actually built the one at Temple Combe. Then—fortunately, those who know the Temple Combe architecture may think—the whole estate was bought by Mr. John Noble.

Shortly after his arrival fire damaged the interior of the house, and John Noble virtually rebuilt the house on the same site, though retaining the interior much as before. His turreted mansion, in the Franco-Italian style, was not perhaps an improvement from the aesthetic point of view. But he planted thousands of specimen trees, and developed the gardens as never before. Park Place remained in the possession of the Noble family until after the Second World War, when the estate was once again, and this time perhaps finally, dismembered.

Friar Park, which faces Park Place across the valley, has no such history. One can only say that, to be believed, it needed to be seen as 'a going concern' twenty years ago.

It was built about 1880 by Mr. Frank Crisp, who perhaps had a yearning for the Middle Ages. Even the door knobs were fashioned as friars' heads, and the electric-light switches were friars' noses. Everywhere, inside and out, were friars and texts.

It must not be supposed that the texts were religious, though the carvings and scrolls were often monastic in form. 'Gob(b)-lin(g) Friar', read one, on the east front of the house, outside the dining-room (it had to be outside the dining-room, because nothing at Friar Park was without its laboriously devised *double entendre*), 'with open mouth devouring two boys (Eton boys, a Harrowing sight)'.

The gardens at Friar Park were at first conceived as a serious study of mediaeval gardening. But somehow they ran riot. They strayed into Japanese Gardens, and Alpine Gardens, and Sundial Gardens—which, at Friar Park, did not imply a garden centred on a sundial, but a garden containing a collection of every known variety of sundial. Finally, they strayed right up the Matterhorn. A scale model of the mountain was constructed at one end of the garden, and several men were employed, travelling to and from Switzerland, to ensure that the details were correct. From a telescope on the terrace, outside the house, one could see the model chamois disporting themselves amongst the rocks. There was some doubt as to whether the chamois were actually on the rocks, or inside the telescope. For the construction of the Alpine Garden, at the foot of the Matterhorn, seven thousand tons of Millstone Grit rock were brought from Yorkshire. Henley oarsmen may have noticed, just above Phyllis Court, a boathouse, facing which there is a brick wall which appears to be sprouting rocks for no apparent reason. It seems that seven thousand tons was an over-estimate for the requirements of the Alpine Garden. For this, of course, is the Friar Park boathouse.

Henley is rich in interesting inns, as well as in great houses, but it is scarcely possible to do them justice here. Two of the oldest are the Bull and the Bear, in Bell Street. The Catherine Wheel, in Hart Street, existed as a building, if not as a hostelry, in the sixteenth century, when one John Gough, in his will of 12 May 1541, referred to his 'tenement in Hart Street, called the Catherine Wheel'.

The White Hart, between the Catherine Wheel and the church, is even older, and is mentioned in 1419. From the gallery in the yard, now enclosed, but still recognizable, the guests used to watch bull baiting and cock fighting in the courtyard. In all probability the White Hart gave its name to Hart Street, which used to be divided up the centre by a row of houses, as is its continuation up West Hill to this day. The King's Head is another fourteenth-century inn.

But, so far as history is concerned, pride of place must go to the Red Lion Hotel, by the bridge. For many years it was virtually the headquarters of the Regatta. The date of the Red Lion's building is unknown, but Charles I enjoyed its hospitality in 1632. And the Duke of Marlborough retained and furnished a room of his own, in which he used to sleep, when on his way from London to Blenheim Palace.

William Shenstone, the poet (1714–63), is said to have written, on a pane of glass in the Red Lion, his verses, concluding:

> Who 'er has travelled life's dull round;
> Where'er his stages may have been;
> May sigh to think he still has found
> His warmest welcome at an Inn.

The story that he scratched his poem on a window pane may be apocryphal, for Boswell, in his *Life of Dr. Johnson*, records only that they 'happened to lie this night at the Inn at Henley where Shenstone wrote these lines'. Since there were five verses to the poem, it may be thought that this was rather beyond the capacity of a window pane. But, facing across the river towards Leander Club, the Red Lion turns one blind eye, painted so well to resemble the other windows that few ever notice it. Sometimes I wonder if Shenstone spread his verses over a whole window, and afterwards removed it to his library!

Two

HENLEY'S REGATTA

CHAPTER TWO

The Organization

PERHAPS the most remarkable aspect of Henley Royal Regatta is the way in which it succeeds in mingling the friendly atmosphere of a family reunion with the efficiency of an impersonal business organization.

The story of the development of this remarkable organization is wrapped up in the history of the Regatta. But the racing is more easily understood against the background of the organization, and it is therefore worth trying to disentangle what might be described as the administrative background from the operational history.

On 26 March 1839 a public meeting took place at the Town Hall in Henley. How that meeting came to promote a new regatta is the opening chapter of Henley history. Among the resolutions passed, two set in motion the organizational train, which has not ceased to grow from that day to this.

. . . proposed by W. Brakspear Esq., seconded by Mr. E. Johnson, 'That Thomas Stonor Esq., Wm. P. Williams-Freeman Esq., Wm. Fuller-Maitland Esq., Charles Lane Esq., Edmund Gardiner Esq., and the Mayor of Henley-on-Thames for the time being, three of whom shall be a quorum, be appointed perpetual Stewards for the regulation and management of the Regatta and all affairs connected therewith, with power to add to their numbers as they from time to time shall think fit.'

Proposed by E. Gardiner Esq, seconded by Mr. Grayson, 'That a committee of fourteen persons (five of whom to be a quorum) be appointed to assist the Stewards in preparing rules, receiving subscriptions, and in conducting the general business of the Regatta.'

The first joint Secretaries of the Regatta were Messrs. C.

Towsey and J. Nash, to whom, more than to any other man, Henley owed its inception. The first Treasurer was Mr. P. B. Cooper.

The early Minute Books, if there ever were any, have been lost. It is known that the Committee used sometimes to meet alone, but only for discussion, or for the purpose of making recommendations for consideration in session with the Stewards. In fact, the distinction between the Stewards and the Committee was social rather than functional. The Stewards represented the landed gentry of the district. No doubt some of them showed an active interest in the Regatta; but their role was to lend to it an air of respectability. The Committee represented the townspeople, who had a stake in the Regatta's success.

The only interest which was not represented at all was that of the rowing men. The fact is that Henley Regatta was started as a local fête—today we might call it an 'attraction'. The boat racing was the bait to bring visitors to the town. Mr. J. D. Bishop, of Leander Club, was invited to act as Umpire, and he, no doubt, advised on such purely rowing matters as might arise.

It is not recorded that there was any regular chairman, either of the Stewards or of the Committee. The Earl of Macclesfield was appointed Patron of the Regatta in 1839, and probably so remained until 1843. In that year Thomas Stonor, who had just become Lord Camoys, is described as 'the acting Steward of the Regatta', and in 1844 he became Patron. In 1851, when Prince Albert became Patron, Lord Camoys was described as Vice-Patron. Prince Albert died in 1861, and there was then no Patron of the Regatta until 1912, when H.M. King George V graciously accepted the office. At some date in the 'sixties, Lord Camoys was elected the first President of the Regatta. When he died, in 1881, he was succeeded as President by his grandson, the fourth Baron. He, it seems, did not give universal satisfaction, for *The Field*, in 1889, recorded that:

... They were exceedingly wroth at the arrogant and unruly behaviour of the very young Lord Camoys, who seemed to think that the popularity of his esteemed grandfather, the old Lord, exempted him, the new Lord, from obeying the regulations, and justified his steaming up the course between races until stopped half-way by Lieut. Bell, a check which he met with the remark that 'if its president could not do as he liked it was time the regatta ceased to exist'—a speech worthy of being recorded.

Nevertheless, this Lord Camoys remained President until his death, during the Regatta of 1897. There was then a move to persuade the Prince of Wales, or the Duke of York, to accept the position, which having failed, it was decided to dispense with the office of President altogether. The title was revived in 1951, in favour of Sir Harcourt Gold, who in that year retired from the chairmanship of the Committee of Management. Since the title was intended to be honorary and without duties, the Constitution was not altered.

Henley Regatta continued to be run by the town, and without reference to rowing interests, except in so far as they were represented by the Umpire, until 1868. In that year the Stewards wished to institute a new eight-oared race (The Thames Cup), and they invited H. H. Playford to give his views on a suitable qualification. In December, he and Dr. Warre were elected Stewards, the first oarsmen to be admitted.

From the town's point of view this proved to be the thin end of a very forceful wedge. For with the rapid development of the Regatta, in the 'sixties and 'seventies, they were faced with a flood of more or less technical problems, to cope with which they had to elect more rowing Stewards. Finally, in 1880, a Sub-Committee was set up to report on the organization and finances of the Regatta as a whole.

This Sub-Committee consisted of five rowing Stewards, E. Warre, R. W. Risley, H. T. Steward, J. G. Chambers, and F. Fenner—and one local Steward, W. D. Mackenzie, as owner of most of the land on which the Regatta operated. It reported, *inter alia*, that:

... the managing body of Henley consists of:—
A President
The Mayor of Henley

Twenty-four Stewards
Twelve Committee
thirty-eight members in all, having equal votes. . . .

All these are invited to attend ... but only a small proportion attends regularly. Two consecutive meetings often consist of different persons.

It is evident that, while the whole body is too large for working purposes, it would not be advisable under the circumstances to contract the circle of influence, local or otherwise, which a large body of Stewards ensures.

On the other hand, it is equally evident that, for the conduct of business, and for efficient management, it would be advantageous to have a smaller body, of which all the members would feel the obligation to attend all the meetings, and would be responsible to the larger body for the management of the affairs of our Regatta.

We therefore recommend:—

(i) That a standing Sub-Committee, or Committee of Management, be elected by the Stewards and Committee, the members not to exceed twelve, with a quorum of five.

(ii) That a General Meeting of the Stewards and Committee be held once a year, at which the Committee of Management should present their report and Statement of Accounts for the year.

In the following year, acting on this advice, a 'standing Sub-Committee' was appointed, on which, for the first time, town and rowing were equally represented. Although the old Committee remained in nominal existence and, with the Stewards, retained the final legislative authority, the running of the Regatta passed into the hands of the new standing Sub-Committee.

In 1885 came the next, the most important step, with the adoption of a new Constitution for the Regatta. In point of fact it is questionable whether, before 1885, there ever was a formal Constitution, beyond a series of resolutions and minutes. However, this new Constitution recognized the need for an effective and manageable committee. The old Committee was disbanded, some of its members being elected Stewards, and others retired, and the running of the Regatta was placed entirely in the hands of a new Committee of Management of twelve, who were to be elected by the Stewards from amongst their own number.

This, then, is the system which has been in force since 1885:

1. There is no statutory limitation to the number of Stewards, who are self-elected, by ballot, and for life unless they should wish to retire.

2. The Stewards constitute a council for the general conduct of the Regatta.

3. The Stewards elect, annually, and from their own number, a Committee of Management of not more than twelve members.

4. The Committee of Management exercises control over all matters connected with the Regatta, excepting such as involve the alteration of any of the published Rules of the Regatta. Within this limitation the Committee of Management may publish Bye-Laws.

5. The Rules of the Regatta, and the Constitution, can be altered only by a specially convened meeting of the Stewards.

Although, in 1885, there were six rowing men on the newly formed Committee of Management, the local Stewards still outnumbered the rowing Stewards by three to one. In the next fifteen years the number of local Stewards remained static, but the rowing Stewards increased steadily. In 1900 the rowing Stewards were still in a minority of thirteen to eighteen, but after 1885 they always had a majority on the Committee.

After 1900 the ranks of the local Stewards dwindled rapidly, partly, perhaps, because of the changed status of the Regatta, which had long since ceased to be a local festival, and partly because economic changes were thinning the ranks of the landed gentry. Perhaps jealousy entered into it, too, for in 1900 a resolution was passed,

That it is an unwritten law that local Stewards be proposed by local Stewards, and rowing Stewards by rowing Stewards, and that a note of such custom should be entered in the Minutes for future guidance.

Today the original position is reversed, and out of a total of thirty-eight Stewards, only five, including the Mayor of Henley, who is an *ex-officio* member, are 'local Stewards', though more, of course, are local residents.

Inevitably an organization such as Henley depends, to a very large extent, on the genius and driving force of the personalities who run it. It would be hard to exaggerate the part which has been played by those who have presided, in one capacity or another, over the Henley scene.

First of the Henley personalities was James Nash, who may almost be called its founder. Of his methods as Secretary we know little, but certainly he was a master of tact in his handling of haughty Stewards and vociferous Committee men.

In partnership with Nash from 1839 to 1844, and later as Secretary on his own, from about 1854 until 1883, was C. Towsey. At about the same period Charles Lane was another leading personality. W. B. Woodgate referred to him as Vice-Chairman, and as generally taking the chair at the draw for stations. Both these men were of the 'old school', straight-laced in their traditionalism. Towsey's foible, as we shall see, was an unwillingness to see the old records broken. Lane's, according to Woodgate, concerned the arranging of the programme, which, he considered, ought to suit the spectators—the final of the Grand at 3 p.m., and the Ladies' Plate as a finale—rather than the oarsmen, who had an aggravating habit of entering for too many events. Yet between them they nursed the Regatta through its infancy, and handed over a lusty child to the rowing men, when their turn came to take over the reins of management.

It was J. F. Hodges who became the first Chairman of the newly formed Committee of Management in 1881. But H. T. Steward was the power behind the throne. For all practical purposes he ran the Regatta, and from 1894, when he became Chairman, he carried the organization on his own shoulders. It was he, too, who surveyed the 'New Course' in 1885, and who edited and published the first volume of Henley history.

On H. T. Steward's death in 1915, C. Gurdon succeeded as 'caretaker', but resigned in 1919. In February of that year, W. A. L. Fletcher, one of the most beloved of Oxford oarsmen, was elected

Chairman. But he died a few days after his election, the victim of pneumonia, and of lungs damaged by German gas in the war.

There then followed an era of administration which was different, yet the same. It was different in that the new Chairman, F. I. Pitman, did not directly concern himself with the running of the Regatta. Meetings of the Committee were rare, and Pitman declared his task to be the finding of finance 'if Tom Steward overstepped himself'. And herein lay the similarity with pre-war days. For now the practical management of the Regatta was left to C. T. Steward, the son of the previous Chairman. One of the most self-effacing of men, he was, none the less, the architect of modern Henley. And he further followed his father's example by surveying the Straight Course, and by producing the third volume of Henley records.

F. I. Pitman died in 1942, and no Chairman was elected until 1945, when the mantle fell on H. G. Gold. He again varied the pattern, by making the Committee once more into an active governing body, and the Secretary into a responsible executive officer. To his tact and guidance we owe a Henley recast on pre-war lines, and, even more important in these days of mass-produced mediocrity, to pre-war standards.

As already remarked, Harcourt Gold received a Knighthood in 1948, in recognition of his services to rowing in the Olympic year, and, resigning the Chairmanship of the Committee of Management in 1951, was named President of the Regatta. In the same year H. R. N. Rickett became the new Chairman. His success in the office, which he still holds, is best judged by the high reputation of Henley today.

One of the secrets of success in almost any sphere of activity is to leave nothing to chance. And it is that, perhaps, which makes Henley the envy of other regattas, and the ambition of oarsmen throughout the world. Sometimes there are complaints, of course, and Henley, being steeped in tradition, does not as a rule forestall public demand for changes. But undoubtedly the efficiency of Henley is one of its greatest assets.

I cannot resist repeating one of my favourite quotations in this context. Robert Herrick, the historian of Harvard rowing,[1] wrote of Henley:

When a race scheduled for 3:03 starts, if your watch reads 3:08 your watch is wrong, and you reset your watch. I have never seen a contest where the officials adhere so faithfully to the time schedule. At four o'clock all rowing stops for forty-five minutes, for reasons obvious to all who have been to England.

The outside observer is often best placed to judge what is going on, and Herrick's observation is shrewd indeed.

Certainly at Henley, 'everything stops for tea', and it is by no means the oarsmen who benefit least from the fact that the Stewards run the Regatta in a civilized manner, declining to make a toil of a pleasure. And certainly the races start punctually. Elsewhere it is an axiom that the smooth running of a regatta depends primarily on having efficient Raft Stewards, those energetic men whose duty it is to get crews on the water in time for their races. At Henley the problem has been solved, quite simply, by starting the races rigidly on time, and waiting for no one; as a result, everyone is punctual. Nor is there the delay in getting crews off the start, which is experienced elsewhere. Two factors contribute to make this possible. The first is the provision of linesmen, who hold the boats straight if there is an awkward wind blowing; the second is the fact that the Henley umpires have earned the confidence of the competitors. Knowing that their opponents will not be permitted to start before the word 'Go', and that they themselves will not be sent off when they are not ready, or are pointing in the wrong direction, oarsmen are, in so far as this is possible at the start of a race, relaxed and confident. And that makes all the difference.

The life-cycle of Henley Regatta is somewhat like that of the butterfly. For long months the bones and sinews of the Regatta— the booms, the tents, the piles, the timber, the signal boards, the chairs and the scaffolding—are hidden in the chrysalis, in storage. For a brief week, each year, the Regatta spreads its wings, blossoming into a small town of wood and canvas, adorned with flags

[1] *Red Top*, by Robert Herrick (Harvard University Press).

and flowers, beside the perfectly appointed race-course on the river. And the town itself is transformed from a sleepy market town into the Mecca of oarsmen from all over the world. It is a process which never fails to fascinate, and a task of some magnitude.

Sometimes it is asked why the Regatta cannot erect permanent stands and boathouses, which, in the long run, would certainly save them a great deal of expense. The short answer to this is that the meadows beside the river are all liable to flooding, and that the government departments concerned with building, and with the preservation of rural amenities, will not permit the erection of any permanent buildings.

In charge of the gang which prepares the course is Mr. Len Clark, of Messrs. Hobbs & Sons. He has been working on the course since 1919; his father did the same job before him, and between them they have been at it for sixty-seven years; so it is not surprising that the course is the pride of Henley.

There is a widespread belief that every pile slips into the same hole in the river bed each year. But this is true only of the starting and finishing posts. Their positions are measured from marks on each bank, and the actual holes are located with a rye-peck. The rest of the piles, as a matter of fact, are placed, as far as possible, in slightly different positions each year. This is possible because some of the booms, though all originally sixty feet in length, have been shortened in the course of time, and by placing them in a different order from year to year the positions of the upright piles can be changed. It is desirable to do this, because, although the holes silt up during the winter, it is only with mud, and the piles need a firm bed of gravel to hold them secure. During the Regatta launches are moored to them, and launch drivers are often too careless, or ignorant, to fasten their mooring ropes so that they are free to slide up and down the piles. The wash of the Umpires' launches, passing at speed, lifts the moored craft, and can exert a tremendous leverage on the piles.

The first pile to be driven on the course is the Bucks finishing post. It is followed by the Berks finishing post, and then by the two starting posts. Because they must occupy exactly the same positions every year, these four piles must be driven a little farther each time, to ensure that they are secure. When they are in position, the posts at Fawley are sighted from them, and from marks on the bank, and the rest follow in sequence. There are 169 booms of Oregon pine on the course, and the newest of those in use today were purchased in 1931.

Mr. Clark starts work at the end of April, driving the piles for the landing stages, and then moves on to the course. On his heels comes Mr. C. J. Pike, with twenty-one years of Henley service to his credit. His task is to floor and complete the numerous stages and boxes, and to erect the signals; each year most of his nails go into the holes from which they were extracted after the preceding Regatta. In this way the better part of a standard of wood is used, apart from the booms and piles. The whole operation of preparing the course takes about five weeks, and the dismantling is done in three weeks.

Interest is sometimes shown in the floating stand, at the finish of the course. When it was first used, in 1939, it was truly 'floating', and it was an awesome sight to see how it tilted when the spectators crowded forward to watch a race. In fact, it finished the Regatta lashed with ropes to the trees on the bank. Today the stand floats only when it is lightly laden. When the load increases, the weight is taken by the twelve pairs of springs, each taking a compression of 1,200 lb., with which it is held to the twelve great piles. Nearly five hundred people have been counted leaving the stand after a race.

The erection of the tentage at Henley, the preparation of the Enclosures, the bedding out of flowers, and the provision and running of the luncheon marquee are carried out by contractors.

One of the phenomena of Henley is the transformation scene which occurs at the end of the Regatta. The prize-giving and the fireworks and festivities of Saturday evening are the culmination of weeks of feverish activity. The last set-piece of the firework display splutters and goes out. The lights and clangour of the fair last a little longer. A pall of dust hangs over the Enclosures, already stripped of flowers and shrubs. Along the roads leading out of Henley, queues of cars and buses crawl. Soon after midnight all is over, save where, here and there, a circle of rowing men discuss the events of the week. On Sunday there is a great packing up of boats and luggage. On Monday, Henley is once again a quiet country town.

It may well be understood that the running of a regatta such as Henley is an expensive operation. And, in fact, today, the Committee face a bill of some £13,000 each year, for the erection of stands and tents, the preparation of the Enclosures, and the booming and piling of the course.

Finance has always been a serious problem, with all regatta committees in this country, and for a simple reason. Rowing has never ranked as one of the great popular sports, yet it has probably always had, and certainly has today, a sufficient following to provide for its relatively modest needs. But it takes place, almost without exception, on public waterways, and between banks which are either private property, or public rights-of-way.[1] Such of the general public as have a mind to watch the racing can therefore do so without paying for the privilege. Enclosures, where they exist, are generally erected on sufferance, and are of strictly limited capacity. Nor can overheads ever be particularly low, because tents and stands must be erected annually on land where no permanent building is permitted.

In the early days of Henley Regatta the Stewards relied upon the entrance fees and subscriptions, and had often to dip into their own pockets to make good the balance. About 1880 matters took a turn for the better, with the increasing popularity of the houseboats. Houseboats used to be towed to Henley, and moored along the bank, and at the height of their popularity they stretched in an almost unbroken line from the finishing post to Fawley. In 1884, the Secretary, John Cooper, and Pat Labat, who for many years owned and drove the launch used by the umpires, first made the rounds of the houseboats, asking for subscriptions. With difficulty they collected £27.

---

[1] See the remarks on towing-paths, pp. 7–8.

Two years later these subscriptions had risen to £170, and by
1897 the Committee were drawing £1,000 a year from houseboats and launches. Bearing in mind the value of money at that
time, this is a fair indication of the popularity of the Regatta. It
was, of course, an era of prosperity, and others besides the
Stewards benefited. Concert parties, performing on the houseboats, counted their profits in hundreds of pounds. Others were
less ambitious. Cooper records that on one occasion he found a
young lady 'of prepossessing appearance' in the Enclosure, with
a collecting box for the Hospital. He turned her out, but later the
chairman, H. T. Steward, who, as Cooper puts it, was essentially
a man 'who thinketh no evil', told the gatekeeper to let her in
again, as he did not think she would do any harm, being there
only for charitable purposes. About two months later Cooper
happened to be attending the Quarter Sessions at Oxford, when
the same young lady appeared in the dock on a charge of stealing
a bicycle. It appeared that she lodged in Caversham, and had
stolen the bicycle to come to Henley. In her diary, which the
police discovered when they searched her room, appeared the
following entry:

July 3. Went to Henley Regatta. That's the place for me—Ascot not
in it—got in the best Enclosure but a fool of an Official turned me out.
However a kind old gentleman with a beard (God bless him) let me in
again, and I collected £19. 7. 6 of the best. What ho! the Hospital.

It transpired that she had indeed been in the habit of sending a
shilling or two each week to the Hospital, and that after Henley she
had sent them 7s. 6d., retaining the £19, no doubt, 'for expenses'.

Gradually the houseboats dwindled in number, partly because
the Thames Conservancy were uncooperative in the matter of the
sub-letting of mooring sites, a speculative venture which accounted
for much of the money involved. By 1914 houseboats had ceased
to be a major source of revenue.

The 1914–18 War brought serious problems to Henley. It was
estimated that, from an annual £3,000,[1] the cost of mounting the

[1] In 1914, this sum included about £200 for 'precautions against arson'—the
suffragettes had threatened to burn down the boat tents.

Regatta was going to increase to £8,000. Money had to be found.

The answer to this challenge was the Stewards' Enclosure, and the late H. G. (later Sir Harcourt) Gold did more than any other man to persuade the Stewards of the value of the scheme. He argued that many people would come to Henley if the facilities offered were comparable with, for instance, Royal Ascot, and also that if the new Enclosure were run as a club, the members' subscriptions would come in every year, irrespective of the vagaries of the weather, which is the bane of so many regattas.

For a time there was lively opposition to the scheme, notably from those habitual rebels, Sir John Edwards-Moss and W. B. Woodgate, who complained bitterly in the Press that the old rowing men, who had made Henley, were to be squeezed out, and the Regatta given over to the social butterflies.

Nevertheless, the scheme was adopted, and the Stewards' Enclosure was opened in 1919, with a membership of 300. It is a club to which anyone—today including ladies—may be proposed as a member, irrespective of whether or not they are oarsmen. Those who have rowed at Henley, however, are admitted at a reduced entrance fee. Election is by the Stewards of the Regatta, and members of the Stewards' Enclosure have no say in the running of the Regatta, although many improvements have owed their origin to suggestions made by members. It is no exaggeration to say that the Stewards' Enclosure revolutionized Henley Regatta, and made possible its great expansion. By 1939 the membership had risen to 700. Today it is just over 1,500. The great service which it does to the Regatta, as Harcourt Gold foretold, is that it provides a guaranteed income, wet or fine. Receipts from entrance fees and subscriptions to the Stewards' Enclosure now amount to over £9,000 a year, with a further £7,000 from the sale of Visitors' badges, and £3,000 from catering and car parks. Compared with this, the crews' entrance fees for the racing total only £1,200, and the sale of tickets for the General Enclosure, about £2,000.

GROWTH OF THE RULES

When Henley began, and for many years afterwards, there were no generally accepted rules, and each regatta drew up its own code, to suit its own special requirements. So far as Henley was concerned, this was done on 1 May 1839, when the Stewards issued their rules for the ordering of the Grand Challenge Cup, and the Town Challenge Cup.

These first rules covered every eventuality which the Stewards could foresee. They dealt with the qualifications, entries, course, draw, and even with the method of starting, which was to be 'directed by the firing of a pistol unseen by the competitors, the Starter or Umpire first asking "Are you ready ?", and if answered in the affirmative, he shall then order or make a signal for the pistol to be fired'.

In the whole list of eighteen original rules, only one dealt with what, today, we would call the Laws of Boat Racing. Rule XIV, with admirable simplicity, stated: 'That no fouling be permitted.'

There was, of course, no whisper of what was to constitute a foul; yet even the bare statement was no inconsiderable rule to be passed by a body of non-rowing men, when fouling was still very much *de rigueur* in many quarters. Of a race between two presumed amateurs, Messrs. Campbell and Cookes, of the Lyons Subscription Rooms, in 1833, a newspaper reported that, 'while endeavouring to get his starboard scull over his antagonist's head, [Mr. Campbell] struck him on his forehead, which made Mr. Cookes shake his "knowledge box" '. And *Bell's Life*, writing of a £20 wager match between James Burke—a professional pugilist —and one Shepheard, who was described as 'a landsman of Chelsea', had to report that when Shepheard finally succeeded in giving Burke the slip, Burke's supporters gave chase in a cutter, and would have run him ashore had not his own party hastened to his rescue.

One other notable omission from the first Henley rules was any mention of what the definition of an amateur should or should not be, although, in a sense, the Grand Challenge Cup qualification itself fulfilled this purpose. Yet, of all the rulings applicable to boat racing, this, in the long run, was to prove the most controversial.

A great deal has been written about the old amateur definition in rowing, and no one, perhaps, has ever summed up the case more truly, and with less humbug, than W. B. Woodgate.[1] 'The old idea of an amateur,' he wrote, 'was that he was a "gentleman", and that the two were simply convertible terms.' The question of money did not enter into it, except in so far as an amateur did not make sport his ostensible means of livelihood. But private matches could be, and were, made for considerable sums of money. Until 1861 even the Wingfield Sculls, the Amateur Championship of the Thames, was in effect a sweepstake, in which each competitor risked £5, and the winner took the pool.

Henley, and all the other regattas, managed well enough without a common code of rules, and without any amateur definition, for some forty years. But gradually it became inconvenient to have contradictory rulings by different regatta committees, and in 1878 a meeting of prominent oarsmen took place at Putney, to consider what was required. It was attended by representatives of the Oxford and Cambridge University Boat Clubs, Leander Club, London Rowing Club, Thames Rowing Club, and Kingston Rowing Club. The meeting published the following definition:

An amateur oarsman or sculler must be an officer of Her Majesty's Army or Navy or Civil Service, a member of the Liberal professions, or of the Universities or Public Schools, or of any established boat or rowing club not containing mechanics or professionals; and must not have competed in any competition for either a stake, or money, or entrance fee, or with or against a professional for any prize; nor have ever taught, or assisted in the pursuit of athletic exercises of any kind as a means of livelihood, nor have ever been employed in or about boats, or in manual labour; nor be a mechanic, artisan, or labourer.

---

[1] In 1866 Woodgate himself was in trouble for racing a professional named Hoare for £10 from Putney to Hammersmith—though it was a one-sided bet, since Woodgate was to take nothing if he won. The Henley Stewards, with admirable simplicity, ruled that since Mr. Woodgate was a member of an Amateur Club (viz. Kingston), he must, *ipso facto*, be an amateur himself!

It does not require much thought to see that this was a very poor definition, floundering badly between positive requirement and positive disqualification, which had very little connection the one with the other. In the following year the Stewards of Henley Regatta tried their hands, and produced another definition, which was at least more conclusive than the first, in that it remained consistently negatory throughout. The definition ran:

No person shall be considered as an amateur oarsman or sculler—
1. Who has ever competed in any open competition for a stake, money, or entrance fee.
2. Who has ever competed with or against a professional for any prize.
3. Who has ever taught, pursued, or assisted in the practice of athletic exercises of any kind as a means of gaining a livelihood.
4. Who has been employed in or about boats for money or wages.
5. Who is or has been, by trade or employment for wages, a mechanic, artisan, or labourer.

At this time it was a distinct possibility that the Stewards of Henley Regatta might become the governing body for rowing, in much the same way as the Marylebone Cricket Club became the ultimate authority in cricket, and the Royal and Ancient in golf. But it was not to be.

In 1879 there came into being the Metropolitan Rowing Association, which was formed, not with any idea of laying down rules, but to provide a 'super' club, which could sponsor crews, when necessary, to meet any foreign challenge, drawing on the resources of all the leading Metropolitan clubs. In 1882 this body, having expanded its membership beyond the confines of the London river, changed its name to the Amateur Rowing Association, established an amateur definition—which was virtually the same as that enforced at Henley—and, in 1886, issued general Rules for Regattas.

The rules to which the newly formed Amateur Rowing Association gave effect were borrowed from Henley. The Henley Rules, and the A.R.A. Rules for Regattas, have remained identical ever since, except for occasional minor variations in wording.

But Henley, being so much the senior, never accepted A.R.A. jurisdiction, and the A.R.A. have never sought to enforce it. Henley is thus the only major regatta which is not run under the A.R.A. rules.

The amateur definition has been mentioned already. But it was to prove so thorny a problem that something more must be said about it.

The 1879 definition, as drawn up by the Henley Stewards and adopted by the Metropolitan Rowing Association, seems reasonable enough, and was certainly quite reasonable at the time it was framed. Those engaged in manual labour were excluded because it was then considered that they would derive an unfair advantage from their physical exertions. Such an hypothesis may appear indefensible today; but in the 'seventies there were, in fact, few oarsmen among the 'working classes', except perhaps on the river Tyne, where there was a flourishing fraternity of genuinely professional oarsmen, recruited from the coal mines. And the days when the 'amateur' would devote much of his time to training were still far ahead.

But the popularity of rowing spread rapidly, and soon there was a growing demand that the 'manual labour bar' should be removed. In 1890 this led to the formation of the National Amateur Rowing Association, with rules otherwise similar to those of the A.R.A., but omitting the manual labour bar. In 1891 there was a conference between the two bodies, but the A.R.A.—and Henley Regatta—declined to alter their rules.

In 1896 the A.R.A. redrafted their rules, and Henley followed suit. But the change was for the worse. For the relevant clause now debarred any person 'who is or has been by trade or employment for wages a mechanic, artisan, or labourer, or engaged in any menial duty'.

To modern ears this ruling sounds indefensible and even ridiculous, if one begins to consider how it would be applied to all the possible means of earning a livelihood. And inevitably the use of the undefined term, 'menial', greatly widened the gap between the A.R.A. and the N.A.R.A.

The dispute was, of course, primarily an affair between the two Associations, and only occasionally did it disturb the even tenor of Henley Regatta. One such occasion was at the Peace Regatta in 1919, when *The Times* joined the attack, with a leading article entitled: '"Gentlemen" at Henley.' To say the least, the circumstances were unfortunate, for the Stewards found it necessary, at the first post-war Regatta, to reject the entry of an N.A.R.A. crew for the King's Cup, a race for Service crews, for which H.M. King George V had presented the trophy.

As often happens on such occasions, the Henley Stewards were severely criticized for something which was not really their fault. For they had drawn up the conditions for this race before the King announced his intention of presenting the Cup. And, quite reasonably, they stipulated that the definition of an amateur should be that which prevailed on 4 August 1914, in the country of origin of each contesting crew. The N.A.R.A. sent in their entry, and certified the crew as amateurs 'according to the N.A.R.A. definition'. The Stewards invited them to certify that the men, individually, were amateurs in accordance with the A.R.A. definition, but this they declined to do. And the Stewards considered it impossible to alter the qualification after the other entries had been made and received.

The dispute between the two Associations continued, occasionally with some acrimony, but generally on a basis of *laissez faire*, until 1937. In that year the A.R.A. at last dropped the manual labour bar, and the N.A.R.A. agreed to adopt the wording as then enforced by the A.R.A. As from that year, clubs from either Association were able to compete at each other's regattas. Henley followed the lead of the A.R.A., bringing the new definition into force in time for the Regatta in 1938.

Once the problem of the amateur definition was resolved, the way was paved towards an amalgamation of the two Associations. Even before the war an attempt was made to bring this about, but the war intervened before the various administrative difficulties could be overcome. However, a joint sub-committee of the two Associations was set up, to deal with international problems.

The difficulties in achieving an amalgamation were due, in the main, to the differences in organization and purpose of the two bodies. The A.R.A. was, in effect, a committee consisting of the representatives of clubs, and groups of clubs, all directly affiliated to the Association. The N.A.R.A., on the other hand, was a co-ordinating body, consisting of the representatives of a number of self-governing regional Associations. The administrative difficulties were finally resolved in 1955, and with effect from 1 January 1956 the Amateur Rowing Association became the sole governing body of English rowing. On that date the N.A.R.A. clubs transferred their allegiance to the A.R.A., and the National Amateur Rowing Association ceased to exist. Although this may appear to have been a capitulation on their part, the N.A.R.A. had, in fact, already achieved the object for which it was originally formed—which might perhaps be described as the 'democratization' of English rowing.

THE RULES TODAY

Few of those who watch at Henley today, and few, indeed, even of those who take part in the Regatta, give much thought to the Henley Rules, unless they be club captains or secretaries, who must ensure that their entries are made in due form. The Rules are published officially by the Regatta, and there is no need to reproduce them here. Indeed, to do so would scarcely be worth while. For, despite their reputation for conservatism, the Stewards are regularly altering and adjusting the Rules to meet changing requirements. There are, however, a few which, from time to time, are of special importance, and some understanding of which adds to the interest of the Regatta.

Amateur Status

The history and development of this Rule has already been discussed. The Rule now reads:

No person shall be considered an amateur oarsman, sculler, or coxswain:—

(*a*) Who has ever rowed or steered in any race for a stake, money, or entrance fee.

(*b*) Who has ever knowingly rowed or steered with or against a professional for any prize.

(*c*) Who has ever taught, pursued, or assisted in the practice of athletic exercise of any kind for profit.

(*d*) Who is disqualified as an amateur in any other branch of sport.

An amateur may not receive any contribution towards his expenses in competing at the Regatta except from the club he represents, but it shall be open to any *bona fide* member of such club to contribute to the club funds for the above purpose.

Eliminating Races

Not more than sixteen crews may compete, in the Regatta, for any event excepting for the Thames and Wyfold Challenge Cups, for which the limit is thirty-two. When these limits are exceeded, the Committee select the crews which are to take part in the Eliminating Races.[1]

Coxswains

There is a sliding scale of 'minimum weights' for coxswains.[2]

Average weight of crew	Minimum weight of coxswain
$10\frac{1}{2}$–11 stone	$6\frac{1}{2}$ stone
11–$11\frac{1}{2}$ stone	$7\frac{1}{2}$ stone
$11\frac{1}{2}$ stone and over	8 stone

Deficiencies are made up by deadweight placed on the coxswain's thwart.

Substitutions

It will be seen from the programme that eights are generally entered with five substitutes, of whom one must be a coxswain, and fours with two substitutes. The basic rule is that no substitution may be made for an oarsman who has actually raced in the Regatta. However, the Committee may make an exception in

---

[1] See p. 217. [2] See p. 94.

the case of a man who is prevented from rowing through circumstances beyond his control, and not attributable to his having taken part in the Regatta.[1]

Emergency

In cases of exceptional emergency the Committee shall have the power to abrogate, alter, or suspend any Rule at the instance of any competitor, provided they are satisfied that no other competitor is thereby placed in a less favourable position than he would have been in if such an emergency had not occurred. All questions of eligibility, qualifications, interpretation of the Rules, or other matters not specially provided for, shall be referred to the Committee, whose decision shall be final.

Of all the Henley Rules this 'general absolution' is perhaps the most typical, and important. It reflects, of course, the mutual trust of the body of Stewards in their Committee of Management, and of the whole body of competitors in the organization of the Regatta. Rules are framed, in the first instance, to serve a purpose. Too often they then become 'masters', exercising a stranglehold on those who made them. At Henley, very rightly, Rules remain servants.[2]

The Laws of Boat Racing

The Laws of Boat Racing, as enforced at Henley, are the same as those laid down by the Amateur Rowing Association. Two only require special mention here:

[1] See pp. 230–3.
[2] It was, seemingly, this Rule which gave the Committee of Management the loophole through which they escaped, in 1955, from the apparent deadlock of the Russians' withdrawal and request for readmission. This, of course, is a personal opinion. But it would seem that the dock strike constituted an 'exceptional emergency', and that the readmission of the Soviet crews placed no other competitor 'in a less favourable position than he would have been in if such an emergency had not occurred', inasmuch as, if no dock strike had delayed the arrival of the Russian boats, they would never have withdrawn. In the case of the Diamond Sculls, however, S. C. Rand would have been so placed, since, at the time at which the Russians requested readmission, he had already 'won' his heat against Y. Tukalov 'by default'. Tukalov, therefore, was not readmitted.

Law V. A boat's proper course is such a course as will enable it to reach the winning post in the shortest possible time, provided it allows ample water for every other competing boat to steer its proper course on the side on which such competing boat started, when such competing boat is in a position to enforce its right to such water. Any boat failing to keeps its proper water does so at its peril in the event of a foul occurring.

Law VIII. It shall be considered a foul when, after a race has been started, any competitor, by his oar, scull, boat, or person, comes into contact with the oar, scull, boat, or person of another competitor.

Fouls may be claimed by the competitors, or awarded by the Umpire without a claim being made, if he considers that the encroachment was deliberate, or that the foul clearly influenced the race.

THE HENLEY QUALIFICATIONS

In the early years of the Regatta the qualification rules for the various events were often loosely worded, and, even more often inconsistently interpreted. To quote but one example: in 1863 London R.C., the holders of the Wyfold Challenge Cup, protested that in both the Kingston and Third Trinity crews there were men who had previously competed for the Stewards' Challenge Cup. The Stewards overruled this objection, although the qualifications for the Wyfold Cup had been amended quite recently, expressly debarring all those who had previously competed for the senior event.

Many such discrepancies can be found in the official records of the Regatta. They may be better understood in the light of the early pages of this chapter.

All Henley entries are, and always have been, confined to amateurs, though in the notes which follow, this fact is not repeated in every qualification quoted.

Similarly, all clubs must have been established for at least one year previous to the day of entry, except in the case of H.M. Forces, and the Universities and Public Schools. In connection with the schools it is perhaps worth mentioning that in 1954 a correspondent[1] wrote to *The Times*, suggesting that it was out of tune with English life that the Princess Elizabeth Cup should be limited to 'public schools'. The Stewards replied that the Rules had never been applied in that restrictive sense, and that, were entries to be received from a wider circle of schools, they would assuredly be accepted.

Entries for Henley Regatta close on the Tuesday before Marlow Regatta, which in turn takes place on the Saturday falling two weeks before the final day of Henley. Foreign entries close on 1 June, and are accepted only from those countries which have signed the Henley Agreement.[2]

The final day of Henley Regatta falls on the first Saturday of July, after 1 July. Thus the Regatta can start as early as 29 June, finishing on 2 July, or as late as 5 July, finishing on 8 July.

The Grand Challenge Cup

Instituted 1839. 'To be rowed for on the Henley reach annually, in eight-oared boats, by any crew composed of members of a college of the universities of Oxford, Cambridge, or London, the schools of Eton and Westminster, the officers of the two Brigades of Household Troops, or of members of a club established at least one year previous to the time of entering.'

In 1840 the qualification was widened to include all officers of the Army and Navy, and, in 1869, to include members of any university or public school. The Air Force was admitted in 1928.

The present rule reads: 'Any crew of amateurs who are members of any university or public school, or who are serving in Her Majesty's Navy, Army, or Air Force, or any amateur club established at least one year previous to the day of entry, shall be qualified to contend for this prize.'

The Stewards' Challenge Cup

Instituted 1841, for medals only in that year, the challenge

---

[1] Mrs. H. C. Bentwich, a former chairman of the London County Council Education Committee.

[2] See Appendix A, p. 276.

cup, which was added in 1842, not then being ready. The qualification has always been the same as for the Grand Challenge Cup. The Stewards' Challenge Cup was originally contested in coxed fours, and became a coxswainless event in 1873.

The Ladies' Challenge Plate

Instituted 1845, as the 'new challenge cup'. However, it was not ready, and medals only were presented, the cup, named the Ladies' Challenge Plate, being added in 1846. 'For eight-oared boats, open to college and other amateur clubs, except University Clubs, Subscription Rooms, or clubs similarly constituted.'

In 1848 the qualification was widened to include the clubs of 'other public establishments', and clubs restricted in membership to one particular profession, or class of persons, or to any particular town or place (distant at least seven miles from Westminster Bridge), with the proviso that no member of the crew should at the same time be a member of any other club.

In 1857[1] the qualification was drastically narrowed, to admit only the colleges of Oxford and Cambridge, and the schools of Eton and Westminster. The specific mention of Oxford and Cambridge, and of Eton and Westminster, was dropped in 1869, and at the same time it was ruled that members of colleges and schools must be *bona fide* in residence at the time of their entry. In 1877 it was further ruled that they must have been 'in residence' for at least a fortnight in the term immediately preceding the Regatta. This, of course, referred to the colleges rather than to the schools, and the formula was again changed in 1880, to exclude those who had exceeded four years since commencing residence at the University.

In 1882 the words 'in the United Kingdom' were added after 'schools and colleges'.

In 1884 the non-collegiate boat clubs of the Universities were admitted, and in 1920 the Royal Military College, Sandhurst, and the Royal Military Academy, Woolwich. Today it is the Royal Military Academy, Sandhurst. In the meantime, in

[1] See p. 86.

1910, double entries in the Ladies' Plate and the Thames Cup were forbidden. For some years crews were permitted to enter for both, at a reduced entrance fee, but were required to withdraw from one or the other before the draw. Since 1928 this has not been permitted, and the Princess Elizabeth Cup has now been added to this prohibition.

With the creation of the Irish Free State, Dublin ceased to be 'in the United Kingdom', and in 1924 Trinity College Dublin was therefore specifically added to the list of eligible clubs.

Although in the 1857 drafting it was made clear that the eligible colleges were those of the Universities of Oxford and Cambridge, this was not stated in the 1869 and subsequent revisions. In 1934 the point was again made clear, and at the same time a rule was added, forbidding combinations of two or more Boat Clubs, 'whether of the same or different colleges'.[1]

The present rule reads:

Any crew of amateurs who are members of any one of the following boat clubs shall be qualified to contend for this prize subject to the restrictions hereinafter set out—

(i) The boat club of any college of the Universities of Oxford or Cambridge;

(ii) The non-collegiate boat clubs of the Universities of Oxford or Cambridge;

(iii) The boat club of any public school in the United Kingdom;

(iv) The boat club of Trinity College, Dublin;

(v) The boat club of the Royal Military Academy, Sandhurst.

(a) Two or more boat clubs, whether of the same or different colleges, shall not combine to make an entry.

(b) With regard to members of any of the colleges or non-collegiate clubs:

No one shall be allowed to row who has exceeded four years from the date of his first commencing residence at the university, unless, his university being Oxford or Cambridge, he has rowed in the last preceding summer races of his university, or, his university being Dublin,

---

[1] In 1940, finding it impossible to maintain two separate clubs, Trinity College Cambridge amalgamated their First and Third Boat Clubs, under the title 'First and Third Trinity B.C.'. Thus, although the title 'First and Third' commemorates two separate clubs, it is not a 'combination' within the meaning of this rule.

he is at the time of entry taking a professional course at one of the schools of his university, and no one shall in any case be allowed to row after five years from the date of his first commencing residence as aforesaid.

(*c*) With regard to members of the public schools:

Each member of a crew shall at the time of entering be *bona fide* a member *in statu pupillari* of such school.

(*d*) With regard to members of the Royal Military Academy:

Each member of the crew shall be a cadet at the Academy, or shall have completed a full course at the Academy not more than one month previous to the day of entry.

(*e*) No one (substitutes as per Rule XI and coxswains excepted) may enter, and no one (coxswains excepted) shall compete for this Plate and the Princess Elizabeth Challenge Cup, or Thames Challenge Cup, at the same Regatta.

The Thames Challenge Cup

Instituted 1868. For any amateur clubs, excluding University crews, amalgamations of college or club crews, and individuals who had previously rowed for, or were entered for, the Grand Challenge Cup, or the Stewards' Challenge Cup, or who had rowed in the head boats at either University in the current year.

In 1869 the qualification was made the same as for the Grand Challenge Cup; but no crew or individual member of a crew (other than the coxswain) was permitted to enter for the Thames Cup and the Grand or Stewards' Challenge Cups at the same Regatta. This ruling was modified in 1880, to exclude only those who had actually won either of these events.

In 1910 it was ruled that no crew might compete for both the Ladies' Plate and the Thames Cup at the same Regatta, though they were permitted to enter for both, providing they declared for one or other before the draw. This concession was withdrawn in 1928. In December 1949 the ban was extended to the Princess Elizabeth Cup.

The prohibition on past winners of the Grand and Stewards' Challenge Cups was withdrawn in 1950, to take effect for the 1951 Regatta, and in December 1954 a further relaxation permitted double entries in the Thames and Stewards' Challenge Cups.

The present qualification therefore reads:

The same as for the Grand Challenge Cup; but no one (substitutes as per Rule XI excepted) may enter, and no one (coxswains excepted) shall compete for this Cup and the Grand Challenge Cup, or Ladies' Challenge Plate, or Princess Elizabeth Cup, at the same Regatta.

The Princess Elizabeth Cup

Instituted 1946, in which year the race was contested over a shortened course of about a mile, for school crews, except those which reached the final of the Ladies' Plate. Competition for the Princess Elizabeth Cup started on the Friday, and those schools which reached, but did not win a Ladies' Plate semi-final, were given a bye through the first round.

In the following year the full course was used, and this concession was dropped. Before the 1949 Regatta, double entries in the Princess Elizabeth Cup and the Thames Cup were barred. For the 1949 Regatta schools were permitted to enter for, but not to start in, both the Princess Elizabeth Cup and the Ladies' Plate. But in December 1949 this concession, too, was withdrawn. The qualification now reads:

Any crew of amateurs who are members of a boat club of any public school in the United Kingdom shall be qualified to contend for this prize, subject to the restrictions hereinafter set out:

(i) Each member of a crew shall at the time of entering be a *bona fide* member *in statu pupillari* of such school.

(ii) No one (substitutes as per Rule XI and coxswains excepted) may enter, and no one (coxswains excepted) shall compete for this Cup and the Ladies' Challenge Plate, or Thames Challenge Cup, at the same Regatta.

Visitors' Challenge Cup

Instituted 1847, in which year the trophy (previously the *District Challenge Cup*) was offered as a special prize for a race added to the programme at the last moment. In 1848 it was placed under the same qualifications as the Ladies' Plate, and has so remained ever since. Originally contested in coxed fours, the Visitors' Challenge Cup became a race for coxswainless fours in 1874. The qualification now reads:

The same as for the Ladies' Plate, omitting Clause (e); but no one (substitutes as per Rule XI excepted) may enter, and no one shall compete for this Cup and the Wyfold Challenge Cup at the same Regatta.

The Wyfold Challenge Cup

Instituted 1847, and presented to the winners of the trial heats for the Grand Challenge Cup. In 1855 the Wyfold Challenge Cup was made over to a newly instituted race for fours, for any clubs not composed of resident members of either Oxford or Cambridge.

In 1857 the qualification was altered to admit any amateur crew, excepting only those individual oarsmen who had entered, previously or currently, for the Stewards' Challenge Cup. This ruling was relaxed in 1869, to debar only those currently competing for the Stewards'. The Wyfold Cup became a race for coxwainless fours in 1874.

In 1880 all previous winners of the Stewards' Challenge Cup were debarred, as well as those currently competing for that event. The same disqualification was extended in 1932 to past winners of, and current contenders for the Grand Challenge Cup. The qualification was redrafted in 1950, removing the disqualification from past winners of the Grand and Stewards' Cups. In December 1954 the ban on rowing in the Grand and Wyfold Cups was also removed, but double entries for the Wyfold and Visitors' Challenge Cups were barred. The qualification now reads:

The same as for the Grand Challenge Cup; but no one (substitutes as per Rule XI excepted) may enter, and no one shall compete for this Cup and the Stewards' Challenge Cup or the Visitors' Challenge Cup, at the same Regatta.

The Silver Goblets and Nickalls' Challenge Cup

Instituted 1845, as the *Silver Wherries*, for presentation prizes, 'for amateurs in pair-oars, open to all England'.

In 1850 presentation goblets were given instead of the silver wherries, and the name of the event was changed to the *Silver Goblets*. The *Nickalls' Challenge Cup* was presented in 1895. The present qualification reads: 'Open to all amateurs'.

The Double Sculls Challenge Cup

Instituted 1939, as the *Centenary Double Sculling Race*, for presentation prizes only in that year. At the next Regatta, in 1946, the Challenge Cup was added. The present qualification reads: 'Open to all amateurs'.

The Diamond Challenge Sculls

Instituted 1844, for a presentation diamond scarf-pin. 'Open to all England, for amateur scullers.'

The present trophy, the Diamond Challenge Sculls, was presented in 1850, when the scarf-pin was replaced by a presentation goblet. Present qualification: 'Open to all amateurs.'

The following Henley events are no longer contested :

The Town Challenge Cup

Instituted 1839, for four-oared crews whose members resided within a five-mile radius of Henley-on-Thames.

In 1852 the radius was extended to admit all clubs on the Thames between Windsor and Oxford (excluding resident members of the University, and members of the University Boat Club). Subsequently, various alterations were made in the distance restriction.

In 1869, as part of the general revision of the Rules, the qualification was made: 'Any amateur club established at least one year previous to the day of entry, of any town or place within twenty-five miles of Henley-on-Thames, and whose members reside within five miles of such town or place respectively, shall be eligible to contend for this prize, Universities and Public Schools excepted.'

In 1884 the Town Challenge Cup was withdrawn from competition, and given in trust to the Henley Town and Visitors' Regatta.

The District Challenge Cup

Instituted 1840, 'For four-oared crews or clubs belonging to the towns of Maidenhead, Marlow, Reading, Wallingford, and Henley, whose members reside within four miles of their respective towns'.

In 1842 the qualification was extended to include Windsor and Oxford, but excluding resident members of the University, or members of any university club. In 1847 the District Challenge Cup was withdrawn from competition, and the trophy altered and used for the newly instituted Visitors' Challenge Cup.

Local Amateur Scullers' Race

Instituted 1846, for a presentation prize. In some years this took the form of a silver wherry, 'a model of one of Searle's new racing boats', and the event was sometimes referred to as the *Silver Wherry for Henley Amateur Scullers*.

In 1848 the qualification was extended to include scullers resident within twelve miles of Henley. The race was discontinued in 1858.

District Goblets

For pairs. Instituted 1858, 'For amateurs residing within twenty-five miles of Henley, but excluding the Universities and public schools'.

In 1861 the restriction on university and public school oarsmen was removed. In 1868 the race was discontinued.

Public Schools' Challenge Cup

Instituted 1879. For coxed fours, open to 'The Boat Clubs of Public Schools only . . . each member of the crew, at the time of entering, to be *bona fide* a member *in statu pupillari*'.

In 1885 the Public Schools' Challenge Cup was withdrawn from competition, and acquired by Marlow Regatta, where it is still presented for a similar race.

THE COURSE

The first description of the Henley course, in the rules drawn up for the Grand Challenge Cup in 1839, was 'That the distance rowed should be about one mile and a half, commencing near the island, and terminating at the bridge'.

No doubt someone expressed the opinion that it was 'about a mile and a half' from Temple Island to the bridge. The distance actually rowed in the first Regatta was, in all probability, about one mile and six hundred yards, for there is every reason to suppose that the races started near the head of the Island.

In 1840 *Bell's Life* recorded:

The course commenced opposite the Temple on the island, and extended for about a mile and 550 yards upstream, the finishing post being within 50 or 60 yards of the bridge, which was an improvement on last year, when the boats had to proceed under the bridge to conclude the heat.

Another newspaper account, quoted by H. T. Steward, put the finish only ten yards from the bridge, but Mr. Steward concluded that the finish was probably at the steps on the Red Lion lawn, as it certainly was for many years thereafter. These steps were about forty yards below the bridge.

A glance at Plate I (p. 68) will reveal the shortcomings of the Old Course.[1] For the bend at Poplar Point must have been worth at least half a length, and perhaps more, in the last two minutes of the race. Nor was the advantage to the Berkshire station solely a matter of geometry. For the aerial photograph reveals—what the eye on the towpath sometimes misses—that the Berkshire bank falls away into a series of bays below Poplar Point. By keeping

---

[1] Throughout this book the various courses are described as C. T. Steward named them, i.e. the Old Course (1839–85), New Course (1886–1922), Experimental Course (1923), and Straight Course (1924 onwards).

close to the shore, between Remenham Club (which, of course, did not exist at that time) and the Point, the Berkshire crew was able to avoid the strength of the stream.

An account in *Bell's Life*, in 1851, believed to have been written either by Arthur Shadwell or Tom Egan—it matters little which, since they were the two leading coxswains of their day—described the set of the stream thus:

> The natural course of the stream is direct from the bridge upon the projecting wall of Phyllis Court grounds, nearly opposite Poplar Point (not upon the Point itself, as so many have supposed); thence it flows obliquely towards the gate below the Point (i.e. opposite the *White House*), and then it proceeds still more obliquely and more quietly to the boughs near Fawley Court, leaving comparatively dead water for some distance below the grounds of Phyllis Court. The stream becomes stronger as it approaches the channels on either side of the Island, but is much stronger on the Buckinghamshire side than on the barge channel, or Berks side, while at the head of Temple Island are the remains of a small 'eyot' or 'ait', which acts as a breakwater.

Since the widening of the Berkshire channel, past Temple Island, the stream is more evenly distributed at this point, though the greater volume of water still flows down the Bucks side. And the small eyot has long since disappeared. Apart from that, the 1851 assessment still stands today.

The conclusion is that, on the original Henley course, the Berkshire station enjoyed a great advantage. It had less stream at the start, and much less, together with the inside of the one and only bend, at the finish.

Statistics confirm this opinion. In the twenty years before the course was changed (1866–85), in the Grand, Ladies', and Thames Cup racing, the Berks station won 90 times, against 45 by the Centre station, and 21 by the Bucks station. When there were only two crews racing, the Centre station was not used, so that, to make fair comparison, Bucks and Centre wins must be combined against Berks wins. Even so, 90 to 66 is a significant advantage.

Furthermore, it is very probable that the old rule as to right of stations[1], operated in favour of the Bucks station. For if for any reason the Bucks crew did manage to get ahead, it was entitled to cross over to take the inside—Berks—station, at Poplar Point. A fair proportion of Bucks wins were certainly achieved in this way. Under the revised Laws of Boat Racing there would probably have been an even higher proportion of Berks wins.

Attempts were made to even up the course, by roping poles across the bays below Poplar Point. But they were never successful. There were even proposals for cutting off Poplar Point altogether. But a sub-committee, appointed in 1884, to consider the practicability of such a scheme, reported 'that having regard to the probable cost of cutting off the Point and that it would after all only remove to a limited extent the unfairness of the course, the Sub-Committee do not feel justified in recommending the Stewards to undertake the work'.

But they had a better idea, which was to move the finish down to Poplar Point, and the start to the bottom of the island.

This, of course, was by no means a straightforward proposition, nor a universally popular one. For one thing, it deprived the townspeople of their fine view of the finish, from the roadway outside the Little White Hart Hotel. And it relegated Henley bridge to the background, as no longer a suitable vantage point from which to watch the racing. And, by no means least inconvenient, it deprived the Stewards of their pleasant grandstand, which used to be built out into the road in front of the Red Lion, whither they could retire, through an upstairs window, when refreshment was needed.

On the strength of the replies received to a questionnaire, which was sent to the captains of the leading clubs, the sub-committee also suggested that only two crews should row abreast. This, of course, meant a three-day Regatta.

Nevertheless, both proposals were accepted, and put into effect for the 1886 Regatta.

The finish was now opposite the top of Phyllis Court, almost as it is today. The start was just below the tail of Temple Island,

[1] See p. 97.

on the Bucks side, and the length of the course was the same as before. There were two slight bends, one above the Island, and the other at Fawley; but the stations were nominally equal, because the starting line was staggered. The course was 150 feet wide, and was piled, but not boomed, on both sides.

To replace the grandstand, the Exeter College barge was moored at the finish, also serving as a Committee Room.

Soon after the adoption of the New Course, it became apparent that the advantage had now shifted to the Bucks station, by virtue of the fact that the first half of the course hugged the Buckinghamshire shore, and therefore offered more shelter from the prevailing wind. The prevailing wind at Henley, in June and July, is from the south-west. It was in this era that the term 'Bushes Wind' became current in Regatta circles, to describe the south-west wind, blowing off the Bucks shore below Fawley.

In an attempt to minimize the effect of the Bushes Wind the course was progressively made narrower, and pushed farther out from the Buckinghamshire bank, towards the middle of the river. From the original 150 feet it had narrowed, by 1914, to 100 feet, tapering down to only 80 feet at the finish. Booms were introduced in 1899, rather to keep the spectators off than the competitors on the course.

Another important innovation came in 1891. In that year it was pointed out that since the crews started with their sterns level, and were judged at the finish by their bows, the longer boats had an advantage. So the practice was introduced of measuring all the boats, and arranging for the longer craft to be pulled back, on the stake boats, so that the crews should start, as well as finish, by their bows.

Incidentally, it is this practice which explains why the Henley course is still described as 'about a mile and 550 yards'. In fact, the distance from the starting posts to the finishing posts is perfectly well known. It is 1 mile 570 yards. The average length of an eight is 60 feet, or 20 yards; and a boat of that length therefore covers exactly 1 mile 550 yards when rowing over the Henley course. A shorter boat rows a little farther; but in any given race both boats row the same distance.

In retrospect one cannot help wondering whether the 'New Course', as introduced in 1886, was, in fact, an improvement on the old course, finishing at the bridge. Obviously it looked a fairer proposition, because there was no large bend to be rounded at Poplar Point. And contemporaries certainly thought it was an improvement. But statistics do not support them.

John Cooper quotes Dr. Warre, who was one of the experts on whose advice the change was made, as saying of the new course, 'Given a calm day there is nothing in the stations except this—any duffer can steer the Bucks station, keeping a course, say 12 feet away and perfectly parallel to the piles. But it takes a real good cox to steer the Berks course as he leaves the head of the Island until the half-way mark'.

Cooper explained that few coxes on the Berks station kept close enough to the Bucks crew before Fawley, or took full advantage of the slack water on their own station at the finish. On the wide course there was more room to wander about than there is today.

Dr. Warre's opinion deserves respect. But statistics show that the expectation of success shifted, with the change of course, from Berks to Bucks, in no uncertain fashion. For, taking the racing in the same three events, over the next twenty years (1886–1905), we find 189 wins from the Buckinghamshire station, and 131 from the Berkshire station. This gives a rather larger advantage to Bucks than was previously enjoyed by Berks.

With the resumption of rowing after the 1914–18 War thoughts turned again to the problem of improving the course, and this time centred on the Berkshire channel past the island. But a survey showed that even if the course were narrowed to 75 feet, the start would have to be some 185 feet above the old line, which would have meant, in effect, reducing the Henley distance to a mile and a quarter. Some might say that this would have been the logical thing to do. Certainly it would have been a convenience to those amateur mathematicians who like to calculate the speed of the boats. But the consensus of opinion was that it would not have been 'Henley'.

None the less, the Stewards decided to try the experiment of a straight course in 1923, even though it meant racing over a shorter course. It was a calm week, and the advantages of moving the course further from the Bucks shore were not proved. But in every other respect the Experimental Course was voted a success.

And so the bold decision was made. Lord Hambleden, who owned the land on the Berkshire bank, and Mr. W. D. Mackenzie, who owned Temple Island, both generously agreed to give up the necessary land, and contractors began the arduous task of cutting off a slice of the Island, and part of the projecting Berkshire bank, and of dredging out the river channel. In all, some 10,000 cubic yards of soil were removed, and 800 feet of new camp-sheathing erected.

By the spring of 1924 the work was finished, and at the 1924 Regatta the modern Straight Course was used for the first time. It is 80 feet wide, and, of course, the correct Henley distance of 'about a mile and 550 yards'.

The Henley trumpet has sometimes been blown very loudly in extolling the merits of the Straight Course. It has been described as perfect, and as the finest course in the world. It may, indeed, be the best-appointed course in the world. But it is highly problematical whether there is a perfect course anywhere. Nearly every course is affected, to some extent, by the 'conditions'; and Henley is certainly no exception to this rule.

A poll of opinion in the Enclosures would doubtless reveal many differing views as to the fairness of the present course. On the one hand, the reputation of the Bushes Wind is by no means dead. On the other, the value of the slack water, particularly near the finish, is strongly urged in favour of Berks.

If there is a moderate to strong Bushes Wind, the Bucks station still offers an appreciable advantage over the middle section of the course. If the stream is running hard, then the Berks station benefits in the last quarter mile, and, perhaps to a lesser extent, between the quarter-mile and half-mile signals. No one can put a definite value on either of these factors, which vary according to the strength of the stream, and the strength and exact direction of the wind. Also, the two factors may tend to cancel each other out. The operative question, in considering the fairness of the course, is what may be the average, and the greatest advantage, likely to accrue to either station, on any given day. There are many days in the winter when the wind would give an overwhelming advantage to Bucks; and there are days, generally in the early spring, when the stream would offer an equally overwhelming advantage to Berks. But fortunately, at the time of year when Henley takes place, such conditions are most unlikely to occur. It is probably fair to say, therefore, that in the great majority of races, the advantage offered by either station is not more than a quarter of a length. In unfavourable conditions, the advantage might rise as high as three-quarters of a length of an eight.

These remarks suggest that the Henley course, even today, is not really a fair one. The statistics given in the table below seem to bear this out.

NUMBER OF RACES WON FROM EACH STATION, IN
THE GRAND, LADIES' PLATE, AND THAMES CUP

	Bucks	Centre [1]	Berks
Old Course 1866–1885	21 + 45 = 66 =	42.3%	90 = 57.7%
New Course 1886–1905	189 =	59%	131 = 41%
Straight Course 1924–1955	702 =	53.3%	614 = 46.7%

The table shows that the Old Course, finishing near the bridge, conferred a great advantage on the Berkshire station. The New

[1] On the Old Course, when only two crews raced, the Centre Station was not used. In demonstrating the Berks advantage, these statistics therefore compare Berkshire wins with wins from either Bucks or Centre, since crews on either of these stations had to row outside the Berkshire crew at Poplar Point.

Course, adopted in 1886, shifted this advantage to the Bucks station, making it even more emphatic than before. And the modern Straight Course still gives a decided, though now much less excessive, advantage, to Bucks.

Perhaps a final word on this subject is necessary. The statistics from year to year differ very considerably. In the slow years, and in particular when the Bushes Wind is misbehaving, the advantage to Bucks is very noticeable. On particular days there can be a high proportion of Bucks wins. In the fast years, and the drought years, Berks fares better. The overall advantage to Bucks probably reflects the fact that slow years outnumber the fast years. In the ten years 1946–55 there have been 494 races in the three events covered by the table. It may sound too good to be true, and is certainly too good to risk a recount, but it seems that Berks and Bucks have each won 247 of these races.

This may seem to be a remarkable contradiction, both of the statistics given in the table, and of the reasoned arguments made in favour of Bucks. Yet it probably reflects the opinion of the average Henley oarsman, that although, in theory, he should watch the draw for stations, and the conditions on the course, with some concern, in fact he rarely does so. Some prefer Bucks, some, and among them the author of this book, prefer Berks; but very few consider that their chances of success are decided at the draw.

In conclusion, it is just possible that the dredging, carried out during 1955, may have had some effect on the stations, probably tending to help Berks. Furthermore, the Stewards now own the land on the Bucks shore, where grow the famous 'bushes', which are now mostly trees. Judicious thinning may here still further reduce the Bucks advantage.

CHAPTER THREE

Early Days. 1839–50

TODAY it is hard to think of Henley Regatta as anything but a rowing occasion, organized by rowing men, and for rowing men. Yet it was not so when the idea first germinated in 1839.

We do not, and probably never shall know for certain, whence the proposal to hold a regatta first came. It could have originated in the Mayor's parlour, or over a shop counter. It might have come from one of the great houses of the district. But perhaps it is most likely to have been inspired by a summer evening's stroll in the Lion Meadow, or down the towing-path towards Remenham, beside that stretch of water which was destined to become one of the most famous in the world.

This much we do know. On 26 March 1839 a public meeting was called in the Town Hall, and to it flocked 'the landed gentry of the neighbourhood and the principal townspeople'. And it is at least highly probable that it was James Nash who brought the meeting together, that it was he who persuaded the 'gentry' to attend, and he who consulted the London clubs about the requirements for a rowing match.

To W. P. Williams-Freeman, seconded by Captain E. Gardiner, fell the honour of proposing the first resolution: 'That from the lively interest which has been manifested at the various boat races which have taken place on the Henley reach during the last few years, and the great influx of visitors on such occasions, this meeting is of the opinion that the establishing of an annual Regatta, under judicious and respectable management, would not only be productive of the most beneficial results to the town of Henley, but from its peculiar attractions would also be a source of amusement and gratification to the neighbourhood, and the public in general'.

Are we, perhaps, already on the scent of a minor mystery? What were these boat races which had already excited 'a lively interest'? We know, for certain, of only three, spread over a period of ten years. Of these, two are well documented. The first was the original Oxford and Cambridge Boat Race,[1] held over a course from Hambleden lock to Henley bridge in 1829. Eight years later, in 1837, Oxford having declined a challenge from Cambridge, the Lady Margaret B.C., as head boat on the Cam, sent a crew to race against their opposite number, the Queen's College Oxford. The two colleges met on 3 June, over a distance of two and a half miles, starting 'rather more than a mile below the Island'. J. F. Bateman, of St. John's College Cambridge, wrote[2]: '. . . about 3 o'clock . . . the two boats took up their positions in front of a rope stretched across the river. The Queen's men soon began to draw ahead, and eventually won by six or eight lengths, covering the distance in 13 minutes. . . .'

The third of these early races at Henley seems to have been forgotten,[3] and lost to history for more than fifty years. In 1882 W. B. Woodgate was talking to George West, the Oxford waterman, when West remarked that he had once steered the University eight in a race. Thus was the forgotten race revealed. It was a challenge match for £200 a side between Oxford and Leander, and it took place in June 1831.

The only account of this race appeared in *Bell's Life* on 26 June 1831. There is no record of the start, but Oxford won the toss, and chose the Berkshire station. However, Leander gained a length in the first dozen strokes, and soon led by two lengths.

---

[1] *The Oxford and Cambridge Boat Race*, by R. D. Burnell (Oxford University Press) pp. 25–9.

[2] *Aquatic Notes*, by a Member of the C.U.B.C. (J. Deighton and G. Bell, 1852).

[3] The strange thing was that in 1879 there was a Jubilee Dinner, to celebrate the fiftieth anniversary of the first University Boat Race, and although requests were received from dozens of oarsmen, who had rowed for one or other University, yet were not Blues, not having competed in an official Boat Race, yet no member of the 1831 Oxford crew applied.

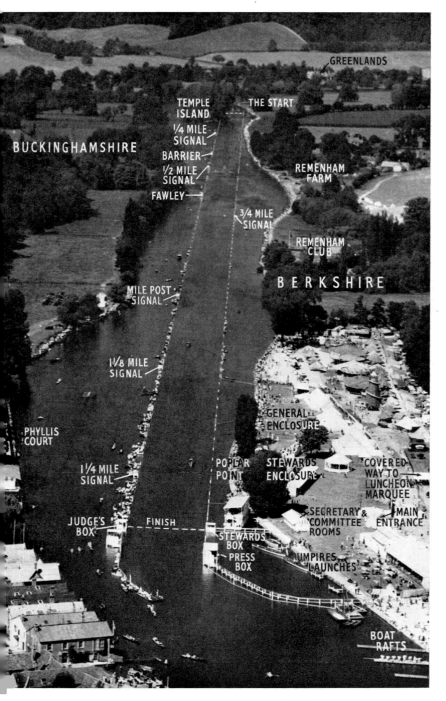

I. THE COURSE FROM THE AIR

Over the second half of the course the Oxford men pressed so hard that Noulton, the Leander steerer, shouted that if the Londoners did not 'give it her' it would be all over with them. Thus exhorted, Leander got home by two lengths, in 11 min. 15 sec. One of their crew nearly fainted, and another had to retire immediately to bed. However, a few days later they were able to row their boat back to London, where they were greeted with cheering and cannon, and, at Searle's Boatyard, by a *feu de joie*.

It is not impossible that there were other contests, of which no record remains. But it seems probable that it was these three, which had brought 'the world' to Henley, which were the spur to those who saw the possibilities of a regatta. It was to attract similar crews that the Grand Challenge Cup was put up for competition. At the same time, it is highly probable that there had been other races on the Henley reach, of a more local character. It is much more likely that the Town Challenge Cup was created for crews—such as the *Wave*, the *Albion*, and the *Dreadnought*—which already existed, than that these crews were formed only after the cup had been offered.

Whatever their justification for believing in the public interest in boat racing, Williams-Freeman and Gardiner were assuredly right in urging the benefits which would accrue to the town from sponsoring a full-scale regatta. Indeed, neither they, nor any of those who entered the Town Hall on that March day, could have foreseen the full harvest which their resolution was to bring in— a harvest which would carry the fame of their town to the four corners of the world, and bring them visitors from California and Moscow, and from Norway and New Zealand, and make the name of Henley synonymous with boat racing throughout the globe.

At the same meeting, further resolutions were passed:

(2) That a subscription be forthwith entered into for the purchase of two cups (or pieces of plate) . . . the one to be rowed for by Henley amateur crews in four-oared boats . . . the other to be rowed for by amateur crews in eight-oared boats . . . open to all challengers, and rowed for annually on the same reach . . . .

(3) That Thomas Stonor Esq., Wm. P. Williams-Freeman Esq., Wm. Fuller-Maitland Esq., Charles Lane Esq., Edmund Gardiner Esq., and the Mayor of Henley for the time being, three of whom shall be a quorum, be appointed perpetual Stewards for the regulation of the Regatta. . . .

(4) That a Committee of fourteen persons (five of whom to be a quorum) be appointed to assist the Stewards. . . .

Significantly the meeting closed with a vote of thanks to Mr. Stonor for taking the chair, and 'to Mr. Nash, for his exertions in promoting the success of the undertaking'.

1839

During the past week [reported the *Herald*] great preparations had been made in the Town of Henley, for the reception of the company expected to be present at the Regatta; but, unfortunately, after a fine week, on Thursday night a storm arose and for some time the rain poured in torrents, amidst the most terrific thunder and lightning. The chimney of Mr. Cooper's Assembly Rooms in Bell Street was struck by the electric fluid and fell . . . several people were knocked down by the fluid in various parts of the Town, but happily none . . . sustained any serious injury . . .

Every possible care was taken by the Committee to provide against accidents. Drags and other apparatus were procured from the Humane Society in London . . . but we are happy to say were not wanted.

At 11 o'clock the Stewards and Captains of the different boats attended at the Town Hall, and tossed for the choice of places, the [Berks] . . . being considered the most advantageous. . . . For three hours the two Cups, although in an unfinished state, were shown to the public in the Town Hall: The Challenge Cup weighs nine pounds. . . .

About 11 o'clock the Leander Club arrived from London, drenched in rain. They rowed the distance each heat with the racing boats, in good style. . . . About 3 o'clock the weather cleared in a slight degree, and the Spectators to the amount of 9,000 or 10,000 assembled on the Bridge, and on either bank of the river, also in stands which had been erected. . . . The bells of the Parish Church were ringing the best portion of the day, and cannon fired at intervals, and two bands of music on the water playing popular airs alternately.

The course was from just above Temple Island to the bridge, and there were four entries for the principal race. At 4 o'clock the Oxford Etonian Club, dressed in white guernseys with pale blue facings and rosettes of sky blue, defeated an even more resplendent Brasenose crew, which sported blue striped jerseys, blue caps with gold tassels, and rosettes of yellow, purple, and crimson. They were followed immediately, by Trinity College Cambridge, soberly attired in blue striped guernseys with French blue rosettes, who beat Wadham, whose colours were white guernseys with narrow blue stripes, dark blue caps with light blue velvet bands, and light blue scarves. Wadham gave Trinity a hard race to Phyllis Court, but, being on the Bucks station, could not hold them round the outside of the bend at Poplar Point, and lost by a little over a length.

At 5 o'clock there was a special match for the London watermen, which was not part of the Regatta, for a purse subscribed by members of Leander. They raced from Henley bridge, round the island and back, and the winners were H. Campbell and J. Phelps.

At 6 o'clock the Town Challenge Cup was hotly contested by three local crews, the *Wave* defeating the *Albion* and the *Dreadnought* after a good race. And at 7 o'clock came the final of the Grand. 'Each crew led alternately to the Point', wrote H. T. Steward, 'and eventually Trinity College won by half a length'. They again had the advantage of the Berkshire station.

1840

The following year the Regatta was held a fortnight later, and occupied two days, or rather two afternoons. Before the Regatta it was rumoured that the Oxford college authorities had forbidden their undergraduates to compete. But it transpired that the veto lay only on their using the names of the colleges, and the various crews duly entered under assumed names. These were the names borne by the boats in which they rowed, and many are still familiar. The *Child of Hale* (Brasenose College Oxford), the *Black Prince* (First Trinity B.C. Cambridge), the *John Crosse*

(University College Oxford), and other names are still carried
by the college boats today.

Bell's Life records that 'the kindness of the Thames Com-
missioners in directing the pound locks to be closed ... that
barges might not interrupt the racing ... was duly appreciated'.

The course was moved a little downstream, starting opposite
the Temple, and finishing short of the bridge. This was a safer
arrangement than in 1839, when the boats had to shoot the bridge
in finishing.

Mr. J. D. Bishop umpired, as he had in 1839, but this time from
a cutter manned by London watermen, whereas in the previous
year he had ridden a horse. Watermen continued to perform this
task until replaced by a steam launch in 1869. They must have
had a strenuous time, for in addition to following all the races,
there was generally a purse subscribed for a watermen's race,
sometimes in fours, and sometimes in wager boats or wherries.

Six crews entered for the Grand Challenge Cup, which was
won easily by Leander. An additional race was included in the
programme, 'it having been intimated that a wish had been
expressed by the Neighbouring Towns to join in the amusements
of the day'. It was called the District Challenge Cup, and was
open to crews from Maidenhead, Marlow, Reading, Wallingford, and Henley. Reading and Maidenhead competed, but there
was an all-Henley final, the *Dreadnought* winning both this and
the Town Challenge Cup.

1841–2

The next year, 1841, saw the institution of what was to become
one of Henley's most important races, and the blue riband of
four-oared rowing. The Stewards' Challenge Cup was offered
under the same qualification as the Grand; but in this year the
cup was not ready, and medals only were given. The race was
won by the *The Midge*, Oxford Club, London.

Taking advantage of the broadened qualifications, the Cambridge Subscription Rooms entered for the Grand, beating
Leander on a foul in the final. The *Dreadnought* rowed over in

both the Town and District Challenge Cups, and as a result, in 1842, the qualifications for the District Challenge Cup were altered to include the towns of Windsor and Oxford, 'whose members shall not be resident members of the University . . .'.

For the first time, both Oxford and Cambridge entered representative University crews for the Grand, but an unhappy dispute led to Oxford's withdrawal.

They drew the Cambridge University crew in the challenge heat, and then learned that, if beaten, Cambridge proposed to draft several of their men into their Subscription Rooms crew, which, as holders, did not have to race until the final. The Oxford president inquired whether this would be permitted, and the Stewards adjudicated that there was nothing in the existing Rules to prevent it. In fact, Cambridge won through to the final, beating King's College London and the Oxford Aquatic Club in the heats. In the final they raced against their own Subscription Rooms, so that the question of substitutes did not arise. But T. S. Egan coxed the University crew in the heats and the Subscription Rooms in the final.

The University crew lost by feet, but the Subscription Rooms were nearly beaten, too. *Bell's Life* recalls that '. . . the Umpire's admirable crew of watermen (assisted by a well-known member of the Leander Club), who had hitherto been rowing in the rear, on coming round the corner on the Berkshire shore on the outside of the competing boats attempted to get on level terms with them, so that on approaching the Stewards' stand all three boats were stem and stem. The shouting was deafening—the shrieks of exhausted runners—the clearer words of encouragement from the fixed spectators—the guns—the bells—the hoarse voices of the three coxswains exciting on with a last gasp their various crews.'

1843

Consequent upon the dispute about substitutions, the Stewards met in the autumn of 1842, and made various small amendments to the Rules, of which the most important was:

That no member of a club shall be allowed to be substituted for another who has already rowed a heat, nor shall any member of a club be allowed to row with more than one crew in any of the races for the same cup.

Although consistent with later practice in most amateur sports in this country, this was an uncompromising rule, of which we shall have more to say later. As fate would have it, it was to be dramatically invoked in its first year of operation.

The Cambridge Subscription Rooms had now won the Grand twice in succession, and were naturally desirous of completing the 'hat trick', thus early in the Regatta's history. They were able to produce a crew, all of whom were, or were to become, Blues. But in spite of this it seems that they were not well together.

Oxford again entered their University crew, which won through to the final quite easily, there to meet the Cambridge Subscription Rooms. But all was not well. F. N. Menzies, captain and stroke of the Oxford crew, was suffering from a fever. Nor was his treatment for it such as would commend itself to the medical profession. On the Wednesday evening he personally drove his crew over, the twenty-two-odd miles from Oxford, by coach, and then rowed over the course in 8 min. 29 sec., which, incidentally, was faster than any time hitherto recorded in the Grand.

On the Thursday Menzies won two races, though obviously unwell. On Friday he was reported better, though still feeling sick and faint. But when he came down to embark for the final, he fainted.

Consternation filled the Oxford camp. A deputation asked permission to replace Menzies with a substitute, but this was not permitted because of the new rule. Oxford then asked for a postponement, and were given an hour's grace.

In the meantime Menzies was carried to the Red Lion and put to bed, not without protest it seems, according to a verse written by Tom Hughes, brother of a member of one of the crew:

> Within a darkened chamber,
> Wrapped in his tartan plaid,

Fevered in mind and body,
  Our captain brave is laid.
To keep him from the river
  They've ranged stout waiters four,
And they've barred the windows firmly,
  And firmly locked the door.

Having thus safely disposed of their captain, Oxford then moved their number seven to stroke, and their bow to seven, and announced their intention of racing with seven men. Against this Cambridge protested, but Lord Camoys, for the Stewards, declared that there was nothing in the Rules to prevent them so doing.

This, the celebrated 'Seven-Oar Race', has persistently enjoyed the best of two worlds, creeping, or rather bursting into both Boat Race and Henley history. But it was not a University Boat Race, because the Cambridge Subscription Rooms were not a representative University crew, and Henley is its proper home.

There is not much to say of the race itself. Oxford had the Bucks station, which was fortunate on the day, since there was a Bushes Wind blowing. At Remenham the crews were level, and then, in the sheltered water, Oxford began to forge ahead. At the notorious Poplar Point they had sufficient lead to cross over to the Berkshire side, and they went on to win by nearly two lengths. In *Henley Records* H. T. Steward recorded the verdict as 'nearly a length', but other authorities agree that there was nearly a length of daylight between the boats.

Oxford's supporters went mad with excitement, and, amongst other exploits, stormed the toll gate on Henley bridge, and threw it bodily into the river.

1844

The year 1844 is important in Henley annals for the institution of the Diamond Sculls, which were to become the best-known sculling trophy in the world. *Bell's Life* described the prize thus:

At the top of a long gold pin are a pair of well-executed sculls crossed, and from these are suspended a valuable drop diamond. On the guard pin, attached to the other by a neat gold chain, are green stones representative of a wreath of laurel.

There were ten entries for the Diamonds, and nine starters, ample proof of the demand for a scullers' race. In the final, T. B. Bumpsted, of the London Amateur Scullers Club, won a good race by a bare length.

For some reason the Grand entry dropped to two, the Oxford Etonian Club beating Caius College Cambridge by three lengths.

1845

In 1845, trying to widen the appeal of the Regatta, the Stewards introduced two new events. The first of these was a challenge prize for eight-oared boats, which it was originally intended to call the 'College Cup'. It was bought by public subscription, but was not ready in 1845, medals only being given. There is no clue as to why, in 1846, it was named the Ladies' Challenge Plate.

The second new race was for the Silver Wherries, which *Bell's Life* described as 'perfect gems of their kind, being about nine inches long . . . and made from one of Searle's models of pair-oared racing boats'. The Wherries were presentation prizes, and were won by J. Mann and F. H. Arnold, of Caius College Cambridge.

For the first time the Grand produced a straight fight between the two Universities, there being no other competitors. Cambridge won by more than two lengths. In the Diamonds, J. W. Conant, of St. John's College Oxford, appeared in an outrigged boat, the first to be used at Henley. The outrigger, which was probably the most important single innovation[1] in the history of racing-boat design, is ascribed to Henry Clasper, who had thus rigged a four in 1844.

'In a few strokes', reported *Bell's Life*, 'Mr. Conant led by over a length, showing in an extraordinary manner the superiority of the outrigging boat over others, for such an advantage could not

[1] *Swing Together*, by R. D. Burnell (Oxford University Press), Ch. I.

be accounted for in any other way. Mr. Bumpsted fairly turned round on his thwart to see what had become of Mr. Conant. . .'.

But the advantage was not enough to see him through the final, in which he finished last.

The outstanding race of the year was the final of the Stewards' Challenge Cup, between Oxford University and St. George's Club, London. At Fawley, St. George's led by less than a canvas, and at the Point the crews were level. St. George's had the advantage of the station, but rowing stroke for stroke they could only gain a few feet, and in the last few yards the Dark Blues came back to them. 'A Mr. Forest', as H. T. Steward charmingly puts it, 'about whose appointment [as judge] there seems to have been some informality, declared the race a dead heat. Mr. Bishop, the Umpire, however, stated he was certain the Oxford crew had won, and the race was awarded to the Oxford crew'. George Treherne, the Boat Race historian, states that no judge at all was on duty, and that it was possible to give a decision only because Arthur Shadwell—the Oxford coach [*Honi soit*]—'seeing the race . . . to be a very close thing, ran in front of the boats, and, by covering both posts with his eye, was able to discern that Oxford passed the goal first . . .'.

After this, says Treherne,[1] there was always a judge nominated by the Committee. But of what St. George's said there is no record!

1846

In 1846 another local race was added, this time a Silver Wherry for Henley Amateur Scullers. The Thames Club, no relation[2] to the Thames Rowing Club of modern times, broke the university monopoly of the Grand, which had only once previously been won by a Metropolitan club, and that by Leander in 1840. It is interesting to note that, being on the Berks station, the Thames Club beat First Trinity by more than three lengths. In the Ladies' Plate, on the Centre station, they lost to the same Trinity crew by a quarter of a length.

[1] In fact, Judges were not officially appointed until 1847.   [2] See p. 283.

In the Stewards' there was a dead heat, but the local Dread-nought Club declared that they had won, and refused to row again. Consequently the race was awarded to Guy's Club, who, however, were easily defeated by Oxford in the final.

1847

Eighteen-forty-seven was a busy year. A new challenge cup was presented by Mr. Donkin, of Wyfold Court. The Stewards allotted it to the winners of the trial heats for the Grand, and named it the Wyfold Challenge Cup. H. T. Steward records that it was 'so given each year until 1855, when it was made a challenge prize for a four-oared race'. It was not a very satisfactory arrrange-ment, because only in the first year was there a 'trial race'—that is to say, a heat—to be won. A word of explanation is perhaps necessary. The Grand, and, indeed, all the Henley events, were then truly 'challenge races'. The 'winner' became the 'holder', and was required to defend his title only once. If there were more than two 'challengers'—and therefore more crews than could be accommodated in a single race—trial heats were held to eliminate the surplus challengers.

The Thames Club desired to enter for both the Ladies' Plate and the Grand Challenge Cup, but the Stewards ruled that they were ineligible for the junior event. Their reasoning is obscure, since the Thames Club had been accepted for both events in the previous year, and Royal Chester were to enter for, and win, both events ten years later. In the following year the qualification of the Ladies' Plate was elaborated, so that it still included clubs, but expressly debarred those within a seven-mile radius of Westminster Bridge.

St. George's Club intended to enter for the Stewards', but failed to do so in time, and Worcester College Oxford entered but withdrew, leaving Christ Church to row over. There was only one entry for the Town Challenge Cup, and, for the second year in succession, none at all for the District Challenge Cup. Thus there would have been no four-oared race at the Regatta at all, and the Stewards, at the last moment, decided to offer a

special prize for any amateur four-oar, to be called the Visitors'
Challenge Cup. For this purpose they allocated the District
Challenge Cup trophy. St. George's were thus able to compete,
and were narrowly defeated by Christ Church.

It was a good year for Oxford, for besides the University crew
winning the Grand, Brasenose took the Ladies' Plate, and Christ
Church both the Stewards' and Visitors' Challenge Cups. The
following year was as good, for the University again won the
Grand, whilst Christ Church carried off the Ladies' Plate,
Stewards', and Visitors.

<h2 style="text-align:center">1848–50</h2>

There can scarcely have been a race worth watching in 1848,
except the Ladies' Plate, in which Christ Church had to work
very hard, round the outside of Poplar Point, to keep ahead of
Worcester. In both the Stewards' and Visitors' they rowed over
without opposition.

Eighteen-forty-nine was another lean year, but with a little
excitement provided by the rivalry between Second Trinity B.C.
Cambridge and Wadham. In the Grand, Trinity just got home
first, on the Berks station, after a level race all the way; but there
had been a slight foul, and the umpire gave the verdict to Wadham. In the Ladies' Plate, Wadham had the station, and won by a
third of a length. These two races took place, one on each day of
the Regatta, at nearly 8 o'clock in the evening, because the Oxford men were not allowed away until 4 p.m. Since they had
twenty-two miles to cover by coach, they cannot have wasted
much time.

The lowest ebb since the start of the Regatta, or for many
years to come, was reached in 1850. As usual, the Regatta was
advertised for two days, but with only fifteen entries, of which
five were for the restricted local events, it occupied only one.
Oxford University rowed over in the Grand and Stewards', and
Lincoln College Oxford rowed over in the Ladies' Plate. There
was not a single Cambridge crew, nor even a club one, except in
the Town Cup.

Nevertheless 1850 was not without some importance, for the
Stewards adopted the new Laws of Boat Racing, which had been
codified by the two Universities and the principal Metropolitan
clubs in the previous year. These rules were substantially the
same as those in force today, with the important exception, already mentioned, that if a crew took its opponent's water it
thereby became entitled to keep that water.

Another change in 1850 was that, in response to the requests of
the competitors, the Stewards agreed to give presentation cups
for the pair-oar and sculls winners. The Diamond scarf-pin was
superseded by the beautiful pineapple goblet we know today—
surely the most handsome individual prize given annually for any
sporting event—and the present Diamond Sculls were added as
a challenge trophy. The model silver wherries were replaced by
the silver goblets, and the name of this event was changed from
the Silver Wherries to the Silver Goblets.

CHAPTER FOUR

The Royal Regatta. 1851–86

HENLEY REGATTA was still young in 1851, but with a dozen Regattas behind them the Stewards must have felt that they were suffering their full share of headaches.

Above all, it is the eight-oared rowing which must be the backbone of a successful regatta. And the fact was that fewer eights had started in the second than in the first five years of the Regatta, and the initial impetus seemed to be running down. Oxford and Cambridge continued to give their support, probably to the fullest extent of which they were capable, in an era of difficult transport, and with Henley taking place, very often, in the middle of June. But they could only average three or four eights between them, and the clubs seemed to have faded away after the first few years. Only the introduction of the Diamonds and Goblets had helped to swell the programme.

But the primary object of the Regatta must not be forgotten. It was certainly remembered by the townspeople of Henley, who, in July 1849, presented the following address to the Stewards:

We the undersigned tradesmen, and inhabitants of Henley, respectfully avail ourselves of this mode of tendering our best thanks to the Patron and Stewards of Henley Grand Regatta, for their kind, and unceasing exertions during the last Ten Years, in promoting the interests of our town by the establishment and continuance of its Regatta, which from its superior attractions has introduced the Town of Henley to the notice of thousands, and causes so great an influx of visitors during a considerable portion of the year, which may in a degree compensate for the injury the trade of the town has sustained from various causes, and we earnestly hope that the Patron and

Stewards will not cease to give it their countenance and support, affording as it unquestionably does, amusement to many, and benefit either directly or indirectly to the tradespeople of our town generally.

Perhaps some, scanning the entry lists of the past few years, had begun to wonder whether it was all worth while. Here, from the town, came the answer in no uncertain terms.

In 1851, the year of the Great Exhibition, there was still an uphill battle to fight. But the next twenty-five years were to see a remarkable advance.

On the rowing side there was the introduction of the Thames Challenge Cup, the Wyfold Cup given to a four-oared race, and all three four-oared events made over to coxswainless boats; sliding seats, and therefore, to all intents, the modern racing boats we know today, were to follow, and the first school entries, and, later still, the first foreign entries.

On what might be called the administrative side there comes the erection of the Regatta's first permanent building, the definition of the Amateur Status, the formation of the Committee of Management, and the drafting of a new Constitution. The Rules, too, are to be redrafted, and the finish moved down to Poplar Point; and the entries are to rise at an increasing tempo, from an average of 17 in the first ten years, to 21 in the second, 31 in the third, and 42 in the fourth decade.

What could be more appropriate and symbolic of the growing up of the Regatta, than that H.R.H. Prince Albert, in the year of his great Exhibition, should consent to become the Patron of, from henceforth, Henley Royal Regatta?

1851

No doubt because of the advertised visit of Prince Albert, the entries were more numerous in 1851, and the racing was therefore better than in the previous year.

Even so, the Grand Challenge Cup produced only one race, a straight contest between the University crews of Oxford and

Cambridge. Oxford won by six feet, the Cambridge No. 3 having broken his rowlock soon after the start.[1]

Christ Church were in trouble with their College authorities, who would not sanction their entry. They therefore entered for the Ladies' Plate as the 'Westminster and Eton Club', and under assumed names. The Press, however, discovered their true identity, and did them the disservice of reporting them correctly, as the result of which they had to interview the Dean, and, apparently, 'lost a term'. They also lost the race, to Brasenose. Fearing the same fate, but perhaps concluding that they might as well be hung for goats as for sheep, C. L. Vaughan, of Oriel, and J. E. Clarke, of Wadham, entered for the Goblets as 'Messrs Hawkins and Symonds'—the names of the heads of their respective colleges! H. B. Arnaud and H. B. H. Blundell, less provocative, entered for the Diamonds as Mr. Box and Mr. Cox.

1852

In 1852 there was a revision of the Rules, but the competition was again disappointing. Indeed, there were no challengers at all for the Grand. Oxford therefore agreed to enter two crews, the winners to be recorded as the Oxford University B.C., so that they should remain holders, and the losing crew to be recorded as the Oxford Aquatic Club. All the main events went to Oxford, except for the Visitors', in which the Argonaut Club beat Christ Church, and the Diamonds, which were won by E. Macnaghten, of the First Trinity B.C. Cambridge.

1853

Next year the tally of entries was down to twenty, but the competition and honours were more evenly distributed. Cambridge had challenged Oxford to a summer Boat Race, but Oxford suggested that they should meet at Henley, 'which having already shown symptoms of decline, it was desirable by all means

---

[1] Fuller accounts of this and other Henley races between the two Universities can be found in *The Oxford and Cambridge Boat Race* by R. D. Burnell (Oxford University Press).

KEY TO SOME OF THOSE SHOWN IN THE PICTURE OPPOSITE

A, the Radley VIII; B, the Eton VIII: C. W. Graham (bow), W. E. Crum, E. R. Warre, J. A. Morrison, R. O. Kerrison, C. M. Pitman, C. E. Corkran, M. C. Pilkington (str.), M. Barne (cox). 1, J. C. Hawkshaw; 2, R. A. Kinglake; 3, D. H. Maclean; 4, A. D. Flower; 5, R. C. Lehmann; 6, F. I. Pitman; 7, C. Gurdon; 8, T. E. Hockin; 9, Herbert Rhodes; 10, H. T. Steward; 11, C. T. Steward; 12, H. A. Steward; 13, J. H. D. Goldie; 14, Frank Willan; 15, R. H. Lebat; 16, J. C. Tinné; 17, Rev. J. C. Gardner; 18, F. H. Maugham; 19, R. S. de Havilland; 20, Rev. S. A. Donaldson; 21, G. D. Rowe; 22, C. W. Kent; 23, W. B. Woodgate; 24, S. D. Muttlebury; 25 [...] 26, A. D. Heywood Lonsdale; 27, R. P. P. Rowe; 28, J. P. Heywood Lonsdale; 29, J. A. Ford; 30, W. A. L. Fletcher;

III. TEMPLE ISLAND
The Leander Enclosure in 1891

IV. THE SILVER GOBLETS

Top: Vivian and Guy Nickalls, three times winners. (Between 1890 and 1897 Vivian won
event five times, Guy six times)

Bottom: W. G. R. M. Laurie and J. H. T. Wilson win easily (1938): one of the finest pair
modern times

to endeavour to preserve'. A wonderful race resulted. Oxford
were lucky to win the toss and chose the Berks station, for
there was a north-east breeze blowing, so that Bucks had no
advantage from the Bushes. Cambridge gained very slightly and
led by a canvas at the Point, but then, with the inside station to
help, Oxford gradually overhauled them, to win, on the post, by
only eighteen inches.This was the fourth consecutive victory
of the O.U.B.C. in the Grand Challenge Cup, a feat which has
never been bettered, and only twice equalled, by Leander Club,
in 1891–6, and again in 1898–1901.

1854

No university crew entered in 1854, and First Trinity beat
Wadham in both the Grand and Ladies' Plate, the latter in spite
of a crab which nearly lost them the race. The Stewards' and
Visitors' were fought out between Pembroke College Oxford
and the Lady Margaret B.C. Cambridge, the former winning the
Stewards', and the latter the Visitors'. The Diamonds were won
by H. H. Playford, perhaps the first of the great club oarsmen at
Henley. In the next year he was beaten by A. A. Casamajor, who,
at least as a sculler, was his master.

1855

Casamajor also won the Goblets in 1855, and at his first
appearance *Bell's Life* reported:
'A capital race between Messrs Casamajor and (J.) Nottidge
and Messrs (W. F.) Short and (E.) Cadogan for half a mile, when
the great strength, and powerful rowing of Mr. Casamajor began
to tell, and he appeared to be lugging both his boat and his
partner along; indeed, he must have had a skegg on his sternpost,
or Mr. Nottidge never could have kept the steerage against such
continuous hard rowing. In the end they won as they liked.'
Next year he won the Stewards', Wyfold Cup, Goblets, and
Diamonds, and in 1857 the Grand, Stewards', and Diamonds.
In 1858 he held all three, and added the Goblets. And in his last
three years he won, respectively, the Grand, Goblets, and

Diamonds. In all, he won twelve out of twenty-four Henley races, and sixteen out of twenty-one events. He died within a few weeks of his last Henley victory.

The Grand was once again an inter-University race, this time with Cambridge as fairly easy winners. And Royal Chester successfully brought off the first invasion from the provinces, winning both the Stewards' and Wyfold Challenge Cups, which this year became a race for fours for the first time.

1856

Chester returned in 1856, on the 'crest of the wave', as will sometimes happen with a relatively small club. With them they brought the first keelless eight, built by Matt Taylor of Newcastle. It is said that they could not sit her, rolled prodigiously, and were the laughing-stock of Henley. If so, the last laugh was theirs, for they took home the Grand Challenge Cup and the Ladies' Plate, were runners-up in the Visitors' and Wyfold Cups, and withdrew from the final of the Stewards'!

1857

Eighteen-fifty-seven was an eventful year in the history of Henley Regatta. In the first place, and presumably in consequence of Royal Chester having won the Grand and the Ladies' Plate in the previous year, the qualification for the Ladies' was altered, so as to limit the entries to the clubs of colleges of the Universities of Oxford and Cambridge, and the schools of Eton and Westminster.

The qualification for the Visitors' Challenge Cup followed suit. And the Wyfold Challenge Cup, having been won, in its first two years as a four-oared event, by the winners of the Stewards' on both occasions, was closed to any oarsman who had competed or was competing, for the Stewards'. Also the practice of tossing for stations was abolished in favour of a draw.

Another important event, though not directly connected with the rowing, was the opening of the Great Western Railway branch line from Twyford, which, of course, made Henley more accessible. The first plan for a railway to serve Henley had been put forward as early as 1833, with a proposal for a Tring, Reading, and Basingstoke line, which would have run parallel to the Fair Mile. Happily, it came to nothing. The railway has been a great asset to the town and to the Regatta, but on that occasion, as well as in 1896, it might well have been otherwise. In 1896 it was seriously canvassed that a loop line should be built, linking Marlow and Henley. This would have involved three iron-girder bridges, numerous embankments and viaducts, and finally a high embankment up the Henley valley.

It is right, too, to record as an important event the fact that London R.C. first entered for—and won—the Grand Challenge Cup in 1857. Founded in 1856, they had not been in time to compete in the previous Regatta, though their members, rowing as the Argonaut Club, had won the Stewards', Wyfold Cup, Goblets, and Diamonds. London have never failed to enter a crew for the Grand Challenge Cup since 1857, a record which is unique, though they have been surpassed by Leander in the number of Grand wins.[1]

There is not much else to report of 1857, save that the Oxford crews again did well. Exeter beat Pembroke Oxford in the Ladies' Plate, and Pembroke beat L.M.B.C. in the Visitors' and London in the Wyfold Challenge Cup.

1858

In 1858 the entries dropped to fifteen, largely because only two pairs entered for the Goblets, which were won by Messrs. Playford and Casamajor, and because no one thought it worth while challenging Casamajor in the Diamonds. The race for local scullers was discontinued in favour of a District Pairs race.

Cambridge won the Grand for the third and last time. They had to work hard, for in the heat Leander led them for half the distance, whilst in the final London R.C. were three-quarters of a

---

[1] Leander 27, London 16, Thames 8, O.U.B.C. 7, Trinity College Cambridge (1st)—4, (3rd)—1, Magdalen College, Oxford, 4. See Appendix B, p. 278 for notes about the leading clubs.

length up at Remenham, and clear, though on the Bucks station, at Poplar Point. They tried and failed to cross over into Cambridge's water, and in a great finishing spurt the Light Blues got home by just under half a length.

1859

Eighteen-fifty-nine was the last occasion on which a University crew from Oxford or Cambridge competed at Henley. There is little to report of the rest of the racing, save that Third Trinity had a neck-and-neck struggle with London in the Stewards', eventually winning by 'something under two feet'. But in the Grand, London R.C. beat Oxford in a heat, by two-thirds of a length, after rowing level all the way to the Point. In the final, with the Bucks station, they were able to take Cambridge's water above Remenham, and eventually won by three-quarters of a length.

It is said that the two Universities took this double defeat to heart, and concluded that it would be better to leave their honour in the hands of the college boat clubs for the future. The point was, of course, that these 'University' crews were, generally speaking, got together only at the end of the summer bumping races. Although they sometimes comprised a complete University crew of the preceding, or succeeding, Boat Race, they were nevertheless scratch affairs at Henley.

On occasions Leander Club have put on a crew which was, in effect, or very nearly, a complete Oxford or Cambridge crew. But since 1859 neither University has itself entered an official or representative eight. This withdrawal of the two leading Universities from regatta competition has had a profound effect, both on Henley, and on British rowing as a whole. For these two Universities, with large numbers of oarsmen in residence, or on call, throughout the year, have an unrivalled opportunity of producing first-class crews.

1860

There was 'a foul wind and a heavy stream' in 1860, and little to report of the racing, except that the First Trinity B.C. won the Grand, Ladies' Plate, Stewards', and Visitors'. But in considering some of these remarkable performances, in the early years of the Regatta, we must remember the weak state of the entries. On this occasion Trinity beat London, the only other contenders for the Grand. Four men from each of these crews were the only contenders for the Stewards', and in the Ladies' Plate and Visitors', First Trinity found no opponents at all. And so, by virtue of being better men than the Londoners, they carried off four major Henley trophies.

1861

In the following year First Trinity repeated their quadruple victory, against rather stiffer opposition.

There were four entries in the Grand, Trinity Oxford beating London and Kingston in the challenge heat, and losing to First Trinity in the final. In the Ladies', Trinity Oxford beat Eton and Radley in the heat, and again lost to First Trinity in the final. First Trinity also had to contest both the four-oar events. In the Stewards' they beat London, and in the Visitors', Christ Church, B.N.C. and Magdalen. First Trinity need have raced against only one of the Oxford colleges, but they were permitted to row both in the challenge heat, on the first day of the Regatta, so as to avoid having to row four races on the final day.

This was the first occasion on which Eton and Radley raced at Henley. Since then, Radley have scarcely missed a Regatta, and Eton never at all. Radley have come to be regarded as the David, gallantly tilting at the Eton Goliath. The two schools have met twenty-four times, and Eton still remain unbeaten, though they would be the first to admit that there have been some narrow shaves, and that they have been saved, on occasions, by the luck of the draw.

Eighteen-sixty-one was also the début of a great individual, perhaps the greatest Radleian to race at Henley. For W. B. Woodgate was in the Brasenose four, who were runners up in the Visitors', and won the Wyfold Challenge Cup; in partnership with W. Champneys, he also easily won the Silver Goblets.

1862

Woodgate's career is mentioned elsewhere. There is no doubt that he was responsible for the revival of Brasenose rowing, for in 1862 they proceeded to win both the Stewards' and Visitors'. This was the year in which Woodgate won three races on the first day of the Regatta, and covered the course five times on the second day, losing only the re-row of a dead heat with E. D. Brickwood, in the final of the Diamond Sculls. No wonder that *Bell's Life*, commenting on the final of the Goblets, which was the last race of the day, referred to the 'everlasting Woodgate', although it was only his second year at Henley.

There is little else to report of the 1862 Regatta, save that stake boats were introduced for the first time, and that the Regatta was 'threatened on the second day with the indignity of a canoe race, but the list not filling the misfortune was averted' (*Bell's Life*).

1863

Eighteen-sixty-three was a great year for Oxford rowing, University College winning the Grand Challenge Cup, Ladies' Plate, and Stewards', and withdrawing from the final of the Visitors', whilst Brasenose won the Visitors' and Goblets, and were runners-up in the Grand and Stewards'. Oxford successes at this time coincided with a run of nine successive Dark Blue victories in the University Boat Race, clear proof of the connection between Henley and Putney.

H. T. Steward records that 'In consequence of the large number of entries [there were thirty-one] it was suggested the Regatta should be extended to three days, but insuperable objections were found to the proposition, and it was abandoned. The racing started at the early hour of twelve-thirty'.

1864

The entries dropped sharply in 1864, the Visitors' and Wyfold Cup going by default to the only entrants, University College Oxford, and Kingston. Kingston also won the Grand for the first of two successive years. Mr. J. F. Cooper, in his recollections of thirty-seven years as Secretary of the Regatta, refers to Kingston as being a club distinctly '*sui generis*'—a law unto itself, for whose especial benefit, he suggests, the Stewards passed the rule that 'No one shall be allowed to row or steer for a club unless he has been a member of that club for at least two months preceding the Regatta'. For everyone understood that in May and early June the captain of Kingston would be on the look-out for 'young Varsity oarsmen whose colleges were not rowing at Henley'.

The first Kingston crew which won the Grand does not appear, on paper, to have been recruited in this way. But the 1865 crew, which gave Kingston their second win, must certainly have been so. For it included H. B. Middleton, from Magdalen, the great Woodgate, and R. W. Risley, from Exeter, these latter two also being Oxford Blues, whilst F. Willan, who was to gain that distinction later, and R. F. Wade, had been recruited direct from school—from Eton and Radley respectively.

This comment, of course, is offered in no unfriendly manner, for Kingston have always been favourites at Henley, and have certainly had no monopoly in recruiting ready-made oarsmen.

But it is a fact that, for consistent success, a club must teach its own novices to row, rather than rely on an annual intake of experts, and it is perhaps significant that Kingston have never again won the Grand, although they have been three times beaten in the final. By contrast, they won the Wyfold Cup fourteen times in forty years, including a run of six consecutive wins from 1863–8.

Eighteen-sixty-four was otherwise notable on two counts. The Regatta erected its first permanent building, a boathouse, just above the bridge. And Eton won the Ladies' Plate. This was the first win by a school crew at Henley. Only two other schools have ever won the Ladies' Plate, Shrewsbury twice, in 1924 and 1932, and Radley once, in 1938—against twenty-three wins by Eton. But the remarkable aspect of this achievement is the fact that, even amongst the colleges, First Trinity head the list with fourteen wins, and are followed by Jesus, with twelve wins.

Since Eton have been runners-up seventeen times, compared with Trinity's eleven and Jesus' four, this means that in a hundred years' racing for the Ladies' Plate, Eton have been in forty finals, which is only one less than the total of the two next most successful competitors added together.

1865

Kingston and Third Trinity shared the honours in 1865, with Kingston winning the Grand and Wyfold Cup, and Third Trinity the Ladies', Stewards', and Visitors'. In the Ladies' they had a hard race with Radley in the challenge heat, and won the final against Eton on the Umpire's decision, the school having fouled them no less than four times. In the Stewards' they had a tremendous race against Kingston, as far as Poplar Point, when, with the inside station, they got away to win by two lengths. In the final, against London, they had the outside station, and were a few feet down at the Point. Above the Point they managed to draw level; London got their bows in front again, but in the end Third Trinity got home by about two-thirds of a length.

1866

It seems that at this period the Rules for qualification and entry had become somewhat lax, and before the next Regatta there were protests against several competitors. Perhaps the Stewards felt that they were themselves to blame, having allowed similar occurrences to pass without redress in previous years. At any rate, they overruled the objections, but revised the Rules in the autumn, laying it down that no one should row for a club unless he had been a member for three months. There were other amendments, including a ruling against the use of assumed names, and entering twice for the same event.

This last was no doubt aimed at the irrepressible Woodgate, who, not content with entering for three events, entered himself twice for the Goblets, once under his own name in partnership with E. L. Corrie, and once, with M. M. Brown, under the alias of Wat Bradford.

Eighteen-sixty-six was an Oxford and Eton year if ever there was one, for the school won the Ladies' Plate, the Oxford Etonian Club won the Grand, and Christ Church won the Stewards' and Visitors' Challenge Cups. *The Field* recorded that 'out of twenty-eight medals (for eight- and four-oared races) . . . twenty-seven were won by Etonians'. For the Oxford Etonians, this was the first of five Grand victories in six years.

1867

In the following year the holders of all the main events retained their trophies. Once again there was a 'canoe chase', over land and water, open to the Canoe Club and to all Henley entrants. In spite of a prize of an exceedingly fine silver claret jug[1] there was little support for this attempt to 'popularize' the Regatta, and the venture was not subsequently repeated.

1868

Eighteen-sixty-eight, by contrast, was a year of importance, for it saw the inauguration of the Thames Challenge Cup, the last of the main events—with the exception of the Double Sculls, still seventy years in the future—which make up the Henley programme today.

In recent years there has been much controversy about the Thames Cup, chiefly arising from the fact that it has been won so often by crews from the United States,[2] and it may be interesting to see what was in the minds of those who first launched the event. The qualifications were drawn up by H. H. Playford, the Committee having suggested to the Stewards the establishment of an eight-oared race for 'crews not strong enough to contend with any chance of success for the Grand Challenge Cup'.

In the same year the race for the District Goblets was discontinued.

There had, for some time, been dissatisfaction with the Rules,

[1] The race was won by T. K. Rixon, and the claret jug is now the property of Leander Club.
[2] See 'Foreign Entries', p. 244.

or the lack of Rules, governing coxswains. The colleges considered it unfair that the schools, and some of the clubs, should
employ boys, who might weigh only a few stone, to steer them.
Their brief was perhaps weak so far as the schools were concerned,
but in principle it was right, for it is not desirable to have imma-
ture coxswains in important races. And there was a further cause
for complaint, in that, although oarsmen were not permitted to
row in the Grand and the Thames Cup, or in the Stewards' and
Wyfold Cups, there was no rule against coxswains steering in
both, nor, for the matter of that, against steering two different
crews in the same event.

Matters came to a head in 1868, when a boy named Weston
coxed the Oscillators Club and London R.C. in their respective
heats of the Stewards' Cup. Since both reached the final, and
neither would willingly forgo the services of a cox who weighed
only 4 st. 9 lb., something had to be done. With the consent of
University College Oxford, who were the third crew in the final,
the case was referred to the arbitration of H. T. Steward, the
captain of Leander, and he ruled that Weston should steer neither
crew.

Before the next Regatta all the qualifications and Rules were
overhauled, and from thenceforward there was a minimum weight
for coxswains, on a sliding scale according to the average weight
of the crews.

The great event of 1868, however, was the appearance of
Brasenose in a four without a coxswain. Woodgate was the
instigator, having seen, and been duly impressed by, a Canadian
four, from St. John's, New Brunswick, which, rowing in a coxswainless boat, had won two events at a regatta in Paris in the
previous summer. Brasenose therefore announced their intention
of contesting the Stewards' Cup in a similar boat.

A formal protest was made, and the Stewards announced:
'That no eight- or four-oared boat would be allowed at the ensuing Regatta without a coxswain, nor will any steering apparatus
be allowed in any other boat.'

Nothing daunted, Brasenose embarked a cox and declared that

he should jump overboard at the start. And so he did, to the delight of the spectators who had gathered to watch the fun. Brasenose came in first, and were disqualified.

The Oxford Etonians did not enter for the Grand this year, since five of their number were rowing for University College. They were beaten by Eton in a heat, and Eton, in turn, lost to London in the final. Eton again beat University for the Ladies' Plate, whilst Pembroke College Oxford won the newly instituted Thames Cup from Radley and the London R.C. second crew. With Brasenose disqualified for not carrying a coxswain, London also won the Stewards' Challenge Cup.

1869

Apart from the revision of the Rules, already referred to, which took place in the spring, there was no great change in the pattern of the Regatta in 1869. The Oxford Etonians once again won the Grand, whilst Eton carried home the Ladies' Plate for the fourth year in succession. This already established a record sequence for the event, previously held by First Trinity, with three successive wins. Since Eton were to win again in the following year, they were well on the way to that dominant position in the Ladies' Plate which was almost taken for granted in later years.

Incidentally, this run of five Eton victories has only been bettered once, and that by themselves, with seven wins, in 1893–9. It was indeed a year of records, of the statistical rather than the time variety. For University College won the Visitors' for the fourth time in succession—a record which still stands today—and the Oscillators Club, Kingston, beat the Kingston R.C. in the Wyfold Cup, and thus broke through their neighbours' sequence of six wins, which was unprecedented, and is still unapproached.

The Stewards offered a Presentation Cup for fours without coxswains, and this was won by the Oxford Radleian Club from the Oscillators; Brasenose, who might have felt themselves in honour bound to support this new event, did not send a crew to Henley at all.

1870

Trinity College Dublin, made their first appearance at Henley in 1870, entering, with their typical panache, for the Grand, Ladies' Plate, Visitors,' and Wyfold Cup. They reached the final of the Ladies', succumbing to Eton after rowing level for half the distance. From the Wyfold Cup they withdrew, but they won the Visitors' Challenge Cup from University College Oxford, who, as already mentioned, had won the event for the four preceding years.

T.C.D., as they are invariably called, have always held a special place of affection at Henley, and have a great reputation for hard rowing, if not always for a high degree of skill. This is reflected in the fact that they have only once won the Ladies' Plate, but have been six times runners-up. They have also won the Thames Cup once, and the Visitors' three times, and have rowed in six other finals, apart from the Ladies', which is not a bad record for a relatively small boat club, which has not generally the benefit of first-class competition on its own doorstep.

Another important newcomer to the 1870 Regatta was the Thames Rowing Club. We have so long taken it for granted that Thames, together with London and Leander, make up the 'big three' of English rowing, that it may surprise some to learn that Thames arrived on the scene thus, relatively speaking, late. Once they started they wasted no time, for they have never missed a Regatta since 1870, and, since 1874, when they first entered for the Grand, there have been few years in which they have not contested all the major events open to them.

The rivalry between London and Thames has been intense, and sometimes even bitter. Today it is of a more friendly nature. Though Thames have been the more successful in recent years, London, with the earlier start, still hold an advantage in terms of wins and finals contested.

1871

There is not much to be said about the racing in the next four or five years. But it was a period of important changes at Henley.

Eighteen-seventy-one gave the Oxford Etonians the last of their Grand wins, whilst Pembroke College Oxford wrested the Ladies' Plate from Eton, who had won the event for the past five years. And through First Trinity, who won the Visitors', Cambridge gained their first Henley victory for some years. In the ensuing decade they were to outshine their rivals from the Isis.

But essentially this was the era of the flowering of London Rowing Club. They were to win the Grand four times in the next six years. But they set as much store by their fours as by their eights, and won the Stewards' no fewer than eight times in succession (1871–8). Of these crews, F. S. Gulston was the genius. He rowed in every one of them, and was the outstanding figure of Henley in the 'seventies, as surely as was Woodgate in the 'sixties. A. de L. Long, S. le Blanc Smith, and F. L. Playford were his most constant companions, and the London fours in which they rowed were considered well-nigh invincible.

1872

In 1872 the Rules of Boat Racing, as codified in 1849, and adopted by the Stewards in 1850, were revised. The most important change was the abolition of the taking of stations. No longer was a crew, which crossed over in front of its opponents, entitled to take and keep their station. The new rule stated that: 'Each boat shall keep its own water throughout the race, and any boat departing from its own water will do so at its own peril.'

The significance of this change is not hard to understand. It meant that, if a crew was fast enough to cross over, it could still do so. But if its opponents could summon the spurt necessary to close up, and threaten a bump, the leading crew must either give way, or risk disqualification. Under the old rules, having taken the station, they were entitled to keep it, and their opponents had to steer outside them to challenge again.

This change of rules has undoubtedly led, in the course of time, to a change in the ethics of boat racing. We still consider it fair tactics for a crew to change its station, if it can thereby gain an advantage in distance. It is taken for granted, in the University Boat Race for instance, that the leading crew will steer for the inside of all the corners. But crossing for the purpose of 'washing' an opponent—that is to say, of harassing him by forcing him to row in disturbed water—is considered today to be, at the least, doubtful form.

One must be careful in passing judgement on such cases, for, although the present-day Henley course is straight, there is still sometimes an advantage to be gained by crossing over. The wind or the current may be less on one side of the course than on the other.

Besides this revision of the Rules, 1872 saw the end of the holders' privilege of not contesting the challenge heats. And London R.C. brought the first sliding seats to the Regatta. They had already won a private match, against the Atlanta R.C. of New York, using slides. Several other crews fitted them before the Regatta. The results conclusively proved the advantage of slides, though there was a good deal of prejudice against them for some time, and the early patterns, with glass or bone runners, were not always satisfactory.

It will be remembered that in 1868 Brasenose suffered disqualification for rowing in the Stewards' Challenge Cup without a coxswain, and that in the following year a special prize was offered for a race in coxswainless fours. This experiment was repeated in 1877, but again with poor response, for London R.C. were the sole entrants. No doubt concluding that clubs would not provide themselves with boats of this type until there was a permanent race for coxswainless fours in the Henley programme, the Stewards made the Stewards' Challenge Cup into a coxswainless race in 1873; and in 1874 they followed suit with the Visitors' and Wyfold Challenge Cups.

It is easy to be wise after the event. But one wonders now, whether, if they had not been carried away by their new-found enthusiasm for coxswainless fours, and had retained at least one of the three races as a coxed-four event, the Stewards might not have rendered a greater service to English rowing.

1873-6

In 1873 two tents were erected below the bridge, to provide more accommodation for boats. A dressing-room was added to the permanent boathouse, and a plunge bath for the oarsmen. In the Lion Meadow an area was set aside for carriages, and the carriages on Henley bridge were limited to one rank, an innovation which must have made movement in and out of the town somewhat easier.

There were still no official stands on the Berkshire shore, but in this year a speculative gentleman set about erecting a private stand near Poplar Point. The crews, which trained *en masse* from the Red Lion, watched its growth with consternation, for it threatened to cut off their view of the course from the hotel windows. On the night before the Regatta the stand was completed. After dinner in the Red Lion, the University College eight and the Brasenose four—it seems superfluous to add that Woodgate was there, too—sallied forth, and proceeded to dismantle the stand with their bare hands. Before long the populace of Henley were there to cheer, with half a dozen policemen standing stolidly by. But the Law did not intervene, until, with the last timber lying flat on the greensward, one of the University men attempted to heave some planks into the river. Then, at last, the Sergeant courteously suggested that floating timber might be a danger to navigation, or foul the weir at Hambleden. After this episode the Corporation secured tenure of the meadow, to prevent any repetition of such a *contretemps*.

Two races in 1875 are worth special mention. The first was the final of the Grand Challenge Cup, between Leander, Molesey, and First Trinity B.C. Cambridge. Going away very fast, First Trinity snatched an early lead of a quarter of a length from Molesey, with Leander another quarter of a length astern. At Remenham Farm Molesey caught First Trinity, and led Leander by half a length. Then Leander began to close the gap, passing Trinity and being only a quarter of a length behind Molesey at Fawley. A great race ensued as far as the White House, when

Molesey had apparently shot their bolt. They held their lead over First Trinity, but Leander rowed right away to win by two lengths.

The other race of interest in 1875 was the final of the Silver Goblets. Long and Gulston had won the event for the past three years. But Gulston was one of those who flourished on the old Rules. 'He loved', so John Cooper records, 'to give his opponents some backwash, and to play the cat and mouse game with them.'

This time he played the 'cat' once too often. The London pair were opposed by W. Chillingworth and C. Herbert, of the Ino Boat Club—'a pair of selling platers', Cooper called them—and soon had a comfortable lead. They duly crossed over to the Berkshire station, and proceeded on their way, unperturbed, towards Poplar Point. By the time they got there, 'Gully' was taking life so easily that there was a bare half-length of clear water between the two boats. The inevitable happened. The Ino pair spurted gamely, Gulston could not reply in time, and the London pair were bumped and lost the race on a foul. Under the old Rules they would have been safe, for the Ino pair would have been forced to come up on the outside of the corner.

1877

In 1877 Cheltenham College joined the ranks of 'Henley Schools', the third to do so. They asked to be placed in the same heat as Radley, but the Stewards would not agree to any interference with the draw. They did, however, say that if the two schools did not meet, they would permit them to row a private match. In the event they were both beaten in their heats, and in a special match, on the second day of the Regatta, Radley beat Cheltenham by several lengths, and were presented with medals recording the fact.

Cheltenham entered for the Ladies' Plate in 1878, and for the Public Schools' Challenge Cup, which was instituted in 1879, for the following three years. They won in 1879, but after 1881 disappeared from the Henley scene as suddenly as they had come.

1878

In 1878 there came a positive invasion from the United States, which was to have far-reaching repercussions, not only on Henley but, indirectly, on English rowing as a whole.

The first foreign entry to be accepted at Henley was that of E. South, of New York, who entered for the Diamonds in 1872. He won one race, but was beaten in his second heat. Then, in 1878, there came two clubs and two scullers. The Shoe-wae-cae-mette B.C., Monroe, entered for the Stewards', and Columbia College entered for the Stewards' and Visitors', whilst G. W. Lee, of New Jersey, and J. Lee, of Boston, entered for the Diamonds. The Bostonian came in last in his heat, but G. W. Lee lost by the narrowest possible margin to T. C. Edwards-Moss, the ultimate winner. Lee held a slight lead all the way to Poplar Point, where, having the inside station, he drew away to one length. Then Edwards-Moss began a tremendous spurt, driving his rating up and up, and steadily overhauling his opponent. But his task still seemed impossible, and Lee was a canvas to the good within a few strokes of the finish. According to C. T. Steward, the American was steering too close to the Berkshire shore, and touched the bottom with his right scull. R. C. Lehmann (in *The Complete Oarsman*) thought that he lost his head, and looked round for the flag. At any rate he faltered, and Edwards-Moss caught him on the post.

In the Stewards', the two American crews were drawn together, in a heat with Dublin University. Dublin led off the start, but at the half-distance Monroe passed them and went on to win very easily. Short of the finish there was a foul between the other two crews, the fault of Dublin. Columbia claimed to row in the final, but this was not allowed, since Monroe had won by such a large margin.

In the final, Monroe were faced by London (S. le B. Smith (bow), F. S. Gulston, A. Trower, F. L. Playford (stroke)), and it is easy to imagine the tense excitement of the crowd before this, the first Stewards' final ever to be contested by a foreign crew. The 'Shoes'

were a crew of Canadian lumberjacks, Monroe being a town with
a paper and wood-pulp trade. They had no style, but had rowed
together for a long time, and could command a high rate of
striking. Incidentally, they rowed with swivel rowlocks, the
noise of which 'might have been heard from one end of the course
to the other' (*The Complete Oarsman*). In a cloud of spray they
started at a terrific pace.

Playford made no attempt to match Monroe's pace off the
start, and lost ground at once. But it was soon apparent that
London, rowing a long, smooth stroke, and beautifully together,
were losing no more, despite the fact that their opponents were
rowing about eight strokes a minute faster. Then London began
to creep back, never attempting to spurt. By the White House
they had their bows in front. Then, quite suddenly, it was all
over. One of their crew 'not feeling well', as H. T. Steward put
it, the American crew stopped, and London paddled in.

In the Visitors' Cup there was a great race between Columbia,
University College Oxford, and Jesus College Cambridge. At
Remenham, Columbia were leading University by half a length.
Then Jesus came up to take University's place. At the half-distance they challenged, and drew level with the Americans. Then
their steering broke down, and they dropped back. Just below
the Point they tried again, and actually had their bows in front,
when the same thing happened, and a gallant crew was forced to
drop out of the race. In the final, Columbia had a close race with
Hertford College Oxford; but Fortune did not smile on the
Englishmen that day, for, just below the Point, they steered into
the bank, and Columbia finished alone, the first foreign crew to
carry off a Henley trophy.

1879

It was unfortunate that the first effective foreign participation
at Henley should lead to recriminations. But the fact was that at
that date there was little organized international sport, that conditions and ideas varied very much in different countries, and that

the requirements for international contests had scarcely been considered.

It was said that the Americans were not amateurs according to the Henley Rules, and it transpired later that G. W. Lee certainly had no good claim to that title; subsequently he became an avowed professional, racing for money. Shoe-wae-cae-mette doubtless considered themselves to be amateurs in their own country. Perhaps they came a year too late, for it was in 1878 that a meeting of oarsmen at Putney had issued a definition of the word amateur, which expressly excepted those engaged in manual labour. It is, indeed, quite evident that the American club did consider its members to be amateurs, and they sent in their entry again in 1879. But by then the Henley Stewards had published their own definition of an amateur, and the 'Shoes' second entry was not accepted.

I have said that the American entries in 1878 had far-reaching repercussions, and this was so, because they focused the spotlight of publicity on the amateur definition at the very moment when English oarsmen were codifying their rules, and at a time when fears were being expressed about the future of amateur rowing. Indirectly, at least, this had a bearing on the new rules, the rigidity of which was to result in our having, for seventy-five years, two separate governing bodies of rowing. But that is a story which must be told elsewhere.

The immediate effect of the invasion was the tightening-up of the Henley Rules governing foreign entries, which, for the 1879 Regatta, stipulated that: 'The entry of any crew out of the United Kingdom must be made on or before March 1st, and . . . accompanied by a declaration made before a Notary Public with regard to the profession of each member of the crew . . . and such declaration must be certified by the British Consul, or the Mayor, or the chief authority of the locality'.

A new four-oared race was instituted in 1879—the Public Schools' Challenge Cup. It produced entries from Radley, Bedford, Cheltenham, and Derby, and was won by Cheltenham.

In this year, too, Twickenham R.C. won the Thames Cup at

their first attempt. They had entered only once before at Henley, when, in 1866, they were defeated by Kingston in the final of the Wyfold Cup. Now suddenly they struck a six-year era of success, which was quite spectacular. In the following year they lost the Thames Cup to London, but in 1881 they were successful again. In 1882 they did not reach the final, but for the next three years they aspired to, and very nearly won, the Grand.

How does it happen that a relatively small club rises in this remarkable fashion? Twickenham were, at first, essentially a local club, teaching their own men to row. They were fortunate in getting J. H. D. Goldie to coach them. Then, in 1883, they imported the Hertford College four (G. Q. Roberts, E. Buck, D. E. Brown, J. Lowndes), who had won the Stewards' two years running. They beat a strong Leander crew in their heat, and held London to Poplar Point in the final, when, being on the Centre station, they were beaten by a length.

In 1884 Twickenham again beat Leander to reach the final, and again drew the outside station against London. They led by three-quarters of a length before the Point, but London passed them, and their number 7 fainted before the finish. The Twickenham second eight won the Thames Cup. For the third time they beat Leander in 1885, and for the third time they drew the wrong station in the final. This time it was Jesus College Cambridge who caught them from behind, on the inside of the bend.

And so Twickenham were, in John Cooper's words, *proxime accessit*. They never won the Grand, and, as yet, they have not again won the Thames Cup.

1880

There were a number of minor adjustments to the Rules in 1880, when Leander won the Grand, and Trinity Hall, then on the threshold of a period of success, the Ladies' Plate. This also was the first occasion on which a foreign crew (Germania Ruder Club, Frankfurt) entered for the Grand.

1881

In 1881 the organization of the Regatta was changed, experience having shown that the Stewards and Committee were too large a body to manage the Regatta efficiently. The solution was to set up a standing Committee of Management of twelve members. Their powers, however, were not clearly defined, and no sooner had they been appointed than they found themselves overruled by the Stewards.

On 25 May a cable was received as follows: 'Cornell Univ. four's entry for Visitors' and Stewards' delayed through misunderstanding. Will you accept now? Passage engaged for Saturday next.'

The Committee of Management decided that they must stand by the new Rule that foreign entries should close on 1 March. But Cornell duly arrived, tendered their entry again, and petitioned the Stewards to overrule the Committee. In this they were supported by the Press, and by many club captains. In the end the Stewards, by the President's casting vote, agreed to accept their entry for the Stewards', but not for the Visitors'.

Cornell were still dissatisfied at being unable to compete for the Visitors', and challenged Hertford College to a private match. This was accepted, and took place on the day after the Regatta. However, Cornell hit the bank twice before reaching Fawley, and Hertford paddled home. It seems that the authorities went out of their way to help the visitors, for in the Stewards', when they and London were involved in a foul, the umpire took all three crews back to the start. This time the Americans led, but Thames passed them at Remenham Farm, and London before the White House.

Bedford Grammar School won the Public Schools' race, their boatman having fitted wide seats—it was a fixed-seat event—and instructed the crew to grease and slide upon the thwarts. In consequence of this infringement, a Rule was passed limiting the seats to a width of six inches.

1882-4

In 1882 Exeter College reached and won the final of the Grand, for the only time in the club's history. The racing was otherwise uneventful. But the Committee, wishing to guard against any future argument as to whether an American 'College' was really a 'University' in our eyes, altered the qualifications for the Ladies' Plate and Visitors', by inserting the words 'in the United Kingdom' after the words 'Colleges and Schools'. They were no doubt right in deciding that it was impracticable to decide whether an establishment many thousand miles away was, according to our ideas, a university or a college, or even a school.

As we near the end of this chapter of Henley history, a chapter which covers the formative years, during which the Regatta grew from small beginnings to its undisputed position as the premier Regatta of the world, we cannot fail to sense the quickening tempo of events. The racing goes on as usual. To our eyes, seventy years later, it may appear now more, now less exciting. But we may be sure it was all 'needle business' at the time. Yet the really important events were being thrashed out on the bank, and in the committee room.

At last, and perhaps for the first time, the Stewards were realizing that they had on their hands a fully grown Regatta, of world-wide importance. And at last they were ready to put it into the hands of those who knew what was wanted.

In March 1884 a sub-committee was appointed to reconsider the course, and, in particular, the practicability of cutting off the Point.[1] In due time they reported that this was impracticable, but suggested that the races should be started below the Island, and the finishing post should be placed opposite the top of Phyllis Court. The full Committee did not accept this recommendation, but decided that the bays on the Berkshire shore should be piled off, to keep competitors out of the slack water.

[1] See 'The Course,' p. 59

In the same year the Town Cup was withdrawn from the programme, and given in trust to the Henley Town Regatta.

1885

The Constitution of the Regatta was altered again in 1885, the old Committee of fourteen being altogether abolished, and the running of the Regatta placed in the hands of a Committee of Management of twelve, who were to be elected by the Stewards from amongst their own number. The Committee of Management elected in 1885 comprised, for the first time, an equal number of rowing and local Stewards.

The race for the Public Schools' Cup was discontinued, and this cup was acquired by Marlow Regatta. C. T. Steward recorded that 'More magnifiicent days could not have been desired . . . houseboats and launches extended in an unbroken line from Phyllis Court, down to the starting place'.

This was the third successive year in which Twickenham were beaten in the final of the Grand. 'The unfairness of the course', wrote H. T. Steward, 'was more than ever manifest.' However, Eton managed to win the Ladies' Plate, for the second year running, from the Bucks station.

In the autumn another sub-committee was asked to consider the unfairness of the course and the Laws of Boat Racing, as recently drawn up by the Amateur Rowing Association. In February 1886 they recommended, *inter alia*, that the course should finish at Poplar Point, and should commence just below the tail of Temple Island. Their recommendations were accepted.

It was also suggested that the Thames Cup should be discontinued, partly in order to cut down the racing, and partly to keep up the standard. But this proposal, not unnaturally, met with violent opposition, and was dropped.

The alteration to the course, and especially the piling of both sides, was voted a great success, though, as we have seen, it hardly had the desired effect of making the course a fairer one. The new course was 150 feet wide, to accommodate three crews. But in response to numerous requests from the clubs—who no doubt felt that the crew on the Centre station would always be at a disadvantage—it was decided to row only two crews in a heat, although this entailed a third day's racing. There were two slight bends in the course, the first above the Island, and the second at Fawley. But the start was staggered, so that the distance to the finish was the same on either station.

As for the racing, the honours were, for once, very evenly distributed. Trinity Hall won the Grand for the first time.

CHAPTER FIVE

The Great Days. 1887–1914

THE division of Henley history into chapters is necessarily some-what arbitrary. The new Constitution of 1885, and the change of course in 1886, were, in many ways, more significant than any-thing which occurred at Henley in 1887. Yet this was a year, like 1851, which opened the previous chapter, in which an important social event took place, greatly adding to Henley's prestige. In 1851 it was the visit of the Prince Consort. In 1887 it was the visit of another royal party.

The Field recorded that:

On the third day the Regatta was honoured by the presence of the Prince and Princess of Wales, the King of Denmark, the King of the Hellenes, the Princes Albert Victor and George of Wales, the Prin-cesses Victoria, Sophie and Margaret of Prussia, the Hereditary Princess of Saxe-Meiningen, the Duke of Sparta, Prince George of Greece, the Duke of Cambridge, and the Indian Princes staying in England. The Royal party was received with enthusiasm.

The year 1887 has often been referred to as the *annus mirabilis* of Cambridge, and in particular of Trinity Hall, rowing. For the 'Hall' carried off the Grand, Ladies' Plate, Thames, Stewards', and Visitors' Challenge Cups, a feat which is quite unique in Henley history. In addition, Pembroke College won the Wyfold Challenge Cup, C. T. Barclay and S. D. Muttlebury, of Third Trinity, won the Goblets, and J. C. Gardner, of Emmanuel, completed the discomfiture of the Oxonians by beating Guy Nickalls in the final of the Diamonds.

Mr. Cooper recalls that he played some part in making the Trinity Hall success as sweeping as it was. For, on the day on which the entries closed, he was talking to C. J. Bristowe and S.

Swann, on Henley bridge. They told him that they wanted to encourage their second eight, but feared that it lacked the experience to survive in the Ladies' Plate. Cooper suggested that they should enter the crew for the Thames Cup as well, to give them, so to speak, a second string to their bow. And so it came about that the Hall made a clean sweep of all three eight-oared events.

1888–90

The crowd of spectators, watching the racing from pleasure craft on the river, was now steadily increasing. Already it presented a serious problem. The first piling of the river was aimed more at keeping this fleet of boats off, than at keeping the competitors on, the then not-so-straight-and-narrow course. In 1888 the course was further reduced to 120 feet. Next year it was tapered down to 110 feet at the finish.

In spite of the piling, accidents have sometimes occurred. Thames R.C. hit a skiff, in 1888, just before the finish of the Grand Challenge Cup final, but although No. 3's rigger was damaged they managed to get home first. In the semi-final of the Diamonds, E. Doëring, of Hamburg, was less fortunate, for he struck a boat moored at the side of the course, and capsized. In the following year Leander ran into a pleasure boat in the semi-final of the Stewards'.

Each year the Committee issued appeals to the public to keep clear of the racing, and from 1889 launches were used to police the course. In 1891 electric bells were attached to the piles, at quarter-mile intervals. This proved most successful on the first day, but during the night someone with a strange sense of humour fished up the cable from the bottom of the river, and cut it. In 1892 boxes were erected on piles, at the quarter-mile marks, in which men were stationed with bells.

Strange to relate, after their year of triumph, the Hall could win only one event, the Stewards', in 1888, and in 1889 they did not send a single crew to Henley. The Grand was won by Thames R.C., after a great struggle with New College Oxford. On and off, New College led up to Fawley, but the crews were level at the mile post, and Thames got away to win by a bare length. There was another magnificent race in the final of the Goblets, which J. C. Gardner and S. D. Muttlebury won by two feet, from Lord Ampthill and G. Nickalls.

In this year the first official grandstand was erected, on the Berks shore, in an enclosure at Poplar Point.

Personalities mean much at Henley, and we are now to meet many of the great names, which are still familiar, though legendary, to the present generation of oarsmen. In the 1890 programme there appeared the names of Guy Nickalls, and his brother Vivian,[1] still a boy at Eton, S. D. Muttlebury, W. A. L. Fletcher, G. C. Bourne, and others as distinguished, amongst them C. W. Kent, who, like Lord Maugham, of Trinity Hall, is still with us today.

This was, in fact, Kent's third year at Henley, and he had already won the Visitors' in 1888, rowing bow in the Brasenose four. But 1890 was his first year as a stroke, and it is on his stroking that his reputation stands. In that year he took Brasenose into the final of the Grand, in which they were beaten by London R.C. And he won the Stewards' and Visitors'.

H. T. Steward's account of the first heat of the Stewards' seems to me to be couched in such masterly terms of understatement that it would be unthinkable to attempt any embellishment.

Brasenose [he records] seemed ahead half way up the Island, but at the top of it Leander were ahead, and led by a quarter of a length at the quarter-mile mark. Brasenose, however, led at Remenham, but the crews were again level at Fawley. Brasenose led slightly at the three-quarter mile post, but the boats were alongside at the mile post. Off Phyllis Court Leander seemed to be getting the best of it, but Brasenose passed the post first by two feet.

That was the way C. W. Kent liked his races. He weighed 10 st. 10 lb., and stroked Leander in the Grand for the next five years. Four times in succession he led them to victory, and on the last occasion, as we shall see, his record was broken only by an untoward occurrence.

[1] See photograph facing p. 85.

1891

'Tuesday' [of the 1891 Regatta], commented *The Field*,

A gale of wind from the south-west, with torrents of rain, the whole atmosphere reeking of damp, a never-ending downpour, were the climatic conditions under which Henley commenced. Wednesday. As the racing commenced a thunderstorm broke over the town, and for nearly an hour and a half a perfect deluge of rain descended—more like a tropical storm than anything else—which for a time killed the wind. After this the wind breezed up again, and the sun shone for two to three hours, but another deluge of rain descended from five to six o'clock.

But the final Thursday was 'a really fine summer day'. And the racing throughout the Regatta was magnificent.

At the draw somebody pointed out to the Committee that one of the boats was six feet longer than usual, and that since crews were started with their sterns level, and judged by their bows, this was unfair. As a result, all boats were measured, and arrangements made to draw back the longer boats at the start, so that bows should be level. This practice has been followed ever since.

The first heat of the Grand, between Leander and Thames, gave promise of what was to come. Leander, on the Berks station, led by a length at Remenham, and by three-quarters of a length at Fawley. But Thames were closing fast, and at the mile Leander had only a quarter of a length in hand. At the bottom of Phyllis Court Thames got their bows in front, but on the winning post Leander came back to force a dead heat.

Cooper suggests that this was the strongest Leander crew he ever saw.[1] Every man was an Oxford Blue. Thames were boating four Cambridge Blues—P. Landale, A. M. Hutchinson, S. D. Muttlebury, and J. C. Gardner—so there was an inter-university flavour to the race.

[1] Leander 1891: W. F. C. Holland (bow), J. A. Ford, V. Nickalls, Lord Ampthill, G. Nickalls, W. A. L. Fletcher, R. P. P. Rowe, C. W. Kent (stroke), L. S. Williams (cox).

This race is interesting as an example of the value of stations on the New Course, for there was no doubt that Leander were considerably the faster crew. But the heat was rowed in a gale of wind off the Bucks shore. In the re-row, on the next day, when there was little wind, Leander won by two lengths.

In the final they were led by London to the three-quarter-mile post, but went away up the Enclosures to win by a length, in the record time of 6 min. 51 sec. This time, though twice equalled, was never to be beaten on the New Course.

The year 1891 marked the revival of Leander rowing, for they were to win the Grand twelve times in the next fifteen years. That is another record which has never been equalled, and is hardly likely to be in the future, with the fiercer competition we face today.

The excitement in 1891 was by no means confined to the Grand. In the Ladies' Plate the crowd were brought to their feet by one of those periodical clashes between Eton and Radley, in which the latter, so far, have always just lacked the luck or skill to get home. On this occasion Eton led by three-quarters of a length at the quarter-mile, but Radley brought them back and were level at the three-quarter-mile. The crews raced level to the mile; then Eton began to edge their way to the front again, finally winning by half a length. In the final, after being led by Balliol all over the course, they drew level opposite the Enclosures, only to fall back again to lose by a quarter of a length.

In the Thames Cup there was excitement of another sort, for London, leading Twickenham by three-quarters of a length opposite the grandstand, caught a crab and hit the booms. Even so, they managed to scramble home by three feet. Later they were easily beaten by Molesey, the ultimate winners.

There were other close races, of which the most notable was the final of the Goblets, in which Lord Ampthill and Guy Nickalls, after being two lengths down on F. Wilkinson and W. A. L. Fletcher at Remenham, 'made a rush' at the finish, and won by one foot.

1892–4

In 1892 the weather was almost as unkind as in the previous year, without the compensating excitements. In the following year, 1893, the Stewards entered into an agreement with the Union des Sociétés Françaises de Sports Athlétiques, exempting their affiliated clubs and scullers from sending in their entries before 31 March. The new date was 1 June, and this agreement was the pattern for subsequent agreements with the governing bodies of other foreign countries.

Unfortunately, at their first appearance, the French were involved in an unlucky clash. In a heat of the Stewards' Cup, Thames R.C. suddenly sheered off their course, and the Société de Basse Seine, giving way, rammed a pleasure boat which was lying just off the course. The French claimed a foul, which Baron de Coubertin, of Olympic fame, insisted should be withdrawn. Next day Thames were summoned before the Committee 'to explain their conduct', and a subsequent statement by the Committee, that 'having heard their explanation, the Committee accept their assurance that the deviation of their boat from its proper course was not intentional', failed to close the matter. Correspondents in the Press said that Thames' behaviour was 'disgraceful'; others said that the Committee's action was 'disgusting', and both sides declared that the umpire had no right to bring the matter before the Committee.

Apart from this unusual display of bad temper, 1893 had little to offer. The weather was better, but there were few close races, and too many fouls. The entries, however, were substantially up, numbering, according to the annual report, fifty-three, as compared with an average of forty-two for the previous ten years.

As a result of the increased entries there was a proposal, in 1894, that the Regatta should be extended to a fourth day. But the Stewards, always unwilling to extend the length of the Regatta, decided not to add another day, but to state that they reserved the right to require some of the preliminary heats to be rowed on the day before the Regatta, a formula which they have copied in later years.

In this year there were alterations to bring Henley's amateur definition, and Laws of Boat Racing, into line with changes made by the Amateur Rowing Association.

For the first time the swans, which had been interfering with the racing, were removed from the reach during the Regatta. The swan on the Thames is deemed a Royal bird, and no one may own swans on the river, except by grant from the Crown. Today there are only three owners; the Crown, the Dyers' Company, and the Vintners' Company. Each year the Swan Masters of these two city companies, led by the Queen's Swan Master, row up-river from London, checking the swans, and marking the young cygnets. The swan-mark of the Dyers' is a notch[1] on one side of the beak; the Vintners' swans are notched on both sides of the beak. The Royal swans are unmarked, and therefore include any which escape the annual 'upping', as the process is called.

In the racing, Leander won the Grand, rather more easily and for the fourth time in succession, whilst Eton won the final of the Ladies' Plate by 'five or six lengths'. But the most remarkable performance of the Regatta was that of the Nickalls brothers, Guy and Vivian, who together won the Silver Goblets, and, in opposition, fought out the final of the Diamond Sculls, Guy being the winner. In the following year, no doubt prompted by this unequalled feat, but ostensibly in commemoration of his sons having won the Silver Goblets for the past five years, either together or with others,[2] Mr. Tom Nickalls presented the Nickalls Challenge Cup, which now goes with the Silver Goblets.

[1] Properly known as a 'nick', or 'neck'. Hence the Inn name, 'The Swan with two Necks'. The old penalty for stealing a swan was this: the swan was hung up by the beak, just clear of the floor, and the felon had then to cover the swan with wheat, by pouring it over the bird's head until it was completely covered. It is said that the same penalty used to be enforced on those who stole cats, and that this resulted in the breeding of long-tailed cats and long necked swans!

[2] 1890–1, Lord Ampthill and Guy Nickalls. 1892–3, V. Nickalls and W. A. L. Fletcher. 1894, V. and Guy Nickalls.

1895

By contrast with the preceding three years, 1895 brought ample excitement, and one of those unfortunate episodes which occur even in the best-run regattas.

Leander had now won the Grand four years in succession, thus equalling the record of the Oxford University B.C., which had won in 1850-3. And they seemed well placed to win again. Cornell University were their opponents, and no doubt the Englishmen were confident, as they sat on their stakeboat, for the day was still far ahead when the best that we had to offer would feel serious qualms at facing the Americans.

When the umpire asked 'Are you ready ?', several members of the Leander crew called 'No.' But there was a strong wind blowing, and apparently they were not heard.

On the 'Go', Cornell started, and some of the Leander men rowed a stroke. The rest waited, expecting the Umpire to recall Cornell. H. T. Steward charitably records that the umpire thought Leander had made a bad start, and therefore let Cornell go on. But since Leander, for all practical purposes, did not start at all, this is hard to accept. The fact must be that the umpire lost his head, for at any time within the first ten strokes he could well have signalled to the Americans to stop.

Thus Leander lost the opportunity of winning the Grand five times in succession, and, more particularly, C. W. Kent lost his chance of stroking five successive winning crews.

But the damage was more serious than that, for the natural displeasure of the Henley crowd was vented on the unhappy Americans, who, many felt, and some said, ought to have stopped rowing when they saw what had happened. Perhaps the chivalry of the day demanded this, but it would have been a lot to expect of a foreign crew, rowing at Henley for the first time. And no doubt they, like many crews before and since, had strict instructions from their coach to take no notice of their opponents, 'and devil take the hindmost'. The real trouble was that they had a professional coach, and, through keeping his crew overmuch to

V. THE GRAND CHALLENGE CUP, 1897

New College, on the Bucks station, win from Leander by 2 feet, equalling the record time of 6 min. 51 sec,

VI. THE GOLDEN DAYS

Top: The Graphic's artist's impression of Henley in 1891

Bottom: The Royal Barge conveys their Majesties King George V and Queen Mary to Enclosure in 1912

themselves, he had not endeared himself to the rowing fraternity, who were, therefore, only too ready to find fault.

Next day there was yet greater excitement, when Trinity Hall, who were not thought to have much chance, rowed Cornell to a standstill in the semi-final. At Fawley the Americans led by half a length, but at the mile post the crews were level, and Cornell stopped. Even Mr. Cooper felt constrained to recount that 'Henley was pretty noisy that night', both with the all-too-obvious distortion of the battle-cry, 'Cornell, Cornell, I yell Cornell,' and the newly coined counter-cry of 'The Hall, the Hall, I bawl the Hall'.

The final proved to be another great race, between Trinity Hall and New College, in which there was never more than half a length between the boats, with each crew leading in turn. Trinity Hall were popular winners by a third of a length.

Such grim doings in the Grand naturally overshadowed the other events, but there was plenty of excitement, and it was, perhaps, in the Stewards' that the best race of the Regatta took place. It was in the very first heat between London R.C. and the Argonaut R.C. of Canada.

London were stroked by Guy Nickalls, with his brother Vivian at three. Up to the mile post the two crews raced almost level. Then London spurted, and led by three-quarters of a length at the bottom of the Enclosures. But the Canadians had by no means shot their bolt, and, fighting back, they drew level and were actually leading London opposite the grandstand. Literally 'on the post' the Londoners 'came again', to win by two feet. They went on to win the final from Thames.

For the Nickalls brothers it was a busy week, for they won the Goblets together for the second time. And Guy Nickalls was beaten in the final of the Diamonds by the Hon. Rupert Guinness, now Lord Iveagh, by only a length, after sculling level for most of the distance.

As though to point the lesson to Cornell, St. John's College Oxford stopped after starting in the final of the Ladies' Plate, because they saw that Eton had caught a crab. In this case, of course, the fault was with the crew, rather than the umpire. St. John's paid the penalty for their quixotic gesture, but may have felt that this was preferable to winning in such circumstances, for Eton beat them by no less than eight lengths.

1896

Eighteen-ninety-six was a year of hot, thundery weather, and the crowds at Henley were, by general consent, greater than ever before. Henley Regatta, now well established as the oarsman's regatta *par excellence*, was becoming also one of the great social occasions of the summer.[1]

Leander, now stroked by Harcourt Gold, made no mistake about winning the Grand, though they had a hard-fought, half-length victory over New College in one of the heats. The Nickalls brothers won the Goblets for the third year in succession. In the previous year, it will be remembered, their father had presented the Nickalls Challenge Cup, as an additional trophy for the Goblets. By the close of the 1896 Regatta his two sons had won three times in partnership, whilst Guy had won twice with Lord Ampthill, and Vivian had won twice with W. A. L. Fletcher. There was to be one more victory for Guy, in the following year, in partnership with E. R. Balfour, bringing the total, in

---

[1] On this point, however, there was still some divergence of opinion. *The Athletic News*, a few years later (14 July 1903), under the heading 'An Over-rated Function', wrote: ' . . . I am not alone in applying this term to Henley. It is neither more nor less than a gigantic middle-class water-picnic. In spite of what is written about it, smart society do not patronize it, but leave it to those whom our Gallic friends call *les bourgeoises*, the would-be smart folk. It is a wonderfully pretty sight, but unless one has friends who own a houseboat, or has the *entrée* to one of the enclosures owned by a "catering club", it soon palls.'

Perhaps the correspondent of *The Athletic News* had neither of these advantages. The correspondent of *The Field*, who wrote on 13 July 1889, probably had. But he deplored the junketings for different reasons. 'The curse of Henley', he wrote, 'is the picnicking—we care not a straw whether it is afloat, on houseboats, steam launches, or row boats, or ashore in the meadows. . . . This picnicking, this ostentatious display of female finery, of flowers, of fruit, of wine, of viands, is a modern innovation, and a sign of the luxurious selfishness of the times—a selfishness which is exampled in the total disregard of the competitors, and in the *bon mot* uttered on a houseboat, that "the regatta would be perfect were it not for the horrid rowing men".'

eight successive years, to six wins for Guy, and five for Vivian. The Goblets is the only event at Henley which carries a named trophy of this sort, and no one could grudge the honour to this extraordinary rowing family. Twenty-five years later, G. O. Nickalls, who is today Chairman of the Amateur Rowing Association, was to add the family name twice more to the roll of Goblets winners.

1897–8

There were minor adjustments to the course in 1897, mainly with a view to reducing the advantage of the Bucks station in the prevailing south-west wind. As it turned out, very little wind blew, for a change, and what there was was favourable. The weather was glorious on all three days.

Eighteen-ninety-seven was New College's year, for they went one better than two years previously, and beat Leander by two feet in the final of the Grand, equalling the course record of 6 min. 51 sec. set up in 1891. Leander led by half a length at Remenham Farm, and held this advantage until the mile post, when New College caught them with a fine spurt.[1] It was a fast year, for Eton won the Ladies' Plate in 7 min. 1 sec., Leander won the Stewards' in 7 min. 30 sec., and H. T. Blackstaffe won a semi-final of the Diamonds in 8 min. 34 sec., all record times. In the Diamonds final, Blackstaffe lost by a length to E. H. Ten Eyck, whose time was a second slower. Later, allegations were made that Ten Eyck was not an amateur, and his entry, in 1898, was refused, even though he was then the holder of the Diamonds.

In 1898 Leander began another winning sequence, but they had to work hard for it. They beat Balliol by a length, after being level at the mile post, London R.C. by half a length in the semi-final, and First Trinity by three-quarters of a length in the final, after being led by a few feet at the bottom of Phyllis Court wall.

There was drama of a different kind, in the same year, disputed for the most part with pen and ink, and in the lobbies of West-

[1] New College—J. J. de Knoop (bow), G. O. C. Edwards, R. O. Pitman, A. O. Dowson, C. K. Philips, H. Thorpe, W. E. Crum, A. Whitworth (stroke), C. P. Serocold (cox). See photograph facing p. 116.

minster. For the Great Western Railway initiated a Bill in Parliament, for the opening of a loop line between Marlow and Henley. This line would have crossed the river, on iron girder bridges, no less than three times, and would have culminated in a high embankment up the Henley valley. However, all available resources were mustered against the plan, and in the end the company withdrew the Bill, the main object of which, it later transpired, was only to forestall possible competition in the district.

At the end of the year, in November 1898, a motion was put to the Committee that the standard of the Thames Cup was so low that the race ought to be relegated to fixed-seats. It found no seconder, and it was decided to postpone the discussion 'in order that private enquiries might be made'.

1899

In 1899 the Stewards at last found a satisfactory solution to the problem of interference by pleasure boats. For some years already the course had been marked out with piles, driven into the river bed. Now, on the Bucks side, floating booms were added, forming an effective barrier from the finishing post to below Remenham Rectory.

One result of the booming of the course was that it was found possible, when necessary, to start races within a few minutes of each other. Today we take it for granted that there will often be two races on the course at the same time. But it was then considered a remarkable achievement.

In 1899 Eton won the Ladies' Plate, fairly easily, from Pembroke College Cambridge. The fact is worthy of remark, because this was the last of an unbroken series of seven Eton victories. They were to continue to reach, but lose, the final for the next four years, and then, in 1904 and 1905, to win twice more, bringing their total number of consecutive years in the final of the Ladies' Plate to thirteen.

Incidentally, 1899 was the first year in which preliminary heats took place before the Regatta, there being one heat each of the Thames Cup and Diamonds on the Tuesday afternoon.

1900

The turn of the century seemed to pass almost unnoticed at Henley. It was the sixty-second Regatta. Leander won the Grand, New College the Ladies' Plate, and Trinity College Cambridge the Thames Cup, this being one of the frequent occasions on which Trinity College Dublin failed, but only just failed, to carry home a Henley trophy. In the Thames Cup final they led the Cambridge crew to the three-quarter mile, and lost by a third of a length.

The Diamond Sculls produced a remarkable final, between E. G. Hemmerde, of University College, and B. H. Howell, of Trinity Hall. Howell led to Fawley, but then Hemmerde passed him, and had an advantage of two lengths opposite the grandstand. Howell, although he had been suffering from malaria, made a desperate spurt, losing by only three-quarters of a length. On stopping, he collapsed and fell out of his boat.

Howell does not qualify for the list of outstandingly successful Henley competitors, but his career deserves mention. An American, he learned his rowing and sculling in this country, and won the Wingfield Sculls, the Amateur Sculling Championship, in 1898 and 1899. At Henley he rowed for Trinity Hall four times in the Grand, winning in 1895. And he won the Diamonds in 1898 and 1899, on the former occasion in the record time of 8 min. 29 sec.

It is perhaps not altogether fanciful to say that in 1900 a shadow fell across the Henley scene, of which, at the time, English oarsmen were largely unaware. For Henley was at the zenith of its fame, and English oarsmanship unchallenged. In that year the Fédération Belge des Sociétés d'Aviron was added to the list of foreign Associations with which Henley was 'in agreement'. And in that year the Club Nautique de Gand first entered for the Grand Challenge Cup. They were beaten by Leander, in a semi-final, by three-quarters of a length. But in the next ten years the Belgians were to rock English rowing to its foundations.

1901–2

In 1901 a foreign crew reached the final of the Grand for the first time. It was the University of Pennsylvania, and to get there they defeated both London and Thames. But in the final they met Leander, in the full strength of their great winning era. Pennsylvania led by a quarter of a length at Remenham, but Leander had a canvas at Fawley and, gradually increasing their advantage, won by a length.

After the Regatta there was a good deal of correspondence in the Press, urging the Stewards to close Henley to all foreign competitors. At a special meeting in November it was decided 'that it is inexpedient that any alteration in the rules of the Regatta be at present made'. It was a subject on which much more remained to be said. Nor, I fancy, has the last word been said yet.[1]

In 1902 Third Trinity broke through Leander's victorious sequence, to win the Grand fairly comfortably. All but one member of their crew were Cambridge Blues. It may seem remarkable that 'Third' have won the Stewards' nine times, and yet have been successful only once in the Grand and the Ladies' Plate. The answer is not far to seek. The Third Trinity B.C. was formed of the old Etonians and Westminsters at the College. 'Water'—that is, 'rowing'—started at Westminster in 1813. But its numbers were never great, and in 1884 'Water' ceased to exist until its revival about 1914. The Westminster contribution was therefore never very strong. And the Eton contribution, though often producing first-class fours, was rarely sufficient to man an eight of winning Grand class.

To win the Grand in 1902 was no mean achievement, for this was one of only three occasions in fifteen years when Leander were defeated. Third Trinity also won the Stewards' for the second year in succession, and the Silver Goblets.

Although the decision had been made to continue to admit foreign entries for the Regatta, many were still unhappy about the position, and in December 1902 a special meeting of the

[1] See p. 244.

Stewards was convened to consider a suggestion to bar professional coaches. By a large majority they passed a rule that 'no eight-oar, four-oar, or pair-oar crew shall be allowed to compete, if, within four weeks prior to the commencement of the Regatta, the crew shall have been coached—or controlled—by any person not considered an amateur . . . under the general rules'.

In the following spring a further proposal was made to extend this ruling to scullers. This was not carried.

1903

The entries in 1903 fell lower than for nearly ten years, but this was due, in part, at least, to the tightening up of the rules against professionals. There were, for example, no American entries this year, though two Americans had actually sent in their names for the Diamonds. However, there was excitement in plenty.

Third Trinity made a determined effort to win the Grand again, but were so unlucky as to lose C. J. D. Goldie, their No. 5, on the very morning of the first day's racing. They contemplated starting with seven men, as Oxford had in 1843, and actually had an outing, with their stroke, R. H. Nelson, rowing at five, and the boat 'stroked' by W. Dudley Ward at seven. This peculiar arrangement, which was not very flattering to their spare man, was referred to the Stewards, who ruled that an eight-oar crew might start with only seven men, if so desired. The trouble was that C. H. Chalmers, the spare man, was not in training. In the end, however, he came in at three, whilst W. H. Chapman moved from three to five.

In their first heat Third Trinity were drawn against London R.C. They snatched a lead of half a length at the top of the Island, but could get no more. At Remenham, London were only a quarter of a length behind, but then Trinity managed to gain a little, leading by half a length at Fawley. They actually had a little clear water above the mile, but London chased them home, and lost by only a length.

This row served to shake the crew together in their new order,

and to restore their confidence in Chalmers. In the final, against
Leander, they raced practically level to Fawley. At the three-
quarter-mile Leander led by a quarter of a length. There Trinity
spurted, to lead, in their turn, by a few feet, just before the mile,
and by a quarter of a length opposite the White House. Then
Leander countered, and were on level terms again at the grandstand. In the last few yards Leander forced their way up, to win
by six feet.

The Trinity Stewards' four was unaffected by Goldie's illness,
and carried off the prize fairly easily, taking their revenge on
Leander in the process. In the final they beat the Royal Nether-
lands R.C., who had rowed a most eventful semi-final against the
Victoria R.C. of Berlin. The German crew gained an early lead,
lost it through bad steering and regained it, to lead by a third of a
length at Fawley. Once again the Dutchmen drew them back, and
once again the Germans led, this time by a quarter of a length, at
the mile post. Soon after this the Dutchmen drew level for the last
time, and the Germans, probably exhausted, steered across and
fouled them. Both crews stopped, and from the ensuing mêlée
the Dutch crew got away to win.

Two members of this Berlin four—L. Klaus and A. Ehrenberg
—went on to win the Silver Goblets, the first foreign pair to do so.
In their first heat they were drawn against C. J. D. Goldie and
C. W. H. Taylor. This was the day on which Goldie withdrew
from the Third Trinity eight, but he insisted on racing in the
pair. The Germans led up the Island, but the Trinity pair's good
form took them past, to lead by a quarter of a length at Remenham. Goldie soon began to feel his sickness, and for the most of
the course Taylor kept the rudder hard on against himself. They
managed to be on level terms at the three-quarter mile, but could
not keep up the unequal struggle. The Germans got away to win
by two lengths, and went on to an easy victory in the final.

1904

Third Trinity were still in winning vein in 1904, when they
won three events. In the final of the Stewards', against Winnipeg

R.C., Canada, they equalled the record time of 7 min. 30 sec. Their second four won the Visitors', having a hard race against University College Oxford in the final. And Goldie, fit this year, won the Goblets, with Taylor, without difficulty.

There were plenty of fine races at this Regatta, but the most exciting of all was a heat of the Diamonds, in which L. F. Scholes, of Canada, unexpectedly beat the redoubtable F. S. Kelly, winner in the previous two years.

This was a rude shock for the pundits, for Kelly was reckoned the finest, if not the strongest, sculler the Regatta had seen. He started at a great pace, and led Scholes by two lengths at Remenham, where he crossed over into Scholes' water. Then the Canadian, a rough and ugly performer, spurted and drove him out. Even so, Kelly still led by a length at the mile. But he was nearly finished. At the bottom of Phyllis Court the two were level, with Scholes gaining rapidly. And at the grandstand Kelly stopped, having to be lifted from his boat into a Thames Conservancy launch.

The fact was that Kelly was unfit this year. In the following year, beating H. T. Blackstaffe in the final, he set up the Diamonds record of 8 min. 10 sec., which stood until beaten by J. W. Burk in 1938. On that occasion supporters were stationed down the course, to exhort him to keep his rating down. As a result, Blackstaffe set the pace, and led at Fawley, Kelly sculling right away over the second half of the course, to win by nearly a quarter of a minute.

But we must return to Scholes, whose labours in 1904 did not end with his race against Kelly. In the final he was always ahead of his opponent, A. H. Cloutte. At Fawley he led by two lengths. But Cloutte spurted again and again, and was within a length at the mile. Scholes won a desperate race by one and a quarter lengths, in the then record time of 8 min. 23 sec. After the Regatta the Press reported that the Diamond Sculls were on show in a Toronto bar. Nobody apparently objected to this in itself, for it was well known that Scholes' father kept a 'sporting hotel'. But they did take exception to an alleged remark by

Scholes senior, that 'at times they [i.e. the Diamond Sculls] get mixed up with the cigar boxes'! Perhaps this was not very honourable reporting on the part of some sections of the Press; but it was indicative of the sensitive, and even belligerent feelings of the British public, at that time, as regards foreign, and even Dominion sportsmen.

1905

Theodore Cook, once Editor of *The Field*, and always an indefatigable rowing scribe, wrote (*Henley Races*, Oxford University Press) that, in 1905, 'the houseboats and launches moored on the Regatta reach seem to get fewer in number every year'.

In recent years we have seen a revival of launches at Henley, due to the growing popularity of cabin cruisers. But the houseboat is only a memory. There are a few, up and down the river, but none, I imagine, fit to be navigated to Henley. Until 1939 a few were permanently berthed above Henley bridge, but I cannot recall any houseboat being moored on the course during the Regatta.

John Cooper recalls that 'the first little houseboat, rather of the Arc type' came to the Regatta in the early 'seventies. The first big boat—and some of them were big—was Mr. W. H. Weldon's *Athena*, about 1880. Of her, J. Ashby Sterry wrote:

> I fly to the cheery *Athena* for shelter
> The pâté is perfect, the Giesler is dry.
> And I think while I gaze undismayed at the pelter
> That Henley's still joyous in dripping July.

Many of the houseboats were, indeed, splendid affairs, and their occupants offered lavish entertainment. One of the best known was the *Golden Grasshopper*, owned by Raymond Radcliffe, of the *St. Stephen's Review*. One year he let her to a nitrate magnet by the name of Colonel North. On the last night of the Regatta there was a concert on board. After the show the crowd on the river—Cooper said there were three or four hundred punts and canoes—called for a speech, whereupon the gallant Colonel invited them all to supper. He qualified his invitation by saying that the food might run out, but guaranteed that the drink would not. By way of corroborative evidence he then attempted a hornpipe on the deck, and fell flat on his back.

Whenever the nights were fine there would be a crowd of visitors and sightseers around these houseboats, enjoying the illuminations and music. There is no doubt that, with the passing of the houseboats, Henley has lost a touch of bravado and romance.[1]

To return to 1905, the entries once again took an upward turn. The outstanding performance was that already mentioned, in which F. S. Kelly set up a new record for the Diamonds, which was five seconds faster than the then existing Goblets record. There was excitement in the Grand, too, with a serious challenge from two foreign crews. Theodore Cook considered the Vesper B.C. crew, from Philadelphia, to be the strongest foreign crew to come to Henley to that date. But, unhappily, its arrival heralded another dispute about foreign entries. For after the Regatta, allegations were made that Vesper had no good claim to be amateurs. In January 1906 the American sporting Press countered with a violent attack on English sportsmanship, and on the management of the Henley draw in particular. But worse was to come, for in June 1906 the Committee of Management issued a statement about their investigation into the allegation against the Vesper crew. They stated that the National Association of American Oarsmen had failed to make proper inquiries into the status of the crew before certifying their entry, that the cost of sending the crew to Henley had been met by public subscription, that all the members of the crew had accepted money payments, and that the sworn declarations of several of them were untrue.

This, so to speak, 'put the fat properly in the fire'. The Committee resolved 'that no entry of the Vesper B.C. of Philadelphia, nor any entry comprising any member of that club's crew of 1905, be accepted in future'. W. A. L. Fletcher announced that he would propose that no entry at all be accepted from the United

[1] See illustration facing p. 117.

States, and it seemed that the whole question of foreign entries once again hung in the balance. However, Fletcher's resolution was not accepted, and, later in the year, at their December meeting, the Stewards passed a new Rule governing foreign entries, which, by detailing the exact requirement of the Henley amateur Rule, largely put an end to misunderstandings.[1]

Returning to the Regatta, Leander met Vesper in the semi-final of the Grand. Starting at forty-one, to the Americans' thirty-nine, they led at once, but, gaining by inches, had only half a length at Remenham barrier. Rowing the slower stroke, thirty-four to thirty-eight, Leander continued to gain, except when Vesper spurted, which they did frequently. In the end Leander won by a length, in 7 min. 1 sec. In the meantime, the Sport Nautique de Gand had won the other semi-final easily, against London R.C.

In the final, Leander started at forty-two. The Belgian stroke caught a crab on the fifth stroke, but, even so, he managed to put in forty-four strokes in the minute. Leander, however, gained half a length, and continued to gain until they led by a length at Fawley. For one more year the Grand was safe, and Leander won, in the end, quite easily.

1906

In 1906 the Regatta at last became a four-day affair, though it had been the practice, before this, to row some heats on the day before the Regatta, to avoid the necessity for asking any crew or sculler to compete twice for the same event on the same day. This was also the first year in which official timekeepers[2] were appointed, relieving the umpire of that duty.

What the timekeeping was like in the early days—that is, before rowing men took over the running of the Regatta in the mid-eighties—has been described by John Cooper. In the Stewards' stand there used to be a telescope, trained on the start. Through it the Secretary, Mr. Towsey, would watch for the races to begin. On one occasion, being called away to speak

---

[1] See 'Foreign Entries', p. 246.   [2] See 'Record Times', p. 257.

to one of the Stewards, Towsey left Cooper, then a boy of ten, in charge of the telescope. Almost immediately the race started, and Cooper called 'They're off'. Towsey, however, distrusted youth, and had a look for himself. Satisfied that the crews were really away, he then signalled with his flag to the man in the Lion Meadow, across the river, whose duty it was to fire the signal gun. By this time the man's attention had wandered elsewhere, and it was the better part of a minute before he woke up and fired his gun. Only then, says Cooper, did the clocking begin.

What gave 1906 its historic importance, however, was the fact that the Grand Challenge Cup, premier trophy of the Regatta, was at last carried away from these shores.

Leander had had an astonishing run of success, winning the Grand twelve times in the preceding fifteen years. Now, unhappily, they produced no eight at all. Once again the challenge came from Canada, and from Belgium.

The Argonaut R.C., Toronto, beat First Trinity in the first heat, and Thames R.C. in the second. The Club Nautique de Gand beat Magdalen, and Third Trinity in the semi-final. In the other semi-final, Trinity Hall met the Argonauts. Nobody had much hope that they would win, though they led by a few feet at the top of Temple Island. But win they did, after a terrific struggle, in which they gained, literally by inches, to pass the finishing post with just half a length in hand. After this, British hopes for the final rose perceptibly. But, as will often happen at Henley, the gallant Hall had shot their bolt. Although they started at forty-one, the Belgians, at forty-two, led by a length at the quarter-mile, and won as they liked by three lengths. At least the Hall had postponed, by another eight years, the grim day when no English crew should appear in the final of the Grand.

At the same Regatta Leander won the Stewards', from Third Trinity, by two feet. H. T. Blackstaffe won the Diamonds.

During the Regatta, but not as part of it, there was a private match between coxed fours of the Royal Engineers and Royal Artillery. It was won fairly easily by the Engineers, much to the surprise of the onlookers, who had expected that the presence of J. H. Gibbon as stroke of the Gunners would prove decisive.

1907

Leander put on an eight again in 1907, determined to recover the Grand. But any comfort the British public may have drawn from the belief that the Belgian victory of the preceding year was a flash in the pan, made possible by the absence of Leander, was rudely shattered. For the two crews met in the second heat, and not only did the visitors win, but, horror of horrors, they did it by outlasting the Englishmen.

The race was rowed at a great pace, with Ghent stroking forty-three, and Leander forty-two in the first minute. At the quarter-mile Leander led by a canvas, but although they were on the Bucks station, and there was a head wind blowing, they lost a few feet in the next quarter. At Fawley, D. C. R. Stuart, who was stroking Leander from bow side, spurted in an attempt to shake the Belgians off. He gained half a length before they countered, but still Leander led by only a quarter of a length at the mile post. Above the mile the Belgians pushed the rate up to thirty-eight, and came up fast along Phyllis Court Wall. In a desperate finish they won by a third of a length.

In the final, Ghent, this time with the Bucks station, met Christ Church. Both crews rowed twenty-three and forty-four in the half and full minutes, and the Belgians led by three-quarters of a length at the quarter-mile. All over the course they scarcely dropped below thirty-six, and Christ Church hardly below forty. The Belgians were clear at the half-mile, rather more than clear at Fawley, and a length and a quarter to the good after three-quarters of a mile. From there the gallant Christ Church men were able to hold them, and the race was won by a bare length.

There was a worrying moment in the Stewards' Challenge Cup that year, too, when Ludwigshafener R.C. got their bows in front of the Leander four at the mile, after being led for half the distance. Again there was a great struggle, but the Germans stopped, rowed out, opposite the Enclosures. Leander stopped too, but then paddled on to the finish. The danger was probably not as great as it appeared, for next day Magdalen beat Leander by three lengths in the final.

This was a Magdalen four strengthened by the inclusion of the veteran Guy Nickalls at stroke. But at the same time, the Magdalen second four was winning both the Visitors' and Wyfold Challenge Cups. This is the only occasion in the history of the Regatta when one club has won all three four-oared events. It can, of course, only be done by a college, because of the qualification restriction on the Visitors'.

Blackstaffe was expected by many to win the Diamonds again, but he was beaten in a heat by Captain W. H. Darell, whom he had defeated in the 1906 final. Only for a few strokes, near the mile, did Blackstaffe show ahead, but it was a grim struggle all the way, and Darell's margin of victory was only half a length. He had another stiff fight in the semi-final, until his opponent, B. von Gaza, stopped, rowed out, near the mile. In the final, against A. McCulloch, Darell led all the way, but in the end won by only a length and a quarter.

After the 1907 Regatta, a lady, whose name was not disclosed, complained to H.M. The Queen that the swans—Her Majesty's royal birds—had been housed, during the Regatta, in a pigsty. The Queen was not amused, and Sir Douglas Dawson, Comptroller of H.M. Household, wrote severely to the Stewards. Much acrimonious correspondence followed, before the matter was closed. Then the Stewards, ever men of resource, elected Sir Douglas Dawson to be a Steward himself.

1908

In 1908 the Olympic Games came to Great Britain for the first time, and John Cooper tells a story of how nearly the rowing did not come to Henley. The A.R.A. were entrusted with the running of the Olympic Regatta, and, it seems, originally planned to hold it at Putney, London being the official venue of the Games.

At a meeting in the previous autumn the matter came up for discussion, and Cooper records that he urged the Stewards to make a bid for the Regatta, on the grounds that foreign crews would naturally expect it to take place at Henley. But his plea found little support, the Stewards not wishing 'to interfere with the arrangements of the A.R.A.'. Cooper then obtained some Vincent's Club notepaper, from Oxford, and wrote to *The Field*, under the pseudonym of 'An American Oxonian'. 'How could it be ?' he asked, 'that the Regatta should be held at a place of which he, as an American, had never heard until matriculating at B.N.C. ? Would not the Olympic Games be absurd, in Greece, if not held at Athens ?' and more in similar vein.

At the next Stewards' meeting 'An American Oxonian's' letter was read out, and voted to be fine stuff!

In the previous summer, before the 1907 Regatta, the Stewards had resolved that, in view of the forthcoming Olympic Regatta, no foreign entries should be accepted for the Royal Regatta in 1908. At the time this decision passed without comment, but later the Press was deluged with letters complaining of the unsporting and disgusting action of the Stewards in passing a rule which debarred the holders from defending the Grand Challenge Cup. In vain did the Stewards protest that the rule was passed before the 1907 Regatta, and that Ghent knew the position when they entered. Not until the Belgians themselves wrote, agreeing with the Stewards, and declaring that they would not think of competing at Henley so soon before the Olympic Regatta, did the agitation die down.

Since neither of the eights nominated to represent Great Britain entered at Henley, the Grand, in 1908, looked to be a very open event, if not 'easy money'. It attracted a record entry of ten crews, seven of them Oxford and Cambridge colleges. Eton entered for the Grand this year, for the last time. But the winners were Christ Church, who beat Eton by a length and a half in the final.

The outstanding performance of the Regatta was put up by the Magdalen four, the same which had won the Visitors' and Wyfold Cups in 1907. In the first heat of the Stewards' they had a close race with Thames R.C., winning by a length and a half, in

VII. THE OLYMPIC GAMES

*: 1908: Leander Club, representing Great Britain, beat Belgium in the final of the VIII's (see p. 134)

om: 1948: B. H. T. Bushnell and R. D. Burnell (Great Britain), after winning the Double Sculls

VIII. THE FASTEST SCHOOL AND THE FASTEST COLLEGE CREW

Top: Eton beat First Trinity B.C. Cambridge in the final of the Ladies' Plate, 1911, in 6 56 sec. (This time has never been beaten by a school crew)

Bottom: Lady Margaret B.C. beat Trinity Hall Cambridge in the Ladies' Plate, 1949, in 6 43 sec. (This was a record both for the event and for the course; see p. 189)

record time. In the final, London R.C. lost a length through hitting the booms near Fawley, when the crews were level. Magdalen again won by a length and a half. In the Visitors' final, after a close race for half the distance, Magdalen beat Jesus College Cambridge fairly easily. But they did not slack off, and added the Visitors' record to their laurels.

In the Diamonds, Blackstaffe was put out on a technical foul in one of the heats, and McCulloch won the final without being pressed.

The Olympic Regatta took place at the end of July, and, although it was not a part of Henley Regatta, it was sufficiently closely allied to warrant a place in Henley history.

The course was extended some two hundred and seventy yards downstream, to bring it up to a mile and a half. The piling of the normal Regatta course was slightly adjusted to allow this extension without unnecessary additional work. Apart from this, the arrangements were unchanged, although some extra grandstand accommodation was provided.

It was permissible, then, to enter two crews for each Olympic event, and there were four events: Eights, Fours, Pairs, and Sculls. Including the United Kingdom, seven countries were represented, the others being Canada, Germany, Belgium, Norway, Holland, and Hungary. Only one foreign crew reached a final.[1]

That might have made the proceedings rather monotonous. But, at that time, no Regatta could be monotonous if 'les braves Belges' were present. Already they had shattered the calm of English rowing by twice carrying off the Grand Challenge Cup. And who was to stop them now?

This, indeed, was quite a problem. The pundits said that all was not well with English rowing. I fancy that the United Kingdom selectors were thankful for the rule which enabled them to make two guesses. They felt bound to nominate the Cambridge crew, stroked by 'Duggie' Stuart, which had won the University Boat Race for the past two years. But they were not greatly im-

See Appendix C p. 285.

pressed by the way Cambridge rowed. And so, nominally as their second string, they got together a Leander eight which included many of the great names, almost of the previous generation of oarsmen.[1] Certainly some of them had been in retirement for several years.

Leander won their first race, against Hungary, quite easily. But Cambridge drew the redoubtable Belgians. Stuart struck forty-one and the Belgians forty-three up Temple Island. Cambridge showed ahead for a few strokes, but the crews were level at the first signal. Then the Belgians spurted to thirty-seven, and at the half-distance they led by three-quarters of a length. Cambridge chased them home, but could never make any impression, and Belgium won by a length and a third.

In the meantime Leander had won their second race, against the Argonauts of Canada, by a length. But they had to race hard all the way.

And so to the final, with the honour of English rowing in the hands of a crew which, whilst readily recognized as splendid exponents of the finer arts of rowing, were looked upon as somewhat doubtful 'stayers'.

Once again the Belgians started at a great pace, rowing forty-three strokes in the first minute. Leander were only one stroke behind, and began to forge ahead at once. At the first signal they led by half a length. The Belgians tried their usual early spurt, but still Leander crept up, leading by three-quarters of a length at the half-way mark. At the third signal the 'old men' were striking thirty-six, to their opponents' thirty-eight, and, wonder of wonders, were still gaining slowly. At the Henley mile post Leander had eased to thirty-five, and daylight separated the boats. Up the Enclosures they drew away, to win by a handsome two lengths.

There is, I believe, a lesson to be learned from this race. There is always a tendency for the young to think the 'old' too old.

---

[1] Leander (1908 Olympic Games): A. C. Gladstone (bow), F. S. Kelly, B. C. Johnstone, Guy Nickalls, C. D. Burnell, R. H. Sanderson, R. B. Etherington-Smith, H. C. Bucknall (stroke), G. S. Maclagan (cox). See photograph facing p. 132.

Certainly it is true that the veteran of thirty or more summers needs longer to prepare than does the undergraduate. But if he is willing to face the rigours of racing at Henley, at that age, it is more than likely that he will leave nothing to chance. And there is a lot, too, in stamina and experience. Many men, particularly in the heavier weights, never reach their full maturity of strength until long after they have left the University; and for many that means long after they have given up active rowing. Can it be put thus: Sometimes the old are too old; often the young are not old enough?

Theodore Cook compared the relative times of the 1908 Olympic Regatta with the then records over the Henley distance. He estimated that no eight had ever moved faster over the Henley course than this veteran Leander crew.

The other Olympic events proved a happy hunting-ground for the English crews. The great Magdalen four[1] won comfortably, beating Canada in a heat, and Leander in the final. In the pair-oared race, one Leander pair (J. R. K. Fenning and G. L. Thomson) disposed of the Argonauts, whilst another (G. E. Fairbairn and P. Verdon) beat the Berliner Ruder Club pair. Fenning and Thomson were comfortable winners in the final. In the single sculls final, H. T. Blackstaffe beat A. McCulloch, the Diamonds winner. The only other sculler who might have made a showing was von Gaza. He broke his stretcher, but was already behind Blackstaffe at the time.

1909

Perhaps due to the impetus given by the Olympic Regatta,[2] there were more starters in the 1909 Regatta than ever before. It was the first time the entries had topped the seventy mark, as against an average of fifty-six for the preceding five years.

The Belgians came back, with seven of the men who had al-

[1] Magdalen College (1908 Olympic Games): C. R. Cudmore (bow), J. A. Gillan, D. Mackinnon, J. R. Somers-Smith (stroke and steers).

[2] It is interesting to note that the same thing happened forty years later, after the 1948 Olympic Games, when the Henley starters topped one hundred and fifty for the first time.

ready won the Grand, and they won again, for the third time in four years. Some thought that Magdalen might have stopped them, for they were beaten by only half a length, rowing off the Berks station in a Bushes Wind. At any rate, none could have grudged the Belgians their victory, for they had taught English oarsmen a valuable lesson. They brought many supporters with them, including the Burgomaster of Ghent, and round him they danced in joy after their final race. John Cooper, the Regatta Secretary, escaped the demonstration with difficulty, averring that he was too old to play 'Round the Mulberry Bush'.

Apart from Magdalen's defeat in the Grand, this was a great year for Oxford rowing. St. John's won the Ladies' Plate for the first and only time in their history. Their time in the final, when they beat First Trinity with some ease, was only one second slower than the time which the Belgians recorded in beating Jesus in the Grand final. Wadham won the Thames Cup for the second year in succession, beating Oriel in the final. Christ Church beat St. John's in the final of the Visitors', and Balliol beat Christ Church in the final of the Wyfold Cup. Oxford men today must look with nostalgia on such a state of affairs.

Metropolitan rowing, at this time, was still in eclipse, and a special word is therefore due about the Thames R.C. four, which won the Stewards'. It was a remarkable crew, in that, although it entered under Thames colours, it was, to all intents and purposes, a private four, got together by J. Beresford.

At the time of his victory, Beresford was a few weeks short of his forty-first birthday. He made up the four, consisting of himself at bow, together with K. Vernon, C. G. Rought, and B. Logan, in the autumn of 1907. In 1908 they won the championship of Holland, but lost to Magdalen in the Stewards' at Henley Royal Regatta, forcing them to set up a new record in the process. So they went back to work for another winter. In 1909 they reaped their reward, beating Magdalen, in the final, by a length and a half.

This four were never pretty, but they were by far the fastest club four of the period. In the following year they lost their semi-final to Winnipeg R.C., the ultimate winners. In 1911 they came again to beat Trinity Hall in the final. And in 1912 they lost a terrific final to New College. They were ahead at the mile, but the great R. C. Bourne raced them almost to a standstill, and took New College away to win by two and a quarter lengths.

1910

A Rule was passed in 1910 against dual entries in the Ladies' Plate and the Thames Cup. To be more exact, it was still permissible to enter for both, but now became obligatory to scratch from one or the other before the draw.

The weather was particularly unpleasant, the wind sometimes dropping away altogether, and sometimes blowing strongly off the Bucks shore; rain fell intermittently. But in compensation there were an unprecedented number of close finishes. No less than a dozen races were won by margins of half a length or less, and four verdicts were measured in feet.

Undoubtedly the most interesting race of all was the heat of the Grand, between Leander Club and Magdalen College Oxford.

It is difficult, today, to visualize the true meaning of the dreaded Bushes Wind, though even now, with the start snugly tucked away on the Berkshire side of the Island, and the course not approaching the Bucks shore until Fawley, we still talk of a Bushes Wind as something which favours the Bucks station.

In 1910 a really strong Bushes Wind was reckoned to be decisive, if there was anything like equality between the crews. And that was what Magdalen had to face, drawn on the Berks station, against a Leander crew stroked by R. C. Bourne.

Leander were a very heavy crew, but short of practice, and Bourne took them away at 10—19—37. P. Fleming, stroking Magdalen, fairly leaped from the stakeboat at 12—22—42 strokes in the first minute. Magdalen were clear of Leander in seventy-five seconds, and had a lead of a length and a quarter at the quarter-mile. The start was sensational, but that was not the half of the story. For A. W. F. Donkin, the Magdalen cox, steered straight in front of Leander, without a moment's hesitation appropriating the shelter of the famous 'Bushes'. Less than two minutes from the start the two boats were in perfect line-ahead.

Bourne apparently reckoned that there was nothing he could do about it, and held his spurt for the finish, when the pace would have slowed sufficiently to give his heavyweights a better chance of making themselves felt. Donkin, it is said, never once so much as turned his head to see whether danger threatened, until he reached Fawley. Magdalen then had half a length of clear water in hand.

Striking thirty-six, Magdalen held their advantage, and it was not until the mile post that Bourne attacked. Then Donkin gave way, very slowly, so that he regained the Berks station opposite the Enclosures, just where it offered the advantage of slack water. The Leander spurt was a good one, but they had too much leeway to make up, and Magdalen got home by three-quarters of a length.

This was a particularly interesting race from the point of view of the ethics of steering at Henley. In the heat of battle hard things were said about Magdalen. But in fact, on the day, they faced a Bushes Wind which was estimated to favour the Bucks station by anything up to two lengths. They took a calculated risk, as the price of a chance of winning; and when the excitement had died down, that was generally acknowledged.

The other Grand finalists in 1910 were Jesus College Cambridge, who, in their first heat, got home with only two feet to spare from Thames R.C. Subsequently they beat London by a length, but in the final they were no match for Magdalen, who beat them by two lengths, to win the Grand for the first time.

St. John's Oxford, trying to repeat their victory of the previous year, won a heat of the Ladies' Plate by five feet from Lady Margaret B.C., but then succumbed to Balliol, who, in turn, lost a great final to Eton by a margin of only half a length. In the Thames Cup the Anglian B.C. had only four feet to spare in beating Clare, but went on to win the final from Merton College by a third of a length.

One of the heaviest fours ever to race at Henley appeared in the Stewards' Cup. They were the Mainzer Ruder Club, from Mayence, who boasted three men over fourteen stone. For England there was once again Beresford's Thames four, but this time they went down, after a hard fight, to Winnipeg R.C. The Canadians averaged but little over eleven stone, but in the final they raced the giant Mainzer crew to a standstill, and in the end won quite easily. This was a tremendously popular victory, both because it kept the Stewards' 'in the family', if not 'at home', and also because it was a just reward for persistent endeavour. Three times Canadian crews had crossed the Atlantic to attempt the Grand, and five times to attempt the Stewards'. And this, apart from Scholes' win in the Diamonds, was their first victory.

The two other four-oared events were both taken by Trinity Hall, whilst an old 'Hall' man, G. L. Thomson, stroked the winning Goblets pair. His partner, J. S. Burn, caught a crab when they were leading by half a length at the three-quarter-mile post. But they managed to recover, to win by three-quarters of a length.

1911

Finals day was shifted to the Saturday, in 1911, which proved a popular innovation, as may be imagined. This was the year in which Remenham Club built their bungalow, in the enclosure between the three-quarter-mile and mile signals, where it stands today, 'its position', as Theodore Cook wrote, 'in every way unrivalled, for it is the only place from which it is possible to see both start and finish of every race'.

The subsequent transfer of the start to the Berkshire side of Temple Island deprived the Remenham Club of this distinction. But it is still an admirable place for those who do not like the hurly-burly of the Stewards' Enclosure, and who are more concerned to watch the crews at the critical stage of the race than to witness a few grandstand finishes.

The Remenham Club was founded in 1909, and its membership has always been limited to members of the seven founding clubs—London, Thames, Vesta, Twickenham, Molesey,

Kingston, and Staines. Before building their clubhouse the Remenham Club shared a lawn with the Grosvenor Club, Piccadilly. However, the Grosvenor Club did not long maintain their connection with Henley.

For the second year running the Grand final turned out to be a race between the head-of-the-river boats from the two Universities, and once again Magdalen were the winners. Cook said that this Magdalen crew were the heaviest that had ever sat a boat. Certainly their average of 12 st. $10\frac{1}{4}$ lb. was higher than that of any previous winning eight at Henley, or than any University crew which had then rowed in the Boat Race.

Magdalen had to work hard for their victory, for they rowed through two heats to reach the final. In the first they led New College off the start, but had only a quarter of a length at Fawley, where a tremendous battle began. New College just failed to get on level terms at the mile, when their spurt died away. They tried again, but hit the booms, and Magdalen won by a length and a quarter. This New College crew, and also the Radley crew in the Ladies' Plate, were using 12-feet 6-inch oars, 3-feet 9-inch inboard, with $5\frac{1}{4}$-inch blades.

In the third heat of the Grand there was a sensation, when the Belgian crew stopped at the bottom of the Enclosures, and were beaten by Ottawa R.C. The race was rowed at a great pace—the Canadians were clocked at thirty-eight at the half-mile, when they were a quarter of a length down, and the Belgians were rating thirty-nine at the mile, where the crews were level. Then Ottawa began to draw away, and the end came suddenly, when G. Visser, the Belgian stroke, stopped with a strained stomach muscle. The Belgians considered this to be the fastest of all their Henley crews.

Ottawa put up a great fight in the semi-final, but in the end Magdalen were too strong, drawing away up the Enclosures to win by two lengths. On this occasion, and perhaps with more justification than in the previous year, Magdalen were severely criticized for taking the Canadians' water at the finish. The final was a repetition of this race, with a gallant Jesus crew holding on grimly for three-quarters of a mile, only to be crushed by one of the strongest and finest college crews ever to row at Henley.

Eton had a fast crew this year, equalling the Ladies' Plate record of 7 min. 1 sec. against University College in a heat, which they won very easily. They then set up a new record of 6 min. 56 sec. in the final, against First Trinity.[1] This was six seconds faster than Magdalen's winning Grand time, a remarkable performance, even allowing for the fact that the race was rowed in the afternoon, when conditions had improved.

But in spite of these fine performances, and fast times, 1911 will be remembered chiefly for the Goblets dead heat between J. Beresford and A. H. Cloutte, and B. Logan and C. G. Rought, all of the Thames R.C. Their dead heat was achieved in the record time of 8 min. 8 sec., which was not to be equalled for another twenty-seven years, and not to be beaten until 1952. There was never more than two-thirds of a length between the two pairs, with Logan and Rought leading by less than half a length at the mile. After the race the two strokes tossed up to decide the result, because three of the four men were also rowing in the Thames four. Cloutte won the toss, and in the final he and Beresford beat N. M. Bruce and C. A. Gladstone, of Christ Church, by a length and a half. Thames also won the Stewards', and Beresford, the oldest competitor in the Regatta, thus became the only man to row in two finals, and in a year of sultry heat, which all found exhausting.

One other race is worthy of special mention. In the final of the Diamonds, E. W. Powell spurted at thirty-six, from below the bottom of Phyllis Court wall, in an attempt to catch the holder, W. D. Kinnear, of the Kensington R.C. But Kinnear, always sculling the longer and slower stroke, was too good for him. Opposite the grandstand Powell stopped, completely sculled out, and Kinnear went on to win his second Diamonds victory.

[1] Eton: A. C. Beasley-Robinson (bow), F. A. H. Pitman, A. T. Leather, A. H. M. Wedderburn, C. E. V. Buxton, E. D. Horsfall, F. F. V. Scrutton, S. D. Gladstone (stroke), G. W. E. Elliot (cox). See photograph facing p. 133.

1912

The year 1912 saw the first visit of a reigning Sovereign to the Royal Regatta. On the Saturday, Their Majesties King George V and Queen Mary attended. Arriving by royal train, they were welcomed at the station by the Mayor of Henley, and then embarked in the Royal Barge, and proceeded down to the Royal Enclosure.[1] During the luncheon interval they were taken, again in the Royal Barge, to Greenlands, amidst scenes of great enthusiasm, to lunch with the Hon. W. F. D. Smith (later Lord Hambleden). After lunch the party returned to the Enclosures, amidst scenes of even greater excitement, in which oars, paddles, and punt poles were ceremonially 'tossed' in the great throng of boats which lined the course. Their Majesties followed the final of the Grand in the umpire's launch, and after the last race the Queen presented the prizes.

In the racing there were some surprising results, which were probably due to the fact that the Olympic Regatta, at Stockholm, was to be held soon after Henley. British crews had already been selected, and some were no doubt preparing for the Olympics rather than for Henley. Kinnear, for instance, was put out in the first heat of the Diamonds, by C. M. Stuart, who did not even reach the final. Yet at Stockholm Kinnear had no difficulty with any of his opponents.

Leander, later to win the Olympic eights, were beaten by Sydney R.C. Sydney, however, were certainly a formidable crew, and had already won good races against the Argonauts and New College.

For the third year in succession Eton won the Ladies' Plate, and once again their time was faster than that recorded in the Grand. It is easy to say that conditions changed, but those who know the genius of R. S. de Haviland's coaching sometimes wonder how it was that they always changed the right way. The fact was that, in the preceding six years, college crews, and one Eton crew, had filled nine out of twelve places in the Grand

[1] See photograph facing p. 117.

finals, the other three being the three winning Belgian crews. There is no escaping the conclusion that 'Havi' was turning out crews as good as any in the country at that time. On this occasion they won convincingly from Jesus College Cambridge, who had been runners up in the Grand for the last three years, and who had just regained the Headship of the river in the May Races.

In the Stewards', the famous Thames four were unexpectedly beaten by New College, once again stroked by R. C. Bourne. But the old Thames rivals fought out the final of the Goblets, the victory this year going to Logan and Rought. France scored her first Henley success, through the R. C. de Paris, who won the Thames Cup fairly safely, though they were hunted home by Oriel College Oxford in a heat, and by St John's College in the final.

1913

Perhaps 1913 was something of an anti-climax after the Royal visit, and the Olympic year. But there was plenty of good racing.

After a gap of seven years Leander once again won the Grand. To beat the Argonauts in a heat they had to equal the record of 6 min. 51 sec., and were thought to have covered the second half of the course faster than it had ever been covered before. And so, once again, success eluded the gallant Canadians. Jesus College Cambridge reached the final for the fourth time in five years, but could do no more than give Leander a good race.

The local Marlow R.C. excelled themselves in the Thames Cup, beating Pembroke Cambridge by a canvas, and then rowing a dead heat with Caius. They won the re-row by a quarter of a length, but then succumbed, by a length, to Oriel, the ultimate winners.

In the Stewards' there was a desperately exciting race between the Mainzer Ruderverein, who had previously beaten the Argonauts by many lengths, and Leander. The Germans led by a length at Fawley, but then Leander closed up, in spite of erratic steering. Another spurt at the mile took them level, but the Germans just got home by two feet. Excitement was intense when New College went down to race the Mainzers in the final. Once again the Germans led out at the start, and once again the English crew closed up near the half-mile. Then, unhappily, Mainz steered right across and fouled New College, and the prospects of a grandstand finish were gone. The umpire awarded the race to New College without an appeal.

The brothers A. A. and S. E. Swann won the Goblets. The Diamonds went abroad for the fourth time in their history, the winner being C. McVilly, of Tasmania. He should certainly have been a popular winner but, unfortunately, he suffered for the feeling which had been aroused, in recent Regattas, on the question of steering. He was severely criticized for washing E. D. P. Pinks, of London R.C., in the final, and when he stepped up to receive his prize he was received in silence—neither a very charitable, nor a creditable, performance on the part of the Henley crowd.

1914

And so, in 1914, we come to the abrupt and tragic end of one of Henley's brightest chapters. Though in later years the entries and the attendance in the Enclosures, and the strength of the foreign challenge, were all to increase out of all recognition, yet it was never to be quite the same Henley again. Indeed, the change at Henley, after the war, was but one facet of the change in England as a whole. Above all, the leisured days of the Edwardian era were over.

Nor were the shocks long in coming. For in the first four heats of the Grand Challenge Cup, in 1914, Winnipeg R.C., Canada, beat Thames R.C., the University B.C. of Boston beat London R.C., Harvard University beat Leander, and the Mainzer Ruderverein beat Jesus College Cambridge. All four English contestants for the Grand were thus despatched in their first races. The two American crews won their semi-finals, and Harvard beat Boston, by a length and a quarter, in the final. This Harvard eight were the Junior University crew, and were entered as the Harvard Athletic Association B.C.[1]

---

[1] It is a remarkable fact that on each occasion on which Harvard have won the Grand Challenge Cup at Henley, war has broken out. It has happened in 1914, 1939, and 1950 (Korea).

I cannot refrain from quoting Theodore Cook's prognostication after this débâcle. 'It may with some confidence be predicted', he wrote, 'that not even when the Royal Regatta has celebrated its centenary will such proceedings again be chronicled in its chief race.'

In the years between the wars English rowing had its ups and downs, though we lost the Grand only three times. But in 1939, that very centenary year of which Cook wrote, his prophecy came so near to being disproved that we can hardly escape the conclusion that a mischievous Fate had overheard his rash statement. To be sure, not all the English crews were again beaten in their opening races, but only one, Jesus College, reached the semi-finals, whilst Harvard, for the second time in their history, won the final, their opponents on this occasion being the Argonaut R.C.

There was another odd coincidence between 1914 and 1939. For in the former year Italy won her first Henley trophy, through Giuseppe Sinigaglia, in the Diamonds; and in 1939 came her next, and only other success, when G. Scherli and E. Broschi shared the honour of the Centenary Double Sculls race with J. Beresford, jun., and L. F. Southwood.

Sinigaglia was a giant of 14 st. 10 lb., and he had to work hard for his victory. He first beat E. D. P. Pinks, after a close race to the mile. Then he disposed of J. B. Ayer, of Boston, and R. Dibble, of Toronto, proving too strong for both of them at the finish. In the final he met C. M. Stuart of Trinity Hall. Stuart jumped him at the start. Near the quarter-mile the Italian touched the booms, and was two lengths down at the signal. Sinigaglia was nearly on terms again at Fawley, but a spurt gave Stuart half a length at the three-quarter-mile post. There was a good race for the next quarter of a mile, but then the Englishman, giving away nearly four stone, had had enough. He stopped, rowed out, and Sinigaglia finished alone.

Only in the Stewards' did an English crew give its supporters any real cause for rejoicing in an international race. This was Leander, stroked by Bourne. Their opponents were the now-familiar Mainzer Ruderverein. After half a mile the Germans led by a length. They held this advantage to the mile, though Leander were pushing them hard. Then Bourne started his usual series of spurts. Leander came up fast, and at the bottom of Phyllis Court wall the Germans stopped, their number three having collapsed.

CHAPTER SIX

Changing Scene. 1919–39

HENLEY is said to be a conservative institution. Yet it seldom fails to reflect the times, the changing opinions and fashions, and even the political and social outlook of the world beyond the Thames Valley.

Of no chapter in Henley history is this more true than of the twenty years between the two world wars. It was an era of unrest and feverish activity. The old standards were gone, and the new standards were not to the liking of everyone. The strains of *The Arcadians*, drifting over the evening air, from the deck of the *Golden Grasshopper*, or the *Maid of Perth*, gave way to the insistent grinding of the afternoon gramophone.

From the background pattern of Henley between the wars four changes stand out. Though all become apparent as the story unfolds, they are deserving of mention at the beginning of this chapter.

The four changes are: the inauguration of the 'Straight Course', the opening of the Stewards' Enclosure, the increase in both home and foreign entries, and the collapse of Oxford rowing.

The change to the Straight Course, starting on the Berkshire side of Temple Island, came in 1924, after a year of experiment with a straight but short course, in 1923. The Stewards' Enclosure was opened in 1919, with the object of meeting the increased costs of running the Regatta. Both are dealt with in Chapter Two.

The ever-rising list of entries, and particularly the growing strength of the challenge from overseas, had caused anxiety even before the War. There were those who thought that the ravages of war would have solved both problems, or at least postponed them for some years. But it seems that war acts as a stimulant to sport. Between 1919 and 1939, the number of starters at Henley rose from an average of 67 to an average of 106 a year. And in the same period the foreign entry nearly doubled.

There remains the eclipse of Oxford rowing between the wars. That it took place on a scale which justifies the use of the word 'collapse' is immediately evident from the table below. What, then, of its importance to the Henley story?

Oxford and Cambridge Colleges, and, in the early days, the University crews themselves, have always formed a large, and sometimes a predominant, proportion of the Henley entry, particularly in the eight-oared events.

Without their entry, even today, the Regatta would be a very different affair. In the early days it is doubtful whether it could have survived at all. Therefore the collapse—eclipse—call it what you will, of one of the two partners, must be of importance.

Today a whole generation of Henley oarsmen has grown up without knowing a serious Oxford challenge at the Regatta. The present state of affairs is taken for granted. Yet a glance at the statistics, at the list of Henley winners, even at the few details given in the table below, shows that this was not always so. Since the days when travel ceased to be a major problem, Cambridge, as the larger University, has generally sent more crews to Henley. But quality and quantity do not always go hand in

OXFORD AND CAMBRIDGE EIGHT-OARED ENTRIES
AND WINS AT HENLEY ROYAL REGATTA

	OXFORD			CAMBRIDGE		
	Entries	Finals	Wins	Entries	Finals	Wins
1895–1904	35	11	6	44	14	8
1905–1914	67	17	7	103	22	9
1920–1929	72	10 [1]	6 [2]	125	21	8
1930–1939	87	2	0	155	18	9
1946–1955	84	2	1	178	18	10

[1] Nine of these finalists were between 1920 and 1924.
[2] All these wins were between 1920 and 1924.

IX. TWO GREAT FOURS

top: Third Trinity B.C. Cambridge, 1924: C. R. M. Eley, J. A. Macnabb, R. E. Morrison, and T. R. B. Sanders

bottom: F.C. Zurich Ruder Club, 1935: H. Betschart, H. Homberger, A. Homberger, and K. Schmidt

X. THREE GREAT SCULLERS

Top: R. Pearce beats T. A. B. Brocklebank, Diamond Sculls, 1931 ('a comfortable victor
see pp. 163–4)

Centre: Dr. H. Buhtz, 1934, still the fastest sculler to Fawley

Bottom: J. W. Burk beats R. Verey, Diamond Sculls final, 1939

hand, and a calculation will show that, before 1925, Oxford produced, on the whole, a higher percentage of finalists and winners than their rivals.

Why this Oxford collapse took place is a matter of interest to students of rowing. How the situation can be restored must be a matter of concern to the Regatta authorities.

1919

But we must return to 1919. Within a fortnight of the signing of the Armistice, in November 1918, a letter appeared in *The Field*, urging the revival of Henley Regatta. In January the committee of Leander Club took the initiative in calling a meeting of rowing men. This meeting concluded that it was too soon to revive the Royal Regatta at Henley, but that the Stewards should be asked to run an interim Regatta.

Then, for Henley, came a sudden and tragic loss. H. T. Steward had died during the War, and on 10 February 1919 W. A. L. Fletcher was elected to fill his place as Chairman of the Committee of Management. Fletcher was not at the meeting at which he was elected, for three days earlier he had developed influenza. Four days after the meeting he was dead, and Henley had lost the leadership of one of the outstanding oarsmen and personalities of the time.

Nevertheless, under the Chairmanship of F. I. Pitman, the Stewards set about organizing the Royal Henley Peace Regatta of 1919. It was a time of feverish activity, for everything had to be started from scratch, including the laying out of the new Stewards' Enclosure. But their efforts were rewarded, for what was originally expected to be a two-day stop-gap, became, in the end, a fully fledged four-day Regatta.

Since the standard was unpredictable, and so many oarsmen were still serving in the forces, the traditional Henley trophies were not offered. Instead, the events were:

The King's Cup, presented by H.M. King George V, 'for any crew of amateur oarsmen[1] who, previous to November 11th, 1918, served

---

[1] See p. 46.

in the Army, Navy or Air Force of any country which fought for the Allied cause. . . '. [This cup, which was won by the Australian Army crew, has since become the trophy for the Inter-State Championship of Australia.]

The Fawley Cup, for senior eights 'of amateur oarsmen from the United Kingdom. . . '.

The Elsenham Cup, on qualifications similar to those of the Ladies' Plate.

The Leander Cup, for Allied fours, on the same qualifications as the King's Cup.

The Wargrave Manor Cup, for Service fours, on the same qualifications as the Fawley Cup.

The Public Schools' Cup. [This was the original Henley Public Schools' Cup, which had been transferred to Marlow Regatta in 1885, and was now loaned by them for this occasion.]

The Hambleden Pairs, and the *Kingswood Sculls*, for 'Amateurs . . . of the Allied Countries'.

The Remenham Cup, for clinker eights, and *The Temple Cup*, for clinker fours.

A race was also announced for not more than two crews each from the Oxford and Cambridge University Boat Clubs. But, when both Universities entered for the King's Cup, Oxford, as losers of the 1914 Boat Race, challenged Cambridge to a private match, in the event of their not meeting in the King's Cup.

The King's Cup produced some excellent sport, and a surprisingly high standard of rowing. The Australian Army first crew, after beating their own second eight, won a good semi-final against the Cambridge University Service crew, by half a length. In the meantime, the Oxford University Service crew had comfortably disposed of the Canadian Army, and, less comfortably, of the American Army. The Americans led by three-quarters of a length at Fawley, and by a few feet at the mile. But they were lacking in training, and Oxford got away to win by a length and a quarter. In the final, the Australians were fast away, and were clear of Oxford at Fawley. But they won by only a length.

In the Fawley Cup, both the University crews were beaten, in turn, by Christ Church, who succumbed in the final, after a good race, to Thames R.C., stroked by the veteran Beresford. The Elsenham Cup produced a schools final, which Shrewsbury won from Bedford after a good race. The Public Schools Cup, contested on fixed seats, was won by Winchester. Leander won both the Leander Cup and the Wargrave Manor Cup, quite easily, with the same crew in both events. The brothers C. E. V. and M. V. Buxton were easy winners of the Hambleden Pairs, and D. C. Hadfield had no difficulty in taking the Kingswood Sculls back to New Zealand.

There was difficulty over the Oxford and Cambridge Challenge Match, because, with Oxford rowing in the final of the King's Cup, it could not take place until late in the evening, and then as the second race in the day for Oxford. The problem was put to a committee of three non-University Stewards, who recommended that, in the circumstances, the race could be satisfactory to neither party. It was therefore scratched, but the second crews raced, Cambridge being the winners by a length.

1920

In 1920 conditions had sufficiently returned to normal for the competition to be resumed for the usual Henley Trophies. The standard was variable, but there was plenty of exciting racing.

A strong Magdalen crew, stroked by the veteran E. D. Horsfall, who had rowed for Oxford before the war, won both the Grand and Stewards' Challenge Cups fairly easily.

The qualifications for the Ladies' Plate were amended to admit the Royal Military College, Sandhurst, and the Royal Military Academy, Woolwich. There was a record entry of eighteen crews for this event, including seven schools, and this made it necessary to row two rounds, for some crews, on the opening day. Eton were the only school to survive until the Friday, though Radley and Shrewsbury went down fighting, to Pembroke College Cambridge and Christ's College respectively, both by half-length verdicts. The final was an all-Oxford occasion, in which Christ Church beat Merton by a length and a half.

G. O. Nickalls and R. S. C. Lucas won the Silver Goblets, thus recording Magdalen's third victory at the Regatta, and the twelfth personal success, in this event, for a member of the Nickalls family.

On the sculling scene there appeared a name that was to dominate English sculling for the next twenty years. J. Beresford, jun., won the Diamonds for the first of four times. This in itself does not constitute a record, for three men—A. A. Casamajor, J. Lowndes, and Guy Nickalls—each won five times. But they would certainly have admitted that their successes never involved them in the sort of racing which Beresford had to face in the 'twenties. For example, seven races sufficed to win the Diamonds five times for Casamajor. Beresford had to win fourteen races to carry off the coveted prize four times.

In the same period Beresford won the Wingfield Sculls, the Amateur Championship, no less than seven times, which beat Casamajor's record by one, and is still unequalled. He was also, and, indeed, still is, the only man to have competed in five successive Olympiads.[1] In the first of these, in 1920, Beresford lost the final of the Olympic Single Sculls, by only one second, and thereby spotlighted an interesting situation. For two months earlier his opponent, J. B. Kelly, had been refused admission to the Diamond Sculls.

The case of J. B. Kelly has been quoted, and more often misquoted, many times, in the Press. To the best of my belief the true story has never before been published.

It will be remembered that after the trouble with the Vesper B.C. entry, in 1905, the Stewards passed a resolution that in future no entry from the Vesper B.C. of Philadelphia should be accepted. That resolution still stood on the Minute Book, and it was for this reason that Kelly, who was entered by the Vesper club, was not accepted. In explaining this to the American Rowing Association, the Stewards also pointed out, for future reference, that they thought it doubtful whether, in any case, Kelly could

---

[1] J. Beresford, Jun., Olympic Games, 1920, 2nd in Single Sculls; 1924, won Single Sculls; 1928, 2nd in Eight-oar 1932, won Coxswainless Fours; 1936, won Double Sculls.

have qualified as an amateur under the A.R.A. and Henley definition current at the time. This no doubt gave rise to the miscon-
ception that Kelly's entry had actually been refused on these
grounds. Had the American Rowing Association been aware of
the 1906 resolution they would not have sponsored the entry.
But it was not they, but the National Association of Amateur
Oarsmen, who were involved on that occasion.

1921

The Prince of Wales, later King Edward VIII, honoured the
Regatta in 1921, and presented the prizes on the Saturday. The
weather was fine, and favourable winds resulted in many fast
times. New records were set up in the Ladies' Plate, and in the
Thames and Wyfold Challenge Cups.

The Grand produced no close finishes, but the final, fought
out between Magdalen College Oxford and Jesus College
Cambridge, aroused great excitement. It is perhaps of interest
that there have been only seven occasions[1] when the Grand final
has brought together an Oxford and a Cambridge college crew;
and on three of those occasions it has been Magdalen and Jesus.
This time Magdalen retained their unbeaten record in this respect,
winning by a length, in the fast time of 6 min. 54 sec.

In a heat of the Ladies' Plate, Pembroke Cambridge beat
Trinity Oxford by six feet, to set up a new record of 6 min.
55 sec. Next day they had to equal this time to hold off Shrewsbury, who were rowing forty at the mile post. In the semi-final
there was another great race between Pembroke and Eton. The
school led by a canvas at Fawley, and by a quarter of a length at
the three-quarter mile. Then Pembroke spurted, and were level at
the mile. Eton replied, and drew away to win by a quarter of a
length. In the final they beat L.M.B.C. more comfortably.

The Christiania Roklub, Norway, became the second foreign
crew to win the Thames Cup—the first was the Nereus B.C.,

[1] 1849, Wadham beat Second Trinity B.C. Cambridge; 1854, First Trinity
B.C. Cambridge beat Wadham; 1861, First Trinity B.C. Cambridge beat Trinity
College Oxford; 1895, Trinity Hall beat New College; 1910, 1911, and 1921,
Magdalen College Oxford beat Jesus College Cambridge.

Holland, in 1895. On Wednesday they lowered the record to
7 min. 7 sec., in beating Henley R.C. Corpus Christi College
Cambridge clipped a further second off this time next day, when
they beat Caius. In the semi-finals, the Norwegians beat the
second Magdalen crew by only one foot, and in the final, by a
safe length, they beat Corpus Oxford, who had previously disposed of their record-breaking Cambridge namesakes.

In the Diamonds, Jack Beresford sportingly threw away a
certainty of repeating his 1920 victory, when, in the final, he
stopped and waited for F. E. Eyken of Holland, who hit the
booms at the top of the Island. Beresford led by half a length at
the half-mile, but the scullers were level at Fawley, and Eyken
got away to win by a length and a half.

1922

Next year the weather was as bad as it could be, but by way of
compensation the Thames Cup produced a series of extraordin-
arily close finishes. On the Thursday, Henley R.C. beat Kingston
R.C. by two feet, only to succumb, next day, to Queens' College
Cambridge by the same narrow margin. London R.C. beat Jesus
College Cambridge by four feet. In the semi-final, Worcester
College beat Queens' by a third of a length, after rowing level all
the way to the mile; and in the final they got home from Clare by
only three feet.

This time the Grand was won fairly easily by Leander, from
Thames R.C., and the Ladies' by Brasenose, who were level with
Magdalen at the mile post, but spurted well to open out a lead of
one length at the finish.

A fine Eton Vikings four won the Stewards' Challenge Cup,
and the same men, rowing as Third Trinity B.C., were easy
winners in the Visitors' Challenge Cup.[1]

G. O. Nickalls, again partnered by R. S. C. Lucas, won the
Goblets, recording the thirteenth and last Nickalls success in this

---

[1] Eton Vikings Club and Third Trinity B.C.: C. R. M. Ely (bow) (st.), J. A.
Macnabb, R. E. Morrison, T. R. B. Sanders (stroke). See photograph facing
p. 148.

event; and Beresford once again reached the final of the Diamonds, when he lost to W. M. Hoover of the United States.

1923

Nineteen-twenty-three was the year of the short Experimental Course, which is discussed elsewhere. Conditions were so easy that the advantages of the new course were not fully tested. The racing was, perhaps, less closely contested than in recent years.

Thames R.C. won the Grand, for the first time since 1889. Undoubtedly this was the work of Steve Fairbairn, whose influence as a coach at this period put Metropolitan rowing back on the map, making, thereby, a great contribution to the well-being of English rowing as a whole. Fairbairn was a galvanic personality, and, particularly towards the end of his life, a controversial teacher. No respecter of persons or traditions, he set many tongues wagging at Henley, with dire warnings of what would result from such flagrant disregard for 'Orthodoxy'. But that is another story.[1]

Among the schools there was a rising star, in Shrewsbury. What promised to be the best race in the Ladies' Plate was marred when they broke a slide, racing level with Eton at Remenham Club. It was not a schools' year however, and in the final, Trinity College Oxford beat Jesus College Cambridge.

In the Thames Cup the local clubs made a good showing. Maidenhead beat Henley in one semi-final by half a length. Next day they lost to First Trinity by three-quarters of a length. Third Trinity, with the same four as in the previous year, were easy winners in the Stewards'.

1924

It may reasonably be said that 1924 marks the beginning of the modern era of Henley Regatta, in that it was the first year of the present course. Before the Regatta the qualification Rule for the Ladies' Plate was altered, so as specifically to include Trinity

[1] See *Swing Together*, by R. D. Burnell (O.U.P.)

College Dublin, who might otherwise have been debarred, Dublin being no longer in the United Kingdom.

In the Grand, Leander won a great final from Jesus, by only six feet. And Shrewsbury became the only school, except Eton, to win a race, other than a schools' race, at Henley. But there was more to it than that, for their opponents in the final of the Ladies' Plate were the same Jesus crew which lost to Leander in the final of the Grand. The wisdom of making double entries at Henley is nearly always questionable, and still more so in the rare instances of double entries in the Grand and Ladies' Plate. Naturally, on this occasion, many concluded that Jesus had thrown away a fine chance of winning one event or the other. But others said that Shrewsbury, who won comfortably, by one and a quarter lengths, could have won the Grand this year. Their time was only one second slower than that of Leander, winning their desperate race in the morning.

Maidenhead R.C. at last succeeded in winning the Thames Cup, beating Twickenham in the final by half a length. In their semi-final, against Trinity Hall, they got home by only four feet. The Third Trinity four, still unchanged, and seemingly invincible, again won the Stewards', whilst their second four carried off the Visitors' Challenge Cup.

The most remarkable race of the Regatta, however, came in the Goblets. It seemed that thirteen was to be an unlucky score for the Nickalls family, for that was the full tally of their wins. In the previous year, G. O. Nickalls, partnered by H. B. Playford, had reached the final, only to hit the booms, rowed out, but still leading by a few feet, just below the Judge's Box. In 1924 Nickalls was paired again with his old partner, R. S. C. Lucas.

Nickalls and Lucas had won in 1920, and again in 1922, and when they drew G. K. Hampshire and W. Phillips, of Magdalen College Oxford, in their first heat, Hampshire and Phillips were doubtless the last to expect that the fact that Nickalls and Lucas were also Magdalen men, though rowing under Leander colours, would save them from a severe defeat.

But, as C. T. Steward put it, 'It was not generally known . . .

that as well as being famous oarsmen they were no mean amateur carpenters and always carried a set of tools'. Stroke apparently decided that the boat was too heavy, and cut away some vital timber whilst waiting at the start. On the first stroke Nickalls broke his stretcher, and opened a leak in the skin of the boat.

It was, so to speak, a 'slow puncture', and did not prevent Nickalls and Lucas taking a lead at once. Then the Magdalen pair hit the booms, and Nickalls and Lucas stopped and waited for them. The loss of time, rather than of distance, was fatal. On restarting they soon built up a big lead, and were well ahead at Fawley, but it was then apparent that their boat was dangerously low in the water. At the mile post matters were desperate, and at the bottom of the Enclosures the cut-water disappeared, and the boat sank amidst execrations that were visible, if inaudible, at the winning post.

No one was more surprised than Hampshire and Phillips, when they duly arrived, to find their opponents swimming in the water. Indeed, one might say that no one else was surprised at all, for everyone else, of course, had been facing in the right direction. Hampshire and Phillips stopped, but finally rowed on to the finish, and asked that the race be re-rowed. But the Committee ruled that the race ended as soon as either boat passed the winning post.

1925

Though there was some rain, conditions were favourable in 1925, and fast times were recorded. There were also some close races.

In the Grand, Christ Church disposed of the only foreign crew, the Nereus B.C., Amsterdam, by a quarter of a length, after a great struggle. And Maidenhead R.C., appearing in the Grand for the only time in their history, were beaten by only five feet by London R.C. But it was Leander's year again, and, beating Thames R.C. in the final, they reached Fawley in the record time of 3 min. 17 sec., and the finish in 6 min. 53 sec.

Radley reached the final of the Ladies' Plate for the fifth time, only to fail once more at the last fence. Lady Margaret B.C. beat them by two lengths. It may be remembered that Radley had never yet beaten Eton in a straight fight at Henley, but this must surely have been one of the occasions on which they could have done so, had the two schools met. For in the semi-final Radley beat Shrewsbury, by a length and three-quarters, and Shrewsbury defeated Eton by no less than two and three-quarter lengths.

There was one very fine race in the Thames Cup, in which Twickenham beat Kingston by three feet. And Henley R.C. reached the final for the only time in their career, losing to First Trinity by one length. Third Trinity again dominated the four-oar events, beating Leander in the final of the Stewards', in the record time of 7 min. 27 sec., and Brasenose in the final of the Visitors'. In this race they set up a new record of 3 min. 37 sec. to Fawley, where they were leading by three lengths. Thereafter they took things easily, for two members of the crew, R. E. Morrison and E. C. Hamilton-Russell, were also engaged in the Silver Goblets, in which they beat G. O. Nickalls and R. S. C. Lucas. Morrison and Hamilton-Russell thus completed the 'treble', which has been achieved only once since 1925, and, indeed, only twice since the 1914–18 War.

1926

For some reason the entries for the Grand dropped to four in 1926, and Leander were the winners for the third year in succession. They had a hard race with Thames R.C. in the semi-final, winning by half a length, in 6 min. 59 sec. In the final, clocking 6 min. 56 sec., they won comfortably from L.M.B.C. In the Ladies' Plate, Jesus rowed a dead heat with First Trinity, beating them by three-quarters of a length in the re-row. In the final they got home from Pembroke College Cambridge by three feet.

The only record this year was in the Thames Cup, in which Kingston reached Fawley in 3 min. 24 sec., beating Thames R.C. by three-quarters of a length. However, they lost by half a length in the final to Selwyn, who thus recorded their first Henley victory. The Third Trinity monopoly was at last broken in the fours,

Thames winning the Stewards', and Christ Church the Visitors'. Beresford won the Diamonds for the third time in succession.

1927

Lest Henley's reputation for bad weather should be forgotten, 1927 brought a sharp reminder, with more than three inches of rainfall during the week.

But that was not sufficient to damp the enthusiasm of Thames R.C., for they had a wonderful year, winning the Grand, Stewards', Thames, and Wyfold Cups. In the final of the Grand they beat London by three-quarters of a length, and it may surprise many to know that this was only the second occasion on which these great rivals, and neighbours at Putney, faced each other in the final of Henley's premier trophy. The previous occasion was in 1877.

In the Thames Cup, the Thames second eight had their severest test in a heat, against Kent School, from the U.S.A. This was the first appearance of Kent, who, with Father Sill, their coach for many years, were to become such regular and welcome visitors to the Regatta. In their début they were level with Thames at the mile, and went down by only a quarter of a length. Thames went on to beat Twickenham in the final by the same margin. In the Stewards' and Wyfold Cups, the Thames four had relatively easy victories.

The Ladies' Plate was an all-Trinity Cambridge affair, with the First beating the Third B.C. by three-quarters of a length in the final. In the Diamonds, the Canadian, J. Wright, sculled T. D. A. Collet of Leander to a standstill in one of the heats. In the final, against R. T. Lee, of Worcester College Oxford, Wright was left at the start, but sculled past to lead by a length at the first signal, and by two lengths at Fawley. Lee then spurted, and took back half a length, but Wright replied, and had three lengths at the foot of the Enclosures. Within fifty yards of the end Wright developed cramp in his left arm, and hit the booms. But great credit must go to Lee, for a dogged race, and a well-deserved success.

1928

For Thames R.C. 1928 was almost as good a year as 1927. Indeed, some might say it was better, for they retained the Grand, Thames Cup and Stewards', and substituted the Silver Goblets— through G. C. Killick, and J. Beresford, jun.—for the Wyfold Cup. They had a desperate race with London in the Stewards' final, winning by only two feet.

The volume of entries for the Regatta was, once again, worrying the Committee of Management, and in 1928 they made certain adjustments to the Rules, forbidding double entries in the Ladies' Plate and Thames Cup, and limiting the field for the Thames Cup to thirty-two crews, and for all other events to sixteen. When these limits were exceeded there were to be eliminating heats, on the Saturday before the Regatta. This Rule was invoked at once, as eighteen crews entered for the Ladies' Plate, and nineteen for the Wyfold Cup.

In the Ladies' Plate final, Selwyn pushed Jesus to within half a length; and in the Diamonds, J. Wright earned his revenge over R. T. Lee by a length, which, of course, is a tight finish in a sculling race.

H.R.H. Prince George, the Duke of Kent, presented the prizes.

1929

The weather was again very bad in 1929, with a gale blowing on the Friday. But the racing was excellent, and there were two dead heats.

The first came in the opening heat of the Grand Challenge Cup, in which the Argonaut B.C., of Canada, came from behind to catch London R.C. on the post. In the re-row London held a slight advantage at Fawley, and this time managed to hold off the Canadians' spurts, to win by a quarter of a length. But Leander were the ultimate winners.

The racing in the Ladies' Plate was relatively uneventful, until the semi-finals, when University College Oxford beat L.M.B.C.

by three feet. On the preceding day, University had been allowed to row a substitute, A. M. Emmet, for D. E. Tinne, who had a poisoned hand. Tinne had been rowing number seven, and the change brought N. K. Hutton from three to seven, with Emmet taking Hutton's seat at three. In spite of this, University put up a great fight in the final, being beaten by First Trinity by only half a length.

The Thames Cup, too, brought its thrills, and a very significant final result, for this was the first of many American successes in this event. Browne and Nichols School were the winners, at their first attempt. Another American crew, from Columbia University, beat Westminster Bank by a canvas, but later went down decisively to First Trinity.

The second dead heat came in the Goblets, between G. C. Killick and J. Beresford, the holders, and H. R. Carver and T. R. B. Sanders of Third Trinity. The Thames pair hit the booms early in the race, and were three lengths down at Fawley, yet managed to catch up at the Enclosures. In the re-row, the Trinity pair again led at the mile, though by only half a length, and this time Killick and Beresford got by to win by two and a half lengths. They went on to win the final from A. Graham and H. C. Morphett of B.N.C.

J. Wright reached his third consecutive final, and after another slow start failed to catch his opponent, L. F. H. Gunther of Holland, by a margin of only three feet.

1930

The early 'thirties will be remembered for a series of fine London R.C. crews, and in 1930 they opened well, with victories in the Grand, Stewards', and Wyfold Cups. In the Grand they had little trouble, setting up a new record of 1 min. 56 sec. to the Barrier, and equalling the Fawley record of 3 min. 17 sec., and in the Stewards' they won comfortably from Leander, setting up a new Fawley record of 3 min. 35 sec. But in the Wyfold Cup they had a desperate semi-final heat with Thames, getting home with only six feet to spare. In the final they won easily from Vesta.

Vesta won their first and, indeed, only victory in the Thames Cup, beating Worcester College Oxford without much difficulty.

1931

The high spot of 1931 was the great race between London and the Berliner Ruder Club. It was a semi-final of the Grand. Both crews started at forty, and the Germans led by a few feet at the first signal. London spurted at the Barrier, and gained half a length, but at Fawley Berlin were closing up again. At Remenham Club the Germans began to show in front. London were striking forty at the mile, and making no impression on Berlin, who led by a third of a length. But on the Enclosures the Germans faltered, and at the Grandstand they cracked. London just got by to win by a third of a length, the Germans stopping short of the winning post. The slowness of the conditions is shown by the fact that this great race took 7 min. 30 sec.

In the final, though they led for most of the distance and were at one stage clear, London had another hard fight to beat Thames by the same margin as they had the Germans.

The standard of the schools was high this year, and Shrewsbury pushed Jesus to half a length in the final of the Ladies'. In their semi-final, Shrewsbury had beaten Monkton Combe by a quarter of a length, and Monkton Combe in their turn had previously beaten Bedford by a canvas.

In retrospect, this Shrewsbury and Monkton Combe semi-final is of special interest, for it brought together the two strokes, A. V. Sutcliffe from Shrewsbury, and N. J. Bradley from Monkton Combe, who were later to meet in a memorable University Boat Race.[1] This was in 1934, when, at 14 st. 1½ lb. and 14 st. 2 lb. respectively, Bradley and Sutcliffe were the heaviest strokes ever to meet over the Putney course. In 1931, as schoolboys, Bradley scaled 13 st. 6 lb. and Sutcliffe 12 st. 2 lb. Of the Shrewsbury crew, G. I. F. Thompson was rowing for Oxford in 1934, and M. H. Mosley in 1933. From Monkton Combe, W. G. R. M.

---

[1] *The Oxford and Cambridge Boat Race,* by R. D. Burnell (O.U.P.), p. 191.

Laurie was still with Bradley in the record-breaking 1934 crew, and M. Bradley, a brother of N. J. Bradley, gained his Blue for Cambridge in 1937.

The Thames Cup provided an easy win for London, and two exceptionally close finishes, when Quintin B.C. beat Walton R.C. by one foot, and Magdalene College Cambridge beat Clare by two feet.

The Goblets were won by H. R. A. Edwards and L. Clive of Christ Church. Their final against W. A. T. Sambell and L. Luxton, of Pembroke Cambridge, was won comfortably, but in the semi-final they had a struggle with the brothers T. and J. S. Offer of Kingston, finally getting away when the Offers hit the booms near the mile post. This made H. R. A. Edwards a triple winner, for he was also rowing for London in the Grand and the Stewards'. This was the last occasion on which any individual won three Henley finals at the same Regatta.

The Diamonds were won by R. Pearce, of Canada, a fine sculler who later became a professional. One heat of the Diamonds is, I think, deserving of mention, for those who cannot draw on their personal memories of 1931 may be intrigued, and even perplexed, to read in C. T. Steward's *Henley Records* that, in his heat against T. A. Brocklebank, 'Pearce won comfortably by half a length'. This seems to be a contradiction in terms, and thereby hangs a tale.

Pearce, I suppose, knew that he had the Diamonds in his pocket. He was in a different class from other scullers that year. He himself maintains that he was told to go lightly with Brocklebank, who was a popular and successful Cambridge stroke. At any rate he certainly did so, and for most of the course was sculling comfortably, a length or so in the lead. Whether some third party had put Pearce up to this, with the idea of manufacturing an interesting situation, I cannot say. But Brocklebank was no mean sculler, and emphatically not the sort of man whom any wise opponent would have allowed to remain so close. Coming up the Enclosures he suddenly sprang into a tremendous spurt, and, as is possible only in sculling races, he was on level terms with his opponent before anyone realized what was happening. Pearce just—and only just—had time to recover from his surprise, and to answer Brocklebank's spurt.[1] With another fifty yards he would no doubt have regained a lead which was 'comfortable'. But if Brocklebank had held his spurt for a few strokes he might easily have won.

1932

With nominations for the Los Angeles Olympics depending on their results, the Grand and the Stewards' held more than usual interest in 1932. In the final of the Grand, Thames R.C., though they made repeated attacks, were unable to regain half a length lost to Leander at Fawley. Leander were represented by the Cambridge University crew of that year. In the Stewards' there were only three entries, and Thames won convincingly by two lengths, from the Berliner Ruder Club, who had previously beaten London.

This time Shrewsbury, still stroked by Sutcliffe, were successful in winning the Ladies' Plate, by one length, from Oriel College Oxford. In their closest race, a quarter-final, they came from behind to beat Magdalen by only four feet. Monkton Combe were stroked by W. G. R. M. Laurie, and won a fine race by six feet, from Pembroke College Cambridge, after being led by more than a length at the Barrier. But they were beaten by Clare in the quarter-finals.

There was no shortage of close races this year, for in another heat of the Ladies', New College beat Selwyn by three feet, and in the final of the Thames Cup, London R.C. beat Imperial College by four feet. This was a remarkable race indeed, for London had half a length of clear water over Imperial College at Fawley, yet only just managed to withstand a series of splendid spurts.

But close though they were, these races at least produced decisive verdicts. The Goblets actually produced a dead heat, between H. R. A. Edwards and L. Clive, of Christ Church, and the

---

[1] See the photograph, opposite p. 149.

XI. GRAND CHALLENGE CUP, 1934

Up Temple Island Leander Club, on the Berks Station, row level with Princeton University. (Leander won by $\frac{3}{4}$ length in the record time of 6 min. 45 sec.)

XII. THE CENTENARY DOUBLE SCULLS, 1939

Offer brothers of Kingston. The Oxford pair were a length down
at Fawley, which, of course, does not represent a great deal in a
pair, and, having an advantage of well over a stone a man, were
just able to get on terms at the finish. The row-off was postponed
until the following day, when Clive and Edwards proved considerably the faster.

The Diamonds went to Dr. H. Buhtz, of Germany, one of the
finest scullers ever to compete at Henley.

After the Regatta the qualification for the Wyfold Challenge
Cup was altered, to prevent competitors from rowing in this
event and the Grand Challenge Cup at the same Regatta. This
ruling was rescinded only in 1954.

1933

A problem which came to a head at this time was the
rapid increase in the number of entries, and the consequent overflowing of the programme.

The 'entry' for the Ladies' Plate—that is, the number of crews
starting in the Regatta—was limited to sixteen, and in 1932 it had
been necessary to hold no less than seven eliminating races on the
Saturday before the Regatta. Eliminating races must be unpopular, and particularly so with schools, many of which grant their
boys a holiday when the school eight is racing at Henley. The
schools' case was not helped by the fact that one of the considerations, in limiting the Ladies' Plate entry to sixteen, had been the
reluctance of the Committee to make boys row two races on the
same day. But in 1933 their wishes prevailed. There were, in fact,
twenty-six entries for the Ladies' Plate, which would have
necessitated all but six of the competitors rowing in eliminating
races.

The new ruling was that there should be no eliminating races,
except, when necessary, in the Diamonds.

In the final of the Grand, London R.C. beat the Berliner Ruder
Club by a quarter of a length. Their second eight rowed a dead
heat in the Thames Cup, against Hun School, U.S.A., and won

the re-row by a margin of one foot. But the ultimate winners were Kent School, who beat Bedford R.C. in the final.

A fine Pembroke College Cambridge four were easy winners of the Stewards'. And the Diamonds, which already showed a tendency to be dominated by foreign scullers, brought a pleasant surprise, with an all-British final. The victory went to T. G. Askwith of Peterhouse, with H. L. Warren of Trinity Hall as runner up.

1934

A prolonged drought, coupled with fine weather throughout the week, and keen racing, brought many fast times in 1934.

In the Grand, Leander won a fine race against London, setting up new records all the way—1 min. 55 sec. to the Barrier, 3 min. 15 sec. to Fawley, and 6 min. 45 sec. to the finish. Next day they clipped another second off the overall time, beating Thames by half a length. In the final, against Princeton University, Leander won by three-quarters of a length, in 6 min. 45 sec.[1]

In the Ladies' Plate the times were not exceptional until the last day. Then, in a storming final, Jesus College Cambridge beat Trinity College Dublin by three feet, having rowed past them at the mile. Their time was 6 min. 48 sec. The Thames Cup occasions came earlier, in the quarter finals. Westminster Bank, holding off the Oxford University Isis B.C. by six feet, set up a new record of 6 min. 59 sec. Ten minutes later another neck-and-neck race, between London and Quintin, brought the record down to 6 min. 58 sec. London were the winners. They were beaten by Thames R.C. in the final, but their record still stood.

In the Stewards' the crew was certainly there—the same Pembroke four which won in 1933; but the occasion failed, for their opponents, London R.C., stopped at Fawley, their stroke catching a crab which threw him right out of the boat. Nevertheless, Pembroke saw their record time of 3 min. 33 sec. go up on the

---

[1] Leander Club: J. H. C. Powell (bow), J. M. Couchman, J. H. Lascelles, A. V. Sutcliffe, P. Hogg, K. M. Payne, D. J. Wilson, W. G. R. M. Laurie (stroke), J. N. Duckworth (cox). See photograph facing p. 164.

Fawley signal board, and so raced on, to reach the finish in 7 min. 24 sec., which was another new record.[1]

Most of the racing in the Visitors' and Wyfold Cups was uneventful, but Reading R.C., achieving their first Henley victory, set up a new Fawley record of 3 min. 38 sec. in the final of the Wyfold Cup. In the Goblets, the Germans, H. Braun and H. G. Moller, were pushed by the brothers E. F. and T. S. Bigland to within one second of the famous dead-heat record time of 8 min. 8 sec.

Not the least remarkable performance of the Regatta was that of H. Buhtz. He was suffering from lumbago, and took matters as easily as he dared, his great pace enabling him, in every race, to gain an early lead and then slack off. In the final, against the American sculler, W. Rutherford, he was two lengths clear at the end of the first minute. He reached Fawley, four lengths ahead, in 3 min. 50 sec., which was five seconds inside Kelly's 1905 record, and virtually paddled in, to equal Kelly's 8 min. 10 sec. at the finish. Dr. Buhtz's Fawley time is the only 1934 record which still stands today. Unquestionably he was one of the greatest scullers Henley has ever seen.[2]

1935

The fine Pembroke fours of the preceding two years flowered into a winning Grand eight in 1935. They had hard races against London and Jesus, but won the final more easily, against Leander. In a heat, Jesus won a magnificent race from the F. C. Zurich R.C. by three feet, rowing forty all the way from Fawley to hold them. The stern four of this Zurich crew won the Stewards' with considerable ease, knocking no less than ten seconds off the record set up by Pembroke in 1934.[3] Another member of the eight, E. Rufli, won the Diamonds.

[1] Pembroke College Cambridge: A. D. Kingsford (bow), W. A. T. Sambell, J. H. T. Wilson, N. J. Bradley (stroke).
[2] See photograph facing p. 149.
[3] F. C. Zurich Ruder Club: H. Betschart (bow), H. Homberger, A. Homberger, K. Schmidt (st.) (stroke). See photograph facing p. 148.

In the Ladies' Plate, Eton reached the final for the first time in fourteen years, in spite of the injury of one of the crew, the implications of which are discussed elsewhere.[1] Leading by three-quarters of a length at the Barrier, Eton were gradually rowed down by Trinity Hall, who won, in the end, by a length.

1936

There was a record entry of 109 crews and scullers in 1936, but the only really distinguished performance was that of the Swiss. Indeed, those who remember 1936 will always think of it as the Swiss year.

Their eight was superb, with perhaps the most astonishing boat control ever seen at Henley. And their style provided a fruitful topic of clubroom conversation for the rest of the summer, and for a long time after.

'Here', said the diehards of Orthodoxy, 'is something we have scarcely seen since our youth.' 'This is the logical development of the teaching of Steve Fairbairn,' answered the Fairbairn protagonists. Their claim was strengthened by the fact that the Swiss declared that they had learned to row by studying a film of recent Pembroke crews, and by reading Fairbairn's books.

The Orthodox, of course, could not allow this claim to pass unchallenged, and asked why it was that no other Fairbairn crews looked like this one.

The fact, apparently, was that these Swiss had started as footballers, and had learned to row without any preconceived ideas of how it ought to be done, and with no bad examples to copy. If they had an important lesson to teach us, it was that, despite our sometimes violent arguments about style, there was little difference of opinion as to what constituted a really first-class crew.

The Swiss won the Grand without difficulty, and their four, which was perhaps even better than the eight, retained the Stewards' Challenge Cup. Rufli, who this year was not rowing in the eight, again won the Diamonds.

[1] See p. 230

One other crew must be mentioned in connection with the 1936 Grand, and that is the Imperial University of Tokyo, from Japan. They came for the Berlin Olympics, and raced at Marlow and Henley Regattas as part of their preparation. At Marlow they astonished by their rate of striking, which reached the high fifties, and when, at Henley, they spurted to fifty-six, to beat Quintin by two lengths in their heat of the Grand, tongues wagged throughout the Enclosures. Next day matters were put in their true perspective, for a start of forty-eight strokes in the first minute was not good enough to hold the Swiss, at forty-three, and the diminutive Japanese crew, whose average weight was little over ten stone, were fairly overwhelmed by the Zurich stride. The Swiss won in a paddle, by a very generous six lengths.

The Ladies' Plate was won by First Trinity, in spite of the fact that they almost threw away their chances by catching a crab, in a heat against Shrewsbury, whom they beat by only half a length.

The Thames Cup saw three American crews—Tabor Academy, Kent School, and Browne and Nichols School—in the semi-finals. Kingston R.C., the sole British survivors, went down gallantly but unavailingly to Tabor, who went on to an easy victory against Kent School in the final. This Tabor crew seemed to do almost everything that it is possible to do wrong in a boat. They had no balance, and could not keep their blades off the water; they scarcely even kept time. Yet they fairly ate up the Thames Cup opposition. For them it was the first of three wins in four years.

For the home crews it was a sign of lean days to come. With the exception of 1946, when there was no foreign challenge, no English crew was to win the Thames Cup until 1953. Here there is food for thought, and a problem still unsolved, which must be considered later.

For the rest, Reading R.C. reached the final of the Wyfold Cup for the third year in succession, but were unable to repeat their victories of 1934 and 1935. They lost to London. And the Offer brothers at last won the Goblets, beating the holders, T. S. Cree and D. W. Burnford, in a heat.

1937

With the Ladies' Plate entry standing at twenty-eight, the highest it had ever been, and indeed ever has been, the question of schools racing twice in the day again came up for discussion in 1937. The conclusion was that a school ought not to be expected to race against a college for its second race in a day. It was therefore decided to hold the first two rounds of the Ladies' Plate on the opening day, and to keep schools and colleges apart until the third round.

The Grand went abroad again, this time to the Rudergesellschaft Wiking, Germany. Jesus College Cambridge put up a spirited defence in the final, but were beaten by half a length. In the Ladies' Plate there was a dead heat, between Magdalen College Oxford and Clare College Cambridge. In the re-row Magdalen led by a canvas at the mile, but Clare just got by to win by a quarter of a length. They went on to a comfortable win in the final, against First Trinity.

The Thames Cup produced several narrow verdicts, but Tabor were never in danger of losing the trophy. What should have been a fine race, in the final of the Diamonds, was spoiled when the Canadian sculler, J. F. Coulson, hit the booms near the quarter-mile signal. At the time he held a slight lead over the Austrian, J. Hasenohrl, who went on to win easily.

1938

There were no foreign challengers for the Grand in 1938, which was a pity, as London R.C. had a crew considerably above the average. Only in the semi-final race, against Jesus, were they extended, when the college crew drove them to a three-foot finish. R. Parker, rowing No. 4 for London, at 15 st. 9 lb., was, until 1956, the heaviest man ever to have won the Grand.

In the Ladies' Plate, both Eton and Radley reached the semi-finals, but once again fate intervened to keep them apart, in a year in which Radley must surely have won. Radley went through to the final, there to gain a convincing win against Pembroke, and so to carry off the trophy for the first time in their history. They showed great finishing power, being level at the mile post in their last two races, yet drawing away to win by a comfortable margin. Their final time was 6 min. 56 sec., two seconds faster than that in which London won the Grand, though the club had done 6 min. 52 sec. against Jesus, on the Friday, which was a slower day.

Conditions were never exceptionally fast during this Regatta, though on Saturday there were 'light winds up the course'. Taking advantage of this, an excellent Oriel four lowered the Visitors' record by no less than twelve seconds. In the final of the Goblets, W. G. R. M. Laurie and J. H. T. Wilson equalled the old record of 8 min. 8 sec., set up in the dead heat of 1911. They were unpressed after Fawley, and could certainly have gone faster.

In the Diamonds there appeared a really remarkable sculler, in the person of J. W. Burk, of the Penn Athletic Club, U.S.A.[1] His style, which called for an unusually high rate of striking, was suitable only for a man who had taken immense pains to perfect his physique, both in and out of the boat. But he was certainly as fast as any man who had sculled over the Henley course. In the final, against L. D. Habbits of Reading, he started at forty-four, and shook off his opponent at the top of the island. He continued at thirty-seven to Fawley, where, seeing that his time was 3 min. 51 sec., which was only one second outside Buhtz's best ever, he decided to go on for the course record. Over the second half of the course he never dropped his rating below thirty-nine, and yet never seemed to be exerting himself unduly. His time to the finish was 8 min. 2 sec., eight seconds faster than the thirty-three-year-old record, set up by the great F. S. Kelly.

In the autumn of 1938 the Stewards purchased the remainder of the Lion Meadows, and also the field behind Leander Club, which then, as now, was used as a competitors' car park. They then owned the freehold of all the land between the river and Remenham Lane, as far downstream as the White House, and

---

[1] See photograph (of the following year's race) facing p. 149.

excluding only the site of Leander, and of the houses at the end of Remenham Lane.

Also in this year, the Committee accepted the resignation of Major W. H. Barff, who had been Secretary of the Regatta since the retirement of Mr. J. F. Cooper, after thirty-seven years' service, in 1919. His place was taken by Mr. L. D. Williams, who remains Secretary today. Thus the Regatta has been served by only three Secretaries in the past seventy-four years. The progress which Henley has made in that period is indeed a fine tribute to the loyalty and efficiency of these three men.

1939

The Centenary of Henley Regatta fell in 1939, though it was not, of course, the hundredth Regatta. That tally had dropped behind the calendar during the 1914–18 War. To mark the occasion, H.R.H. the Duke of Kent was invited to present the prizes.

Also to mark the special occasion, the Stewards sent out invitations to all the Dominions, and to all foreign countries which had signed Agreements with Henley Regatta. And they put up for competition a pair of cups, to be competed for, as outright prizes, in double sculls. This was the first and only occasion on which the Stewards have ever invited anyone to compete at Henley and, in the event, the response was disappointing. There were three foreign entries for the Double Sculls, which was no more than might reasonably be expected, from the inclusion in the programme of an event which was already popular on the Continent. There were also three foreign entries for the Wyfold Cup, which, one imagines, had not been looked for; but in all the main events the foreign entries were about normal.

Nor, in spite of the efforts of the Stewards, were other aspects of the Regatta more gratifying. The weather was miserable, overcast, and generally with a stiff head-wind blowing up the course, to which, on Saturday, were added squalls of rain. And the English crews took a drubbing such as they have seldom experienced in the history of the Regatta.

In the Grand, Kingston pushed Sydney R.C. to three feet, and

Thames lost by half a length to the Argonauts. But the satisfaction of a Dominion victory was not to be, for the Canadians beat the Australians by three lengths, and lost themselves, by the same margin, to Harvard University.

The Thames Cup produced an all-American final, for the second time in four years, Tabor Academy being the winners for the third time in the same period. In the Stewards' there was some hope of the previous year's successful Oriel four, but in the final they were overwhelmed, by four lengths, by the Ruder Club Zurich. In the Goblets, strangely, there was no foreign entry. But even so, two Americans managed to contest the final. They were the brothers H. Parker—who had gained a Blue at Cambridge, whither he went from Tabor Academy, and who was now partnered by C. B. Sanford, rowing for Trinity Hall—and R. Parker, who was partnered by P. N. Carpmael, rowing for London R.C.   The Trinity Hall pair were the winners.

Burk was back to defend his Diamonds' title, dissatisfied, so it was said, because he had missed fourteen days' training since the previous year. That event was, therefore, taken as a foregone conclusion, and there was at least some satisfaction in seeing two interesting races. In the first—a semi-final between R. D. Burnell of Magdalen College Oxford and R. Verey of Poland—Burnell came from several lengths astern, to fail by a length and a quarter at the finish. In the other, the final itself, Burk touched the booms near the Barrier, where Verey was leading him by a length and a half. Striking thirty-eight, the American was only a length astern at Fawley, and at Remenham Club, striking forty, he took the lead. At the mile Burk was clear, but up the Enclosures Verey countered, and managed to hold Burk to a length and a quarter at the finish.[1]

The race of the Regatta, however, which went a long way towards enlightening an otherwise depressing week, was the final of the Centenary Double Sculls. Three years before, at the Berlin Olympics, J. Beresford, jun., and L. F. Southwood had come out of retirement to win the Olympic Double Sculls title,

[1] See photograph facing p. 149.

the only aquatic event won by Great Britain that year. Now, at the ages of forty-one and thirty-six respectively, the Thames pair appeared once more.

They reached the final without difficulty, as also did their opponents, G. Scherli and E. Broschi, of Trieste. But against a head-wind, and giving away twenty-four years and three stone in weight, their chances looked slight. Starting slightly the faster, the Thames double gained half a length up the Island, and held their advantage to the Barrier. There the Italians spurted, and took the lead at Fawley. At the mile post Scherli and Broschi led by half a length, but in a tremendous spurt up the Enclosures Beresford and Southwood came up to force a dead heat.[1] Since this was not a challenge race, the Committee decided against a re-row, and gave presentation prizes to all four men.

The only other event in which there was an international final was the Wyfold Challenge Cup, in which Maidenhead R.C. got home by one length, to beat the Tigre B.C. of Argentina. For the rest, Eton reached the semi-final of the Ladies' Plate for the third successive year, but lost to Clare, the winners. And Trinity Hall beat New College in the final of the Visitors' Cup.

[1] See photograph facing p. 165.

CHAPTER SEVEN

Come the World. 1945–56

THE Henley reach was not altogether deserted during the years of the Second World War, for Oxford and Cambridge rowed their wartime Boat Races there, in 1940 and 1945. In 1940, too, it was proposed to hold a Schools Regatta in July, but the plans were cancelled in view of the serious situation following the evacuation of the British Army from Dunkirk. There were, however, Schools Regattas, organized by Eton, in 1941, 1943, and 1944, and a three-sided race, between Eton, Radley, and Shrewsbury, in 1942. And we may be certain that Henley was not forgotten by rowing men engaged in mortal combat elsewhere. They wasted no time in returning in force at the earliest opportunity.

Royal Henley Regatta, so called to distinguish it from the regular Regattas, was held at Henley in July 1945, only two months after the end of hostilities in Europe, and actually before the end of the war in the Far East. It was, indeed, something of an act of faith, for at the time of the meeting which decided to hold the Regatta—that is, on 15 May 1945—there was no Regatta Office, the Enclosures were stacked with timber, it was doubtful whether any tents could be hired, catering facilities were even more problematical, and, of course, no boats could be carted to Henley at all, unless an allocation of petrol could be obtained.

In the circumstances a full-scale Regatta was impossible, and the racing took place on one day only, over a shortened course of about a mile, starting at the Barrier, and finishing rather below the normal winning post. But this course was able to accommodate three crews abreast, so that a lot of racing could be packed into a short space of time.

There were only three events, for specially presented trophies. The Open Eights race, for the Danesfield Cup presented by Mr. A. S. Garton, attracted twenty-three crews. In a semi-final, the Royal Australian Air Force beat Magdalen College Oxford by only three feet, but in the final they lost to Imperial College by a length, with Jesus College Cambridge a length and a half astern. Mr. H. G. Gold presented the Hedsor Cup for School Eights, and this was won by Radley, by one length from Eton, who in turn beat Bedford into third place by three feet. Thus, at last, Radley beat Eton 'at Henley', but were still deprived of the satisfaction of beating them in a straight fight over the full Henley distance, and in the Royal Regatta. The third event was the Barrier Cup for Scullers, presented by Mr. H. A. Steward. It was won by W. E. C. Horwood, from H. P. Henry, by three lengths.

With 1945 we pass into contemporary Henley history, and for that reason it is more difficult to view the scene objectively. Later historians may recognize other trends. But today the most important seems to be the continued and increasing foreign challenge, particularly in the small-boat racing.

1946

For the first full post-war Henley, conditions were favourable, if not particularly fast. The entries dropped a little from the 1939 peak, and there was only one foreign contestant for the Grand. But there were two foreign pairs, one double, and seven single scullers—the highest foreign entry yet received for the Diamonds.

Their Royal Highnesses Princess Elizabeth and Princess Margaret attended the last day of the Regatta, and the prizes were presented by Princess Elizabeth.

A new and positive step was taken, with the introduction of a special race for school crews. In honour of the occasion, H.R.H. Princess Elizabeth graciously gave her permission for the trophy to be named The Princess Elizabeth Cup.

The Committee of Management, feeling their way in this matter, drew up a tentative rule, by which schools were permitted to enter for both the Ladies' Plate and the Princess

Elizabeth Cup, with the proviso that a school which won a Ladies' Plate semi-final should thereby become ineligible for the schools' race. The Princess Elizabeth Cup was rowed over a shortened course, of about a mile, and did not start until the Friday morning. Schools which reached, but did not win, a Ladies' Plate semi-final—Eton and Bryanston were both so affected—were given a bye through the first round of the Princess Elizabeth Cup.

These arrangements were hardly conducive to making Henley less strenuous for the schools. Eton, for example, beat Bedford School in the Ladies' Plate, and lost to them in the Princess Elizabeth Cup two days later, having, in the interim, lost a Ladies' Plate semi-final to Jesus, and won a gruelling Princess Elizabeth Cup race against Winchester. Bedford went on to win an exciting final from Radley, who touched the booms, and broke a blade, just short of the finish.

Mature talent was at a premium, after a gap of six years. In this respect Leander were relatively well off, being able to call upon several pre-war Blues, and notably on N. J. Bradley, stroke of the great Pembroke fours of the 'thirties. Winning their heats without difficulty, they met the Zurich See Club in the final. Before the race the two crews, paddling side by side, escorted the launch in which the two Princesses rode up the course, after lunching at Greenlands.

The race itself proved to be in every way worthy of the Grand tradition. Zurich, starting at thirty-eight to Leander's thirty-seven, took a small lead up the Island, and led by a canvas at the Barrier. They held their advantage to Fawley, but then Leander, increasing the pressure, drew level. At the mile post Leander led by a quarter of a length, and up the Enclosures they drew slowly away, to win by three-quarters of a length.

It was a good year for Leander, for their four won the Stewards', and an excellent pair, the twin brothers J. F. and C. G. Burgess, won the Goblets. This was a remarkable feat, for the Burgesses were not yet nineteen years of age. In the final, against O. Secher and P. Paerregaard of Denmark, they were led by more than a length, yet fought their way back by repeated spurts. The Danes were still in front at the mile, but, completely rowed out, they hit the booms and capsized.

The Double Sculls, instituted as a special race to celebrate the 1939 Centenary, now became a permanent event on the programme. But in 1946 it nearly failed to produce a race at all, for J. H. Neame, who was stroking the Trinity Hall double, injured his hand, and was forced to withdraw. Substitutes are not permitted in the individual events, but on this occasion the Committee asked H. L. Warren, who had sculled for Great Britain in the Berlin Olympics, but who had not raced at Henley since 1936, to take Neame's place, in order to provide a race for R. E. Panelo and E. D. Chafuen, of Buenos Aires, who were the only other contestants. The Argentine double won without difficulty, but the Hall deservedly received a great ovation.

The Diamonds were won by J. Séphériadés, of France. R. D. Burnell, also rowing in the Leander eight, went down to Séphériadés on Thursday, and there were no English scullers in the semi-finals. In the final, J. B. Kelly, of the United States, made a good race to the mile, where the French sculler led by a few feet. But he could not hold on, and Séphériadés went on to win by three lengths.

1947

In 1947 no fewer than five English crews entered for the Grand, a clear indication of the resurgence of rowing after the war. Leander were the favourites, but were unfortunate in losing G. C. Richardson, a Cambridge Blue, who was rowing six, whilst the veteran N. J. Bradley, who had stroked both the winning eight and four in 1946, was also unfit. He continued to stroke the eight but retired from the Leander Stewards' four.

However, it was undoubtedly a Jesus year. They drew Leander in their first heat, and after a level race to the mile, managed to seize the initiative, going on to win a desperate race by half a length. The next day they rowed a similar race against the Ruder Club, Zurich, and, striking forty, again got away at the mile to win by the same margin. In the final their opponents were the Roeivereeniging De Delftsche Sport, Holland. This time Jesus sprang their finishing spurt a little earlier, near Remenham Club. They led by a canvas at the mile, and then drew steadily away, finishing at forty-one, one and a half lengths to the good.

This was indeed an object lesson in Henley racing. It is an old tow-path saying that, in a tight race, 'you must go from the mile'. And it is a very sound one, for there are no prizes for losing a close race. To seize the initiative in the final spurt is half the battle. Too often the supreme effort is delayed until half-way up the Enclosures, when it is likely to be too late.

After the experience of the previous year, the full course was used for the Princess Elizabeth Cup, and no concessions were made to schools which also entered for the Ladies' Plate. Six crews entered for the schools race, Bedford School winning for the second time, whilst five went for the Ladies' Plate, in which Eton reached the final, and were beaten by First and Third Trinity B.C. Cambridge.

After one year of grace, in which there had been no foreign challenge, the Thames Cup reverted to its pre-war pattern of domination by the American schools. The old rivals, Tabor Academy and Kent School, fought out the final, with Tabor winning for the fourth time.

Quintin B.C. gained their first Henley victory, in winning the Wyfold Cup.

There were no foreign challengers in the Goblets, but there was a particularly fine race between J. H. Pinches and E. M. Sturgess, of London R.C., and R. C. Morris and A. Burrough, of Thames R.C. Burrough, a Cambridge Blue, had lost a leg in the war, yet remained a formidable opponent. The London pair led all the way, though never by more than half a length, whilst repeated attacks from Thames brought them back to a few feet. In the end, Pinches and Sturgess got home by six feet, and went on to win the final.

The young American sculler, J. B. Kelly, won the Diamonds fairly easily, this being his second attempt.

In 1947 Lord Nuffield made a gift of two thousand pounds to the Regatta, for the purchase of land. The Stewards used this money to buy Selwyn's Meadow, which proved to be a great boon to them in the following year, when they wished to extend the accommodation in the Stewards' Enclosure. In particular, it enabled them to transfer the luncheon marquee—greatly increasing its size at the same time—from the lawn which now fronts the Bridge Bar, across Remenham Lane to Selwyn's Meadow. The removal of the luncheon tents in turn made it possible to improve the amenities in the Stewards' Enclosure.

1948

In 1948 the Olympic Games came to London, and the Olympic Regatta to Henley, for the second time in exactly forty years. Great Britain thus became the only country to have staged the modern Olympics twice, and Henley-on-Thames the only town to have played host to two Olympic Regattas.

Inevitably the Royal Regatta, in 1948, was influenced by the Olympic Regatta, which was to follow it a month later.

The Committee of Management did not debar foreign entries, as was done in 1908, but there were, in fact, no foreign challengers for the Grand. In the other open events there was just sufficient opposition from overseas to add zest to the occasion. And, of course, there was added interest in the knowledge that Great Britain's representation in the Olympics was to be decided, so far as possible, on the results of Henley.

That has been the avowed intention of the selectors on many occasions. And it must be admitted that it has scarcely ever worked out satisfactorily. For there is no 'seeding' of the Henley draw, and the odds are against the Henley racing providing an indisputable comparison between any two particular contestants.

In the Grand, Leander, based on the winning Cambridge Boat Race crew, Thames, 'Leatham', who were made up for the occasion from the N.A.R.A. oarsmen from the rivers Thames and Lea, and a composite Jesus and Pembroke crew, were all aspiring to Olympic honours. The key race was between Thames and

XIII. THAMES CUP, 1953

The Royal Air Force bring the Cup home to England, beating Princeton University in the semi-final

XIV GRAND CHALLENGE CUP

Leander, but it is perhaps of interest to note that Thames had a Swiss oarsman in their crew. He, of course, was not eligible to represent Great Britain in the Olympic Games.

Leander gained a few feet up the Island, and passed the Barrier, striking thirty-three to Thames' thirty-four, with a lead of nearly half a length. They still led by a quarter of a length at Fawley, and by the same distance at the three-quarter-mile, where the real battle began. Gradually Thames drew up, and the crews were level at the mile. Now striking thirty-seven, Thames drew ahead, and Leander, though they replied at thirty-eight, and then at forty, could not bring them back. Thames won a splendid race, by half a length, in 6 min. 59 sec. In the final they had no difficulty in disposing of Jesus and Pembroke.

The stern four of the Thames eight were also entered for the Stewards' Cup. They were clearly better than any of the other English fours, and their full potential was shown in only one race, against the See Club, Zurich. Steering poorly at the start, Thames lost a length at the Barrier. At the lower rate, thirty-two to Thames' thirty-five, Zurich held their advantage to Fawley. Coming up to the Remenham Club, the Swiss strayed somewhat into their opponents' water. Thames immediately spurted and drove them out, and at the mile the crews were level. Then Thames drew away. At the Enclosures Zurich were finished, and Thames went on to win by two and a half lengths, in the extremely fast time of 7 min. 17 sec.

The Australian, M. T. Wood, had already beaten B. H. T. Bushnell, who was thought to be our only hope in the Diamonds, at Marlow, and it seemed that the outcome must lie between Wood, and Séphériadés.

But in the end Wood's hardest race, and perhaps the hardest race he ever had in this country, came against A. D. Rowe, of Leander, a newcomer to the Diamonds. Both men started at forty, and at the Barrier Rowe led by half a length. At the three-quarter-mile Wood went by him, but Rowe answered at once, and went on attacking, even when Wood crossed over into his water. Rowe lost by a length and a half, and Wood's time was 8 min. 10 sec.—

second only to Burk's record. Bushnell reached the final on the other side of the draw, but, giving away more than two stone, he was no match for the Australian.

The Goblets were distinguished by the return of W. G. R. M. Laurie and J. H. T. Wilson, who had not raced at Henley since they equalled the Goblets' record in 1938. After nearly ten years in the Sudan Civil Service, they had now contrived to arrange their leaves so as to be able to row together once more. At Marlow they failed against a strong Australian pair, F. S. Grace and E. R. Bromley, and the inevitable conclusion was that the veterans were unfit. But in the final at Henley, Laurie and Wilson went right away to win by three lengths. It is only fair to record that one of the Australian pair was unwell, but the subsequent Olympic racing confirmed Laurie and Wilson as an invincible pair.

In the Double Sculls there were three British pairs trying for an Olympic nomination. W. E. C. Horwood and D. C. H. Garrod, the holders, beat J. H. Pinches and E. M. Sturgess, who had won the Goblets in 1947. R. F. Winstone and R. D. Burnell lost a hard race to the Belgian double, P. Piessens and W. A. Collet. In the final, the Belgians beat Horwood and Garrod. To say the least, this was not helpful to the Olympic selectors, and in the end Burnell was paired with B. H. T. Bushnell. They sculled, and won, a trial race against Horwood and Garrod.[1]

The Victoria Lake R.C. four, from South Africa, which was later to row as a coxed four in the Olympics, was criticized for entering for the Wyfold Cup. But not knowing the Henley standards, they had asked for advice and had been told to enter for this event. They won comfortably.

Four schools entered for the Ladies' Plate, and three of them entered the same crews for the Princess Elizabeth Cup. Eton, the only school which did not attempt the double, carried off the Ladies' Plate for the first time since 1921. This was the culmination of a fine run of near successes; for in seven Henleys, Eton had failed only once to reach the semi-final or better.

---

[1] *Swing Together*, by R. D. Burnell (O.U.P.), pp. 98–103.

In the 1948 final Eton raced against Bryanston, thus producing an all-schools final for the first time since 1893. It was a great occasion, and a great race. At the Barrier Eton led by nearly half a length, striking thirty-five to Bryanston's thirty-three, and at Fawley, Bryanston, still striking lower, were level. At the third signal they led by a canvas, but off Remenham Club Eton spurted to thirty-seven and again took the lead. They had only a few feet at the mile, but continued to gain, and held off Bryanston's finishing spurt to win by two-thirds of a length.

1948—THE OLYMPIC REGATTA

The holding of the Olympic Regatta at Henley, in 1948, meant a break in the customary Henley pattern. For instead of the packing up, and dismantling, which usually follows close on the heels of the Royal Regatta, a host of workmen descended on the Enclosures and course, to make them ready for the great event.

Although the organization of Olympic Regattas is the responsibility of the Fédération Internationale des Sociétés d'Aviron, it is their custom to entrust the preparations to the authorities of the country in which the Games are to take place. And so it was that the Henley Committee of Management were entrusted with the preparation of the course and Enclosures, for the Olympic Regatta, which was to open on 5 August. And there was a great deal of work to be done. In particular, a new course had to be marked out. This was necessary because, under the rules of the Fédération Internationale des Sociétés d'Aviron, international contests must take place over a distance of 2,000 metres, on a straight course, and with a minimum of three crews in a heat. As a matter of fact it was not possible to fulfil these requirements in their entirety at Henley, because there is insufficient room on the Berkshire side of Temple Island, and on the Bucks side it is not possible to make a fair, straight course. However, F.I.S.A. agreed to the course being a little short—its actual length was about 1880 metres—since the races were to be rowed against the stream, which was reckoned to compensate for the distance lost.

The Olympic Regatta took place on August 5, 6, 7, and 9, there being a day of rest on the Sunday, before the finals. In the last weeks of July Henley quickly accustomed itself to new faces and to a babel of foreign languages. Eighty-six crews and scullers, from twenty-seven nations, competed in the Olympic rowing.[1] According to the official report of the XIVth Olympiad, Rowing, with 310 individuals taking part, came third, behind Athletics and Swimming, in the final analysis of competitors.

The great difference between the 1908 and the 1948 Olympic Regatta was that Britain was no longer supreme in the world of rowing. From across the Atlantic the United States had become the dominant factor in eight-oared rowing, by virtue, one is tempted to think, of the strength of her university crews. On the Continent, Denmark and Italy were the most consistently successful nations at that time.

The Eight-Oared event was, in fact, completely dominated by the magnificent University of California crew, representing the United States. There was a fine race in the opening heat, when Great Britain staved off a determined challenge from Norway, to win by a length, and an even closer one when Italy beat Switzerland by 1·6 seconds. In the first of the *repêchages* heats, Portugal, Argentina, and Yugoslavia finished, in that order, with less than two seconds separating the three boats.

The final was rowed between Great Britain—represented by Leander—the United States, and Norway. After five hundred metres Great Britain led by half a length, but the United States drew level at the half-way mark. Great Britain spurted gallantly, but the Americans drew away to win by 10·2 seconds, whilst Norway raced in to finish less than a length behind Great Britain.

The Thames R.C. four, winners of the Stewards', started as firm favourites for the Coxswainless-Fours event. But before the Olympic Regatta they seemed to lose the form they had shown earlier. Nevertheless, they were not so far from winning as the result suggested. In a semi-final against Denmark they were level at the Enclosures. Then they hit one of the marker buoys, caught

[1] See Appendix C, p. 286.

a slight crab, and were beaten by 2·5 seconds. In the final, Italy led Denmark by three lengths at the thousand-metre mark, and finally got home to win by 3·5 seconds.

The Coxed-Fours event dragged on interminably through the four days, not through the fault of the crews, which showed some fine racing, but of the system of the draw. In the final, the United States came from behind, to beat Switzerland by three seconds, with Denmark a good third.

Of all the events, perhaps the Coxswainless Pairs produced the best racing, and the most welcome triumph for Great Britain. The competition was intense. Great Britain, represented by Laurie and Wilson, won their first heat from Italy by less than two seconds. Then the Austrian pair, G. and K. Watzke, beat the American pair, F. J. Wade and R. W. Stephen, by one second, and Brazil (C. Diebold and P. Zancani) won by less than two seconds from the Belgians, J. Rosa and C. van Antwerpen. In the semi-finals, B. Boni and F. Fanetti, of Italy, rowed past O. S. Jensen and J. P. Snogdahl, of Denmark, to win by a second and a half. The final was between Italy, Switzerland (J. and H. Kalt), and Great Britain. From the start Switzerland led Italy, with Great Britain a few feet behind. But at the thousand metres Laurie and Wilson took the lead, with Italy dropping back. The Swiss challenged strongly at the finish, but Laurie and Wilson came home by 2·8 seconds, to win Britain's first gold medal.

Coxed-pair rowing is virtually unknown in England, and the opportunity of watching it at the Olympic Regatta is unlikely to have encouraged English oarsmen to take it up. There seems little to be said in favour of carrying a coxswain in a boat which does not require one. Others presumably disagree, so it would be churlish to press the point. However, the only race of interest was a hotly contested semi-final, in which T. Henriksen and F. Pederson, of Denmark, beat Aristide and Ampelio Sartor, of France, by 2·8 seconds. For the rest, those who were not winning generally seemed well aware that they were being asked to pull along far too much dead weight.

As one who took part, I suppose it is inevitable that it should seem to me that the racing in the Double Sculls was exciting. Yet from the official records it appears that it was not so. There were races in which the leadership changed hands, but none in which the actual finish was closely contested.

The final of the Double Sculls was between A. E. Larsen and E. W. Parsner, of Denmark, B. H. T. Bushnell and R. D. Burnell, who had joined forces after Henley, representing Great Britain, and J. A. Rodriguez and W. Jones, of Uruguay. The official version of the race was that Great Britain led at once, were a length and half ahead of Denmark at the thousand metres, two lengths ahead at one thousand five hundred metres, and held off the Danes' finishing challenge 'without effort'. I can only say that it did not seem like that at the time, and refer those who prefer a more exciting story to my account in *Swing Together*.[1]

As this is a history, rather than a book of personal reminiscences, I have tried to keep to the impersonal third person. But perhaps I may be allowed to add one personal note here. The Olympic Double-Sculls title fell to me through a series of, perhaps, fortunate coincidences, not the least of which was the sudden and unforeseen availability of B. H. T. Bushnell as a partner, and the immense psychological advantage of racing on my own home water. Exactly forty years earlier my father was a member of the Leander crew, which won the Eight-Oar title for Great Britain, also at Henley. And I believe that this is the only case, in any sport, of father and son both winning Olympic gold medals.

The only difference—indicative of changing times—is that his gold medal is made of gold, and mine of silver gilt!

Perhaps the most exciting and spectacular race of the whole Olympic Regatta was the Single Sculls semi-final, between G. E. Risso, of Uruguay, J. B. Kelly, of the United States, and A. D. Rowe, of Great Britain. For 250 metres Kelly and Rowe raced level, and at 500 metres the American led by six feet from Rowe, with Risso a length astern. At the half-distance Kelly was just clear, and Risso well astern. During this great struggle between Rowe and Kelly, no one had seriously considered what Risso was

[1] See also photograph facing p. 132.

doing. In fact he, alone of the three, was sculling at an economical pace. At 1,500 metres, Rowe was dropping back, and then, in a squall of wind and rain, which practically stopped the scullers in their tracks, Risso began a sustained spurt, which took him past the exhausted American, literally on the finishing line. His margin of victory was four-tenths of a second. In the final, M. T. Wood, the Diamonds winner, won comfortably from Risso, with E. Catasta, of Italy, third.

1949

After the turmoil of the Olympic year, 1949 brought a welcome return to the old order of things. Yet it was not quite the old order, for many changes were afoot. Appropriately, a knighthood was conferred on Harcourt Gold, in recognition of his services to rowing.

There was a record of 156 starters, nine more than in the preceding year, which, in its turn, had been the highest since the pre-war record of 128. This growing popularity was flattering to the Regatta, but it brought headaches to the Committee.

In its simplest form the problem of the Henley programme is that, with two crews in a heat, and four days of racing, only sixteen crews can be accommodated in any one event, unless two rounds of that event are held on the same day. In 1949 the Committee of Management decided to limit Regatta entries to sixteen, for all events except the Thames and Wyfold Cups, which were to be limited to thirty-two. It was the Ladies' Plate which was immediately affected by this change, and the Committee were doubtless hoping to encourage the better school crews to remain loyal to the Ladies', by doing away with the two races in one day. At the same time they ruled that, whilst a school could enter the same crew for both the Ladies' Plate and the Princess Elizabeth Cup, they could start in only one of these events, having twenty-four hours' grace, after the closing of the entries, to scratch from one or the other.

However worthy the intention of these new rulings, their results were unfortunate. The 'bait' to the schools worked, in the sense that seven of them entered for the Ladies' Plate. But it worked rather too well, for only five schools were left in the Princess Elizabeth Cup, and the total entry for the Ladies' Plate went up to twenty-four, which was eight above the newly proscribed maximum. Consequently, eight eliminating races had to be rowed on the Tuesday before the Regatta. Four schools took part in these races, and three of them were eliminated.

Partly as a result of this, and partly arising from a meeting of the school coaches, at which it was strongly urged that it was the duty of all the schools to support the newly instituted Princess Elizabeth Cup, all but two of the school crews deserted the Ladies' Plate in the following year. It would be unfair to condemn the schools' decision, for it may turn out, in the end, that it was for the good of school rowing as a whole. But their action was certainly contrary to the original hopes of the Stewards, when they added the Princess Elizabeth Cup to the programme. It was then seen as an encouragement to the weaker schools, and even, perhaps, as an opening for the second eights of some of the larger schools. Certainly it would be a pity if any school crew good enough to have a chance of winning, or of reaching the final of, the Ladies' Plate, should forgo it for the lesser prize.

The summer of 1949 was exceptionally dry, and during the Regatta the stream was almost stagnant. The flow over Teddington weir was the lowest since the drought of 1921. The wind, too, was generally favourable, so that it only required some fast rowing to produce record times.

Amongst eight crews contesting the Grand, there was the welcome sight of the first Oxford college crew to do so since the war. And to this crew, Trinity, went the honour of disposing of the first foreign challengers, the Roeivereeniging De Delftsche Sport, Holland. Both crews started at forty, and Trinity led by a canvas at the mile. It was a great race, and Trinity, finishing at forty, won by three feet.

The Cottage Club of Princeton, U.S.A., were comfortably beaten by Thames R.C. in one semi-final, and, in the other, Leander beat Trinity by three-quarters of a length, equalling the course record of 6 min. 44 sec.[1] Leander led all the way, moving fast, but were never able to leave Trinity, who were three-quarters of a length down at Fawley. At the three-quarter-mile they attacked hard, gaining nearly half a length. But Leander waited until their spurt had died away, and then replied, regaining their three-quarter-length lead and rowing in unpressed to the finish. In the final they won comfortably from Thames.

On the opening day of the Regatta, Lady Margaret B.C., beating Eton, lowered the Ladies' Plate record to 6 min. 47 sec. On the Friday, following Leander and Trinity up the course, Lady Margaret not only lowered the Ladies' Plate record a further four seconds, but beat Leander's time, and therefore the Grand and course record, by one second, the new record time being 6 min. 43 sec. The pity was that they could not have raced against Leander. They went on to win the Ladies' Plate by a safe margin, from Pembroke College Cambridge.[2]

In the Stewards', Trinity College Oxford had their revenge on Leander, and went on to win the final by three lengths from London R.C. In so doing they lowered the record to 7 min. 13 sec., one second better than Zurich's time in 1935. This was the first time a college four had won the Stewards' Challenge Cup since the victory of Pembroke College Cambridge in 1934, and it was the first Oxford success since Magdalen won in 1921.[3] Another great success came in the Wyfold Cup, when Lensbury R.C. scored their first Henley win. Beating Corpus Christi College Cambridge in a semi-final, they lowered the record for this event, by eleven seconds, to 7 min. 24 sec.

The lowering of the Wyfold record came not before its time. For, an hour and a half later, the record for the Double Sculls had

[1] Leander Club: J. G. C. Blacker (bow), R. M. T. Raikes, J. R. L. Carstairs, J. R. W. Gleave, W. A. D. Windham, R. D. Burnell, P. A. de Giles, P. Bradley (stroke), Alan Palgrave-Brown (cox).
[2] Lady Margaret B.C. Cambridge: H. H. Almond (bow), D. D. Macklin, D. N. Byrne, A. L. Macleod, W. T. Arthur, P. M. O. Massey, C. B. M. Lloyd, J. L. M. Crick (stroke), R. J. Blow (cox). See photograph facing p. 133.
[3] Trinity College Oxford: J. B. C. Robin (bow) (st.), R. O. Bowlby, A. D. Rowe, C. G. V. Davidge (stroke).

plummeted to 7 min. 27 sec., which was eight seconds below the
then existing Wyfold record. This occurred in a return race between the Olympic finalists—A. Larsen and E. W. Parsner, of
Denmark, and B. H. T. Bushnell and R. D. Burnell, representing
Maidenhead R.C. and Leander. The English double led off the
start, and by half a length at the quarter-mile. But then the Danes
began to pull them back. At the half-mile, Bushnell and Burnell
led by a quarter of a length; at Fawley the pairs were level.
Larsen and Parsner, sculling two strokes a minute more, then
forged ahead, to lead by a length at the mile. Burnell, who was
also rowing in the Leander eight, did not reply until the bottom
of the Enclosures, and the Danes held off the challenge to win by
one length.

1950

The entries in 1950 were a few less than in the preceding peak
year. But it was necessary to hold three eliminating races for the
Wyfold Cup, and one each for the Ladies' Plate, Thames Cup,
and Diamond Sculls. These preliminaries were rowed on the
Friday night prior to the Regatta, an inconvenient arrangement
for those taking part, which led to some adverse criticism. The
whole problem of eliminating races is considered elsewhere.[1]

Nor, in other respects, was 1950 a happy year for English
rowing, with one exception. An English sculler, A. D. Rowe,
brought home the Diamond Sculls for the first time since 1933.
His closest race was against another Englishman, H. J. Renton,
whom he beat with more in hand than the verdict of one and a
half lengths suggests. In the final he beat R. van Mesdag, a
Dutchman, but sculling for Trinity College Dublin, by three
lengths. Almost certainly Rowe was our fastest sculler since the
war.

Four foreign crews, the highest number ever, challenged for the
Grand, but the Canottieri Varese, from Italy, European champions
of 1949, withdrew. And in two memorable races English hopes
were dashed. Lady Margaret led Harvard to beyond Fawley. But

[1] See pp. 217–23.

then the Americans began to close up; they took the lead at the Enclosures, and went on to win by half a length. Then Leander, though starting at forty-one, were led up the Island by the Dutch eight, Studenten Roeivereeniging Njord, and by half a length at the Barrier, which was reached in 1 min. 57 sec., the fastest time of the year. Beyond Fawley there was a great struggle, with Leander closing to a quarter of a length at Remenham Club. But in the end the Dutchmen won by half a length. In the final, Njord again started fast, and led Harvard by a quarter of a length up the Island. But the Americans had their measure, and gradually went by to win convincingly by one and a quarter lengths.

To complete the discomfiture of the home crews, Kent School beat Thames R.C. in the Thames Cup, and Leander hit the booms and damaged a rigger in the final of the Stewards, giving an easy win to the Hellerup Roklub, Denmark. The Belgian pair, J. Rosa and C. van Antwerpen, won the Goblets, and Larsen and Parsner easily took the Double Sculls, for the second year in succession.

It only remains to record that the Ladies' Plate resulted in the first Oxford win for twenty-seven years, when New College beat Trinity College Dublin by a third of a length in the final. The Princess Elizabeth Cup came into its own, as a result of the changes in the Rules in 1949. Out of a field of eleven, Bedford beat Radley by a quarter of a length, to reach the final for the fourth time in five years. But an excellent St. Paul's crew were too good for them, and won a well-judged race by one length.

1951

In 1951 the foreign challenge was even stronger, but this time it was met successfully on all sides, except in the Thames Cup. The total entry was a new record, there being 158 starters. Unhappily, no less than forty-seven of these were in the Thames Cup.

This[1] is the highest entry ever received for any event at

[1] The total entry was actually forty-nine, but two crews scratched before the draw. Generally speaking, the 'entries' quoted throughout this book are 'starters', and may, therefore, sometimes differ from numbers quoted elsewhere, and, in particular, in contemporary newspaper reports.

Henley. The club entry was up, but primarily the great influx came from Oxford and Cambridge colleges, which, at twenty, was more than twice the average for the previous five years. Including the Grand and the Ladies' Plate, there were, in fact, four more college crews than in the previous highest year, which was 1937. But a number of them were certainly driven into the Thames Cup as a direct result of the recent limitation of the Ladies' Plate entry. No doubt they thought there was less danger of being put into an elimination race in the Thames Cup, and a better chance, if the worst should occur, of surviving the ordeal. On the first count they were very wrong, for only fifteen crews entered for the Ladies', and in the Thames Cup there were that number of eliminators. On the second score they were more nearly correct; fifteen colleges and fifteen clubs competed, and nine colleges survived.

There was strong competition for the Grand, including two crews from Holland, and one each from Italy and Spain. Lady Margaret B.C. convincingly disposed of Thames R.C., and of Leander, who had already beaten one of the Dutch crews. The much-fancied Italians failed signally against the other Dutch crew, who went on to beat the Spaniards. In the final, Lady Margaret, who were undoubtedly the fastest college crew for many years, beat the Delftsche Studenten 'Laga' by a length. Though led off the start, they had much the better stride, and looked safe enough after Fawley.

The Stewards' was undistinguished, except for the first heat, which brought together the two best fours. Thames R.C. won a magnificent race from Lady Margaret, by two feet, and went on to win the event with something in hand.

As so often happens, some of the best racing of the Regatta was seen in the Princess Elizabeth Cup, culminating in a dead heat between St. Paul's and Winchester. St. Paul's had already equalled the record of 7 min. 4 sec. in beating Shrewsbury by one and a quarter lengths, whilst Radley, winning by two-thirds of a length from Bedford Modern, had lowered it to 7 min. 3 sec.

The dead heat occurred in the second round. Winchester built up a lead of one and a quarter lengths at the mile post. Then, very nearly too late, St. Paul's sprang a splendid spurt. Along the Enclosures they overhauled Winchester at every stroke, and just caught them on the post. In the re-row, St. Paul's made a determined effort to gain the advantage off the start. At the quarter-mile they led by a canvas, but they had not the pace over the middle part of the course, and Winchester drew level and then forced their bows in front, leading by a third of a length at Fawley and by half a length at the mile. But this time St. Paul's attacked earlier; at the last signal they were level, and went on to win by three-quarters of a length. But in their next race St. Paul's lost to Radley, and in the final Bedford School once again proved their worth, scoring their fourth win since the institution of the Princess Elizabeth Cup in 1946.

The small-boat events, in spite of a strong overseas challenge, proved to be most successful for the home crews and scullers. J. G. P. Crowden and C. B. M. Lloyd, the past and present presidents of the C.U.B.C., won the Goblets from the holders, J. Rosa and C. van Antwerpen of Belgium. P. Bradley and R. D. Burnell, of Leander, won the Double Sculls, beating H. Wilke and W. Neuburger, of Germany, in a heat, and B. G. Davies and A. A. P. Kemp, of Reading, in the final. And T. A. Fox won the Diamonds.

In the Diamonds there was a magnificent race between the youthful J. Guest, jun., of Toronto, son of the Diamonds winner in 1930, and E. Larsen, of Denmark.

Guest was one of the most promising young scullers to come to Henley, but he was badly under-boated, with a span which caused him to pinch his boat. He started at twenty-six, to Larsen's thirty-one, and lost two and a half lengths in the first half-mile. Then he held on, but was still two and a quarter lengths down at the mile post. Then at last he managed to quicken a little and, in a wonderfully sustained spurt, got to within six feet of Larsen at the finish, forcing him to do the remarkably fast time of 8 min. 10 sec.

In the final Larsen led Fox by two lengths at the half-mile, and

Fox then hit the booms. He recovered quickly, and had lost only half a length more at Fawley. Neverthelesss, the race seemed over. But Fox took a look at his opponent and began to attack. This second onslaught in four days was too much for Larsen, and just beyond the mile post he had had his fill; Fox went by to win easily by four and a half lengths.

Altogether, 1951 was a wonderful Henley for Cambridge. For Lady Margaret won the Grand, and Pembroke won the Ladies' Plate from Jesus, whilst Lloyd and Crowden, respectively rowing stroke and seven of these two crews, together won the Goblets. Fox, of Pembroke, won the Diamonds, and P. Bradley, also late of Pembroke, won the Double Sculls in partnership with Burnell, who was the only Oxford man to appear on Saturday. Trinity Hall provided the only English crew to reach the semifinals of the Thames Cup, and won the Visitors' Challenge Cup from First and Third Trinity B.C. Even the Wyfold Cup went to Cambridge, Caius College winning the final from Clare. This was the first Wyfold win for an Oxford or Cambridge College since 1928, and the first time since 1913 that the final had been disputed between two college crews.

1952

In 1952 the Olympic Games were due to be held in Helsinki, and no doubt this contributed to bring the Henley entry down a little on recent years. But the Olympics brought a more than welcome compensation, in the form of the first New Zealand crew ever to come to Henley, as well as a return of old friends from Australia, and a Double Sculls entry from Canada.

Although the total entry was down, it was still necessary to hold ten eliminating races on the Friday before the Regatta, six of these being for the Wyfold Challenge Cup.

During the final week of practice, and on the last three days of racing, the wind was exceptionally favourable. The stream was low, though not abnormally so, and the water was often quite rough. Conditions, in fact, were potentially very fast, but too difficult to benefit any but the best crews. In practice, Leander were credited with rowing to the Barrier in 1 min. 50 sec., which was five seconds—in a short row probably worth one and a half lengths—faster than the best ever recorded in a race. There is, of course, no official record of practice times. But this row was done with reliable witnesses and timekeepers. A similar row, though in slower conditions, by Sydney R.C., who were Leander's only serious rivals—clocked 1 min 54·2 sec., and gave promise of what was to come.

Both won their heats very easily, Leander beating London R.C., and Sydney beating Thames R.C. Leander clocked 3 min. 11 sec. to Fawley, which was two seconds inside the record, and equalled the record of 6 min. 44 sec. all over. Sydney were two seconds slower to Fawley, and one second slower to the finish.

In spite of these well-matched times, Leander went down to the final as firm favourites. Starting at forty and a half to Sydney's forty-one, they led at once, and were just about clear at the Barrier, reached in 1 min. 53 sec. What is more, they continued to gain, and led by one and a quarter lengths at the half-mile signal, striking thirty-three to the Australians' thirty-seven. Most people thought that the race was over. But Sydney started to attack fiercely, and came back to Leander very rapidly. At Fawley they were led by three-quarters of a length, and at the mile, where Leander were up to thirty-seven again, by only a third of a length. There was a breath-taking struggle up the Enclosures, and Leander came home winners by half a length, their time— 3 min. 11 sec. to Fawley, and 6 min. 38 sec. to the finish—no less than five seconds faster than the course record.[1]

It is an interesting postscript to this race that the two crews went on to Helsinki, where the Australians beat the Englishmen, thus reversing the story of 1912, when Sydney R.C. beat Leander in the Grand, and were beaten by them in the Stockholm Olympics. On that occasion, however, they finished first and

---

[1] Leander Club: D. D. Macklin (bow), A. L. Macleod, N. B. M. Clack, R. F. A. Sharpley, E. J. Worlidge, C. B. M. Lloyd, W. A. D. Windham, D. M. Jennens (stroke), J. F. K. Hinde (cox).

second. In 1952 they finished third and fourth, behind the United States and the U.S.S.R.

In the Ladies' Plate no records were broken, but every race on the last three days was won in under seven minutes. Lady Margaret won the final by one and a quarter lengths, and it should be added that this was in spite of releasing several of their best men to row for Leander. In the Princess Elizabeth Cup, Radley, Monkton Combe, and Bryanston all had fine crews. Monkton Combe lowered the record to 7 min. 2 sec. and Radley improved on this by another five seconds. These two schools met in the final, when Radley won by half a length.

For a change the Visitors' produced a faster winning time, and probably a higher standard, than the Stewards'. In the senior event, the New Zealand four from Aramoho B.C. raced well, but lost to London R.C. by half a length. And London lost to Thames in the final, the winning time being 7 min. 24 sec. In the Visitors', half a hour after the Stewards' final, Pembroke Cambridge beat Trinity Oxford by one and three-quarter lengths, in 7 min. 15 sec. This broke the record by three seconds, and was two seconds slower than the course record for coxswainless fours, set up by Trinity Oxford, in the Stewards' in 1949.

The standard of the Thames Cup, as well as of the Wyfold Cup, was well above average, and the English crews at last offered a real challenge to the Americans. In the quarter finals, the University of London beat Tabor Academy by four feet.

The University of Pennsylvania's 150-lb. crew were the ultimate winners, but few crews can have worked harder for their success. Against Corpus Christi College Cambridge they did not lead until after the mile, and won by only half a length. Against University College and Hospital B.C., they led by a canvas at the mile and a quarter, when one of the U.C.H. crew caught a crab. In the semi-final they were led to the last signal, but attacked again and again, and rowed a gallant London R.C. crew almost to a standstill, to win by two-thirds of a length.

In the final they met Christ's College Cambridge in the most dramatic race of all. Christ's led from the top of the Island, and

XV. FOREIGN CHALLENGERS

Top: Harvard University win the Grand Challenge Cup in 1939

tom: Vancouver R.C. beat Club Krasnoe Znamia, U.S.S.R., in the semi-final of the Grand
llenge Cup in 1955. (In the final Vancouver lost by $\frac{1}{3}$ length to the University of Pennsylvania)

XVI. FOREIGN CHALLENGERS (cont.)

were half a length clear at the last signal, in a seemingly unassailable position. Then their number three caught a crab, and in a second the whole race was changed. Pennsylvania dashed by, and won by one and a quarter lengths. For the first time in seventeen years an English crew had been within an ace of winning a Thames Cup final from the Americans. It was a bitter pill, though no one could, for long, grudge Pennsylvania their hard-earned victory.

The 1952 Goblets saw the lowering of the record which had stood since the famous dead heat of 1911. Easily winning the semi-final, H. C. I. Bywater and T. H. Christie covered the course in 8 min. 5 sec. They were only one second slower in winning the final the next day. In the Diamonds, M. T. Wood, over from Australia for the Olympics, was in a class alone. T. A. Fox, the holder, made him work for his final victory—the time was 8 min. 12 sec., with Fox finishing two and a half lengths behind. But of all the others, only one newcomer, S. C. Rand, showed any promise of class.

Soon after the Regatta there came the sad news of the death of Sir Harcourt Gold, O.B.E., the President of Henley Royal Regatta.

1953

The events of 1953 have, to some extent, been dimmed by the excitements and controversies of succeeding years. Yet 1953 must assuredly rank as one of the most successful and memorable of all Henleys. For fine weather—after a shower on the Wednesday morning—for close racing and fast times, and for the astonishingly high-class performance of some of the crews and, above all, of the pairs and scullers, it was unsurpassed.

The only event which might have been described as disappointing was the Ladies' Plate, which attracted only eleven entries, the lowest since 1914. This was the cumulative result of the withdrawal of the schools, and the limit set to the entries. But the standard of those taking part was very level, the largest verdict in four days' racing being a length, whilst out of ten races, seven were won by three-quarters of a length or less. And, to cap it, there was a school and college final, between Radley and Jesus College Cambridge.

The crowd would have loved a school victory, and Radley had so impressed in the heats that many expected it. They were a strong and unusually mature crew. Yet they lacked the attribute most often found in a good school crew—dash and liveliness. It was they who led, and held Jesus at the lower rating. And it was Jesus who spurted to forty up the Enclosures, and finally drew away to win by three-quarters of a length.

The Leander Grand eight turned out to be one of the best ever seen at Henley, and won comfortably, beating the Union Sportive Metropolitaine des Transports, France, in the final, by one length. And in their first heat, beating Lady Margaret B.C. by the same margin, they covered the course in 6 min. 41 sec.[1] This was only three seconds slower than in their desperate race against Sydney, in 1952, when conditions were more difficult but certainly faster for a crew capable of making use of a strong following wind. Leander also carried off the coveted double, winning the Stewards' Challenge Cup for the second time since the war.

In the Thames Cup, at long last, the American challenge was met and repulsed. In speaking thus of the Thames Cup, from time to time, I must not be thought antagonistic to the Americans. On the contrary, they—and particularly Kent School, Tabor Academy, and the Princeton and Pennsylvania lightweights—are old friends at Henley. But the fact remains that it is not good for one crew, or group of crews, to dominate any event for too long. Everyone wants to see these crews at Henley. But it is an accident—if that is the right term—of the Henley qualifications that they are forced to enter for the Thames Cup, for which their standard is, or has generally been, too high.

Two American crews, Kent School and Princeton, entered in 1953; Kent School reached the quarter-finals, and were beaten by

[1] Leander Club: D. D. Macklin (bow), R. M. S. Gubbins, P. A. de Giles, D. A. T. Leadley, E. A. P. Bircher, C. G. V. Davidge, W. A. D. Windham, G. A. H. Cadbury (stroke), J. F. K. Hinde (cox).

Corpus Christi College Cambridge by six feet, a verdict which requires no comment. All but one of the quarter-finals produced fine races. Imperial College beat Maidenhead, who had come through from the eliminating races, by three-quarters of a length. Peterhouse, also from the eliminators, lost by the same margin to Princeton. Only the Royal Air Force had an easy win, finishing three lengths ahead of St. Catharine's College Cambridge, yet another crew which had raced through from the preceding Friday.

In this year, eighteen crews, out of a total Thames Cup entry of forty-one, had to race on the Friday before the Regatta. Of these, Corpus went on to the semi-finals, the three others already mentioned were beaten in the quarter-finals, and two, Queen's College Oxford and Jesus College Cambridge, in the third round. Of the nine winners of eliminating races, four had as easy or easier victories, in the first round of the Regatta.

In the semi-finals, the Royal Air Force made a British victory certain, holding on grimly, after leading Princeton by one and a quarter lengths at the mile post, to win by a third of a length.[1] On the previous day Princeton had lowered the Thames Cup record to 6 min. 45 sec. In the other semi-final, Imperial College beat Corpus by three feet. They led all the way, but Corpus were within six feet at the mile, and were as near to catching them at the finish as any crew could be. The final was another magnificent race, in which Imperial led by a third of a length, or less, all the way to the mile post. But the Air Force, striking forty, finished the stronger, getting their bows in front at the bottom of the Enclosures, and winning by half a length.

Like Leander, the Royal Air Force achieved a double, winning the Wyfold as well as the Thames Challenge Cup. Of the two it was more remarkable, because the junior events attract the larger entry. This was the first occasion since 1901, when Trinity Hall achieved the same distinction, that the same four men had won both events. In a heat, the Royal Air Force lowered the Wyfold record to 7 min. 20 sec.

It remains only to say something of the small-boat events,

[1] See photograph facing p. 180.

which, if they did not on the whole produce such close finishes, nevertheless set a new standard of pair-oared rowing, and sculling, and sent the time records tumbling.

In the Goblets, R. Baetens and M. Knuysen, of the Antwerp Sculling Club, clipped seven seconds off the record, which, it will be remembered, had been set at 8 min. 5 sec. in the previous year. On the following day they lowered the record a further seven seconds, to 7 min. 51 sec., and both these performances were achieved without any sort of competition. The final they won comfortably from H. Kesel and K. Hahn, of Germany.

R. George, a fourteen-stone sculler from Liège, became the first man to scull over the Henley course in 8 min., beating H. Steenacker, of Belgium, in a semi-final. But it did not win him the Diamonds, for T. A. Fox, sculling perhaps his best race at Henley, 'killed' him at the half-mile, and went on to win by four lengths, in 8 min. 12 sec. And in the Double Sculls, E. Schriever and P. Stebler, of Zurich, though quite unpressed, covered the course in the new record time of 7 min. 21 sec. This time was only one second slower than the newly established Wyfold record.

I cannot do better than conclude this account of the 1953 Regatta with a quotation from *The Times*.

Thus ended one of the greatest in the series of great regattas, in which the general standard was probably the highest ever seen, and in which the record was broken in five of the ten events. But the account would not be complete without recording that the prizes were presented by Mrs. G. C. Bourne, who is, in the words of Mr. H. R. N. Rickett, the chairman of Henley Regatta, the 'very embodiment of English rowing'. For Mrs. Bourne, who first saw Henley in 1877, was the wife of Doctor Bourne, who rowed for Oxford in 1882 and 1883, the mother of R. C. Bourne, who stroked Oxford to victory from 1909 to 1912, and the grandmother of R. M. A. Bourne, who, in 1946, became the first rowing Blue of the third generation.

This year's Henley will be remembered for the fine Leander crew, and for the well-deserved successes of the Royal Air Force, and perhaps also for the fact that both they, and St. Paul's, were rowing in a style which owed something to the Americans. But above all it seems to have set us a new standard in small-boat performances. . . .

1954

No doubt, as the Regattas of 1954 and 1955 recede into the pages of history, they will assume their proper proportions. Some future historian, perhaps, will note simply that 1954 saw the first entries from the Soviet Union, and perhaps that it was a year in which the standard was not particularly high.

The entries soared again in 1954, to the new record total of 176. There were nine withdrawals, leaving 167 starters. Numerically, the foreign challenge, too, was the strongest ever; and, whilst there have certainly been better individual foreign crews in other years, and in particular events, there has probably never been such a generally strong challenge from abroad, in all the events at the same time.

Unhappily this coincided with a barren year for English oarsmen. Such a statement must be made with due regard for the dangers of wishful thinking. But it is in accordance with the facts. Only Leander looked capable of producing first-class crews, and they failed signally, in both the Grand and the Stewards'.

Of the Grand there is little to be said, save that Thames R.C. went nearest to making a race with the Russian Club Krylia Sovetov. The verdict of half a length suggests that they succeeded. But the Russians appeared to be unpressed, and the verdict itself was on the ungenerous side. This was in a semi-final. In the final, Krylia Sovetov romped away from Leander, to win by two and a half lengths.

In spite of a record entry of eleven fours, five of them from overseas, the Stewards' Cup was disappointing. Partly due to bad steering, there was only one verdict of less than a length, and that was between Club Krylia Sovetov and their compatriots, Club Avangard, in what did not look to be a race at all, in the usually accepted sense of the word. But there was no doubt that the Krylia Sovetov crew would have given a good account of itself against any opposition. In the final, the Royal Air Force, giving away over a stone a man, and that against a strong head-wind, made a gallant attempt to hunt the Russians home, and lost by one and a quarter lengths.

The Ladies' Plate entry showed a welcome revival, to a total of twenty-one, necessitating five eliminating races, the same number as in the Thames Cup. There were also eliminating races for the Wyfold Cup. They were held on the Saturday morning, instead of on the Friday evening, a change which made matters easier for those taking part. In the eliminators Oxford rowing showed a brief and welcome revival, for no fewer than six Oxford colleges beat their opponents from the Cam. But only Magdalen survived until the Friday of the Regatta, when they had the satisfaction of giving First and Third Trinity their only real race in the Ladies' Plate. Queen's College Oxford reached the semi-finals of the Thames Cup, and there lost to the Royal Navy's first Henley crew by a length. A new challenger from the United States, the Massachusetts Institute of Technology, rowed through to the final on the other side of the draw, and beat the Navy comfortably by two and a half lengths.

As usual, the Princess Elizabeth Cup provided some of the best racing of the year. Indeed, the general standard of the school rowing at Henley has improved so much, since the introduction of the Princess Elizabeth Cup, that few can still doubt its value. On this occasion Winchester were the winners, after winning a hard-fought semi-final from Shrewsbury. Oundle, rowing at Henley for the first time, reached the final, and lost to Winchester by one and three-quarter lengths.

In the Goblets there were seven entries, but two pairs withdrew after the draw. This is always an unpopular, and sometimes a thoughtless action. It resulted in S. L. Blom and R. Gitz, of Holland, reaching the final without having a single race in which to get the feel of the course. But they were no match for the Soviet pair, I. Buldakov and V. Ivanov, who thus gained Russia's third victory.

Only nine scullers entered for the Diamonds, foreign scullers outnumbering the English by six to three. Two races were of the greatest interest.

The first round brought together P. Vlaşic, of Yugoslavia, the European champion, and Y. Tukalov, the Russian victor of the 1952 Olympic Games. Their meeting was therefore pregnant with possibility. Both men started at forty, an astonishing rate for scullers, and both kept going at a killing pace. Vlaşic gained a slight advantage, but there was virtually nothing in it at the Barrier. The time to Fawley, with Vlaşic again showing ahead, was 3 min. 56 sec., only six seconds outside Dr. Buhtz's record, and that on a day which was not fast. No scullers could keep up this pace indefinitely, and soon after Fawley Tukalov had had enough. Vlaşic paddled on, and the verdict was given as 'easily'. Yet few Henley races can have been less easy to win.

A sculler does not quickly recover from this sort of race, and Vlaşic went on to an unexpectedly hard semi-final against S. C. Rand, of the Royal Air Force. In the final he met A. Colomb, of Switzerland.

There then occurred one of those incidents which must happen occasionally on the river, yet are happily rare at Henley. The facts are simple. Vlaşic led up the Island, and was just clear at the half-mile. Then his steering became erratic; several times he infringed on Colomb's water, and several times returned to his own. But up the Enclosures, tiring rapidly, and with Colomb challenging for the lead, he was badly off station. He got home with six feet to spare, and a foul imminent, which, had it occurred, could only have resulted in his disqualification.[1]

What was unusual was not the trespassing, which occurs quite often at Henley, but the fact that it took place so near the finish, thus demonstrably jeopardizing the result. The Swiss lodged a formal protest, but the umpire, of course, was perfectly right in allowing the scullers to finish without interference, and could, in fact, have done nothing else under the Henley code.

It is interesting to note that Vlaşic did not reach Henley until late on the Monday evening, after a week's racing and travelling on the Continent. On the Tuesday he made his choice of several boats and sets of sculls. And on Wednesday, after one day at

[1] See photograph facing p. 197.

Henley, and with borrowed boat and sculls, he won his great race against Tukalov. It was a pity that such a remarkable performance should have been marred by bad steering. But perhaps Vlaşic was taking too many liberties with the blue riband of the sculling world.

The Double Sculls were won by the holders, E. Schreiver and P. Stebler, of Zurich. They were unexpectedly pressed in the semi-final by the London double, consisting of the veteran A. J. Marsden, and T. A. Fox, who had been unable to give sufficient time to prepare for the Diamonds. Though led by one and a quarter lengths at Remenham Club, London raced in gallantly, to lose by only half a length. They had already sculled past the Soviet Double, G. Zhilin and I. Emchuk, and held off their finishing challenge, to win by the same margin.

1955

Until more objective views prevail, 1955 will remain, for many, the year in which the Russian crews scratched at Henley. Did the Soviet oarsmen really want to withdraw, or were they ordered to do so by their Embassy in London? Did they perhaps believe that there was a deliberate plot to deprive them of their boats, or even that the dock strike itself was staged for this purpose? Such a suggestion may sound fantastic to western ears, but would not necessarily be so to the Russians. The true answers to these, and other, questions we shall probably never know. But in the face of much speculation, often ill-informed, it is worth trying to record the facts, in so far as they are ascertainable.

The trouble arose from a dock strike, which held up the arrival of the boats of some of the competing crews, and not only of the Russians, of course. The Canadians, for instance, practised for ten days in a boat loaned to them by Leander, but happily their own boat reached them before the start of the racing. Several of the American crews, too, found themselves without boats, and made the best of borrowing from each other. The University of Pennsylvania obtained their boat, in the end, only with the help of the United States Air Force, which flew it across the Atlantic in a military plane.

For the Russians the position was particularly galling, for their boats were in a Russian ship, which was actually lying in the Thames estuary. And no one, it seemed, could get them unloaded. Yet, in fact, the Stewards did a great deal, which was not generally known at the time. They managed to arrange for a lighter to go alongside the Russian ship and, later, for the ship itself, which was lying thirty-seventh in the queue off Gravesend, to be taken out of turn into the London Docks. There a gang of volunteers—themselves oarsmen of the National Dock Labour Board Sports Association—stood by to offload the racing boats, with the permission of their union. At any time, from the Thursday before the Regatta, the Russians' boats could have been unloaded, with the goodwill of all concerned—but for one factor. Their shipping agent insisted that the whole cargo, and not merely the racing shells, must be unloaded, and required a guarantee that his ship would not then be declared 'black'.

Here again, we cannot know the shipping agent's motives. But there is no doubt that it was insistence on a concession which, clearly, the union would never make that left the Soviet oarsmen without their boats at the beginning of the Regatta. In the meantime, of course, they had borrowed English boats. Their plight earned them the sympathy of all at Henley. But many judged that they still had excellent chances of success. Indeed, their predicament had, in one sense, left them with everything to gain, and very little to lose.

Then, on the opening day of the Regatta, came the following announcement from the Regatta Office:

At 10 a.m. the leader of the Soviet team, the chief coach, and the interpreter dictated and signed the following statement:
'We, the Soviet oarsmen, having discussed the situation which is the result of the fact that the Secretariat of the Henley Royal Regatta has failed in getting our boats off the ship, have decided to withdraw from all events and not to participate in the Henley Royal Regatta'.

And this, in fact, they did, withdrawing the whole of their team to London.

Not unnaturally the wording of this statement caused considerable indignation. But here perhaps—we cannot tell—was an instance of misunderstanding arising from the difficulties of language. The verb 'to fail', after all, is capable of varied interpretation. However that may be, the announcement had one immediate result. It called the bluff—if bluff it was—of the shipping agents. Either it was that, or the wave of comment in the Press. Before the day was many hours older, the Russian boats were unloaded. The rest of the cargo had to wait its proper turn.

At 6.5 p.m. the Committee issued a second statement:

The Soviet crews have requested that they may be allowed to cancel their withdrawal from the Regatta. In the exceptional circumstances the Committee of Management have agreed to the readmission of crews competing in those events which have not yet begun.

The effect of this decision was to readmit all the Russian competitors except the sculler, Y. Tukalov. His race had, as a matter of fact, already gone by default, his opponent having been granted a walk-over.

It was again a bad year for English rowing, and for the first time since the war Leander could not raise an eight at all. But there was some excellent racing.

In the first round of the Grand, Jesus College Cambridge hung on to the Russian Club Krasnoe Znamia, to lose by half a length. In the semi-final the Russians met Vancouver. The Canadians started badly, and lost nearly three-quarters of a length in the first quarter-mile. Then they settled to their task, and gradually began to overhaul the Russians. At Fawley they had their bows in front, and at the mile post they led by a quarter of a length. Then, rising to a great occasion, Vancouver began a storming spurt, and drew right away to win by a length and a quarter.

Like that correspondent of *London Society*, describing the first Oxford and Cambridge Boat Race, which took place at Henley in 1829, 'Never shall I forget the shout that rose away among the hills'. Dearly would the Henley crowd have loved to see the Canadians win the Grand, for which they have tried gallantly but in vain on so many occasions. But it was not to be.

The University of Pennsylvania, who had won both their heats with ease, never led Vancouver by more than half a length. But they never looked to be in serious danger of losing the initiative, and they came home with a third of a length to spare.

The Ladies' Plate racing was less close than usual, and produced a most well-deserved victory for Queens' College Cambridge. It was a fine performance for a crew which had finished fifth in the May Races. It was Queens' first success in the Ladies', and their first Henley win since 1912, when they won the Wyfold Cup.

In a quarter-final of the Thames Cup occurred one of Henley's rare dead heats, between Pennsylvania and the Royal Air Force. In a desperate re-row the Air Force got home by four feet. And, as though that were not enough, they won their semi-final, against Molesey B.C., by only three feet. It was too much for any crew, and in the final they lost to the Massachusetts Institute of Technology by two-thirds of a length.

In recent years, the Princess Elizabeth Cup has grown to be one of the most popular Henley events. And rightly so, for it seldom fails to provide some of the keenest racing. Out of the fifteen races in 1955, seven were won by margins of half a length or less. Shrewsbury won the final by only eight feet, from Oundle. Incidentally, this was only the second year in which Oundle had competed at Henley, and the second occasion on which they reached the final.

Looking to the future, it seems that the popularity of the Princess Elizabeth Cup may soon raise a serious problem. In 1955 the entries numbered seventeen, and one eliminating race was necessary before the Regatta. The Committee may have to decide, therefore, whether schools are to put up with being eliminated before the Regatta, or whether they must return to rowing two races in a day.

In the Stewards', the Italian Moto Guzzi four threw away their chance through faulty steering. At the bottom of the Enclosures they were directly astern of their opponents, Club Krylia Sovetov. A magnificent finishing spurt brought them up fast, but they had to steer out and round, and lost by a canvas. The Russians went on to win the final, against Leander, without difficulty.

In general, the four-oared rowing was not impressive. But special mention must be made of the Kettering R.C., who lost to Thames, in the final of the Wyfold Cup. Prior to 1955 this club had never rowed in, and, in fact, had not owned, a coxswainless four. Furthermore, they practised on an artificial lake, only half a mile long, which is drained every winter. But the Kettering men made good use of the winter of 1954, and built themselves a boat in their spare time, and with no professional assistance. In her they had a successful season, and reached their first Henley final.

The holders, I. Buldakov and V. Ivanov, had no difficulty in retaining the Goblets, but their compatriots, G. Zhilin and I. Emchuk, though greatly improved, won the Double Sculls by only half a length from the Swiss pair, H. Vollmer and T. Keller. The standard of the small boats was lower than of recent years. The Diamonds gave Poland her first Henley win, through T. Kocerka.

1956

It is easy to say that times are unreliable, because of changing conditions. But in practice it is always difficult to divorce the assessment of performances from the evidence of the stop-watch. There is, therefore, some danger of underestimating the standard in slow years. Nineteen-fifty-six was such a year, with head and cross-head winds throughout the Regatta, so that, even though there was no stream running, times were always slow. But even if due allowance is made for the unpleasant, and often very difficult conditions in which the crews were performing, there was fairly general agreement that the standard was lower than usual.

No doubt this was due, in part, to the impending Olympic Games, which were due to take place in the ensuing winter in Australia. This factor certainly reduced the foreign challenge, though in compensation it brought to Henley the French Army crew, which was a welcome exception to the rule, and would have been good Grand winners in any year. The total entry was 175, only one below the record figure of 1954, but an unduly high proportion were Thames and Wyfold Cup crews, necessitating eight eliminating heats for the former and no less than thirteen for the latter event. There were also two eliminating heats each in the Ladies' Plate and Princess Elizabeth Cup.

For the first time since 1861 Eton did not enter for the Ladies' Plate. Having a young and inexperienced crew, they entered, as many had urged them to do in recent years, for the Princess Elizabeth Cup. And yet, as luck would have it, this proved to be a year in which a school might well have won the Ladies' Plate. It can only be a matter for speculation, but many thought that either Eton, or St. Paul's, whom they beat in the final of the Princess Elizabeth Cup, would, at the least, have fared well in the Ladies'. Whether or not a school does better to win the Princess Elizabeth Cup than to reach the final or the semi-final of the Ladies' Plate, must be a matter of personal opinion. But, having had the courage of their conviction that they should enter for the lesser event in 1956, it is to be hoped that Eton will not lack the same courage, when they believe their star to be in the ascendant, and will return to the Ladies' Plate. It is to be hoped, too, that other schools will, from time to time, join them, thus preserving the tradition of the Ladies' Plate.

The racing in the Princess Elizabeth Cup was less close than usual, there being no race during the Regatta in which the verdict was less than two-thirds of a length. Perhaps this was because Eton and St. Paul's were outstanding, and Shrewsbury, who lost a good quarter-final to Eton by three-quarters of a length, the only crew which could challenge them. In the final, Eton led all the way, and convincingly held off St. Paul's finishing spurt, to win by two-thirds of a length.

It would be wrong to conclude, from the fact that the winning time was sixteen seconds slower than that in the Princess Elizabeth Cup, that it was altogether a low-standard Ladies' Plate. What was true was that there was a stronger Oxford challenge than for some years, which added interest to the racing, and that there were lacking the one or two Cambridge college crews, very nearly in Grand class, which are often to be found in the Ladies'. Magdalene made their way into the final with the greatest of ease, for only the second time in their history. Peterhouse, who had never before gone so far, had first to beat Trinity Hall. They gained half a length to the Barrier, and gradually increased their advantage, to win by a length and a quarter. The final was a remarkable race. Level at the half-mile, Peterhouse gained a few feet at Fawley, and led by half a length at the mile post. Both crews then struck a freak gust of wind, which turned them obliquely across the course, and practically stopped the boats dead; this alone could have accounted for the slow time. Peterhouse recovered the quicker, and retained the initiative, which was just sufficient to get them home, in a splendid race, with a quarter of a length to spare.

The disappointment, and surprise, of the Grand Challenge Cup was the complete failure of Leander, who had showed considerable pace in practice. In the first round they lost to Jesus College Cambridge, mainly because, after gaining a slight lead up the Island, they allowed their rating to drop too low, and could not quicken again. Jesus, rowing most gallantly against a gale of wind—certainly not their conditions—passed them beyond the Barrier, and held on to win by half a length.

That, in truth, was the end of British hopes of regaining the Grand, for Jesus, giving away a stone a man, had no chance next day against the very strong French Army crew, which was the heaviest eight ever to race at Henley. Their margin of superiority was shown by the fact that although their stroke came off his slide at the start, so that Jesus were a length and a half clear at the top of Temple Island, the Frenchmen caught them at Fawley, and went on to win quite comfortably. Next day the French Army jumped away from the Swedish Rodklubben Three Towns, and won the Grand rather more easily than the official verdict of one length suggested. This was France's first victory in the premier event.

The Thames Cup produced some fine racing, with thirteen verdicts of a length or less, but culminated in the seemingly inevitable American victory. This time the winners were the Princeton lightweights, and the fact that more English crews than usual seemed to be within striking distance of them served only to emphasize the fact that their standard is consistently a little too high for the Thames Cup. In the final they beat a fit, but rather rough, Royal Air Force crew by one length. The Oxford University Isis B.C. pushed them even closer in the semi-final, losing by only two-thirds of a length.

The four-oared rowing was altogether unimpressive, but, if there was no quality, there at least emerged, from the huge Wyfold field, two crews which provided an astonishing final to that event. The Royal Engineers started at thirty-seven, and Brockville R.C., from Canada, at forty-four, until they hit the booms just above the Island. At the half-mile the Engineers were clear, but at Fawley the Canadians began to close up. At the mile they raised their rating to thirty-nine, and were only a canvas down when they hit the booms again. There followed a tremendous struggle, but although Brockville came in at nearly forty they could not get on terms, and the Royal Engineers won by four feet.

The Stewards' was won comfortably by Thames R.C., their only close race being in the first round, when they won by three feet from Macmillan's crew, drawn from the same club. Merton recorded an Oxford victory in the Visitors', winning all their races with something to spare.

The individual events brought some consolation to English oarsmen, for R. J. Thompson and G. M. Wolfson, of Pembroke College Cambridge, disposed of two foreign pairs, and went on to win the Goblets in convincing style. And the brothers S. C. and W. H. Rand put on a really polished performance to win the Double Sculls.

Apart from the final there was only one worthwhile race in the Diamonds; in it D. F. Meineke, of South Africa, beat H. Kesel, of the Saar, by a length and a half. But Meineke was no match for T. A. Fox on the following day. In the four days' racing there was no other verdict of less than three lengths, a fair indication of the uneven standard.

The final, however, proved the exception to this rule, although, in the end, it was won by the holder, T. Kocerka, of Poland, by four lengths. Losing this final, T. A. Fox sculled one of the finest races of his career, which, be it remembered, included two Diamonds victories. He lacked Kocerka's pace, but very rightly made up his mind to stay with him. Sculling thirty and twenty-eight, for him a high rating, Fox managed to do this, just a length down, as far as the Barrier. Then he began to edge back, gradually whittling away the Pole's lead, until, at Fawley, only half a length separated the two men. The time here, in conditions most unfavourable to scullers, was 4 min. 0 sec., which was perhaps the most impressive performance of the whole Regatta. The race hung in the balance for another quarter of a mile, but then Kocerka began to gain the initiative. Quite suddenly it was all over, and, at the mile post, having done all he could, Fox was out of the fight. A very tired Kocerka sculled on to win a well-deserved victory, and to retain the coveted Diamond Sculls. Another page was written in Henley's history.

Three

HENLEY'S PROBLEMS

CHAPTER EIGHT

Talking Points

THE central chapters of this book set out to tell the story of Henley Regatta. Disputes which have arisen, and controversial decisions which have been made, are a part of that story. But the historical background is not the whole of the pattern which goes to make up Henley today and which will affect the Henley of tomorrow. Besides history, there is something which we might call Controversy.

Let us then consider some of the issues which face the Stewards of Henley Royal Regatta, and which are talking points amongst rowing men.

OVERCROWDING, AND THE HENLEY STANDARD

For many years now, Henley Regatta has grown steadily in popularity. Furthermore, in the past ten years there has been a nation-wide—indeed, a world-wide—awakening to sport, in the widest sense. More and more people get holidays with pay, and transport facilities improve, in spite of local evidence to the contrary. All this means that more crews want to compete at Henley.

This at once raises the question of the well-being of rowing. Sometimes it is argued that Henley ought to expand, and that the Committee should do all they can to encourage crews to come to see and mix with first-class oarsmen. This is an argument with a popular appeal, and it has been used in connection with most of the controversial Henley issues. But it is an argument which is fundamentally unsound. Would it improve the general standard of tennis if all of us could play at Wimbledon? Would it improve the standard of driving if all could race at Silverstone? Of course it would do nothing of the sort. On the contrary, it would lower the prestige of Wimbledon and Silverstone, so that they would cease to be the ambition of aspiring tennis players and racing motorists. It is just because a high standard is demanded that young men make a special effort to improve their own performance. Within reason, the more difficult it is for them to compete, the more they will wish to do so.

This fact is well understood by those responsible for organizing the main sporting events. At Wimbledon the known stars are seeded, and the rest play qualifying rounds; in golf, only those who return the necessary score in qualifying rounds are admitted to the final stages of the Open Championship. It is the same in nearly every great sporting event. The organizers know full well that prestige is all-important, and that it depends on the quality of the contestants.

There is no doubt that Henley, and therefore rowing in general, would suffer if there were no check on the entries. The check is slender enough as it is. For no standard qualifications are demanded, and in practice all entries are accepted, within the limits set for each event. Only when these limits are exceeded does some degree of qualification come into operation. For then the Committee endeavours to pick out the weaker crews, and requires them to take part in eliminating races. That they may not always be successful in their selections, although a point to be considered later, is immaterial to the basic problem. The principle of refusing to extend the Regatta, to accommodate a still wider entry, remains entirely sound.

And there is a further consideration, which sometimes escapes the notice of the protagonists of an extended Henley. The available space on the river, and in the boat tents, is already full to overflowing. Serious congestion, hampering good and bad alike, occurs in the last few days of practice. Even if the principle of trying to make Henley a Regatta for the *élite* be discounted, the physical limitations of the Henley reach cannot be disregarded.

ELIMINATING RACES

From these few remarks it should be clear that Eliminating Races serve a dual purpose. On the one hand, they provide some check on the actual number of entries. And on the other, they provide some sort of qualifying standard. This, of course, is theory. We must still consider how the Eliminating Races measure up to their theoretical tasks in actual practice.

Eliminating Races, eliminating crews before the Regatta itself begins, are inevitably unpopular. But, temporarily ignoring the question of their desirability, as a check on the size and quality of the entry, it is worth considering how, if at all, Eliminating Races could themselves be eliminated.

Assuming the Henley entry to remain at least at its present level, it would be necessary, in order to do without Eliminating Races, either:

  (i) To have a five-day Regatta;
  (ii) To row more than one round a day (or to row two rounds on more than one day, in the case of the Thames and Wyfold Cups);
  (iii) To row three crews abreast.

An extra day's racing would help the Regatta financially. And it must be admitted that the arguments against it are, to some extent, forestalled by the fact that the fifth day, or half of it, already takes place. For whether or not they are rated as part of the Regatta, and whether they are called Eliminating Races, or the First Round, these races actually take place, and the course must be cleared for them. The issue here is therefore whether they should be held on the Saturday, as pre-Regatta eliminators, or on the Tuesday, as part of the official Regatta programme.

There is no seeding of the Henley draw, but, in effect, the Committee's endeavours to place the weaker crews in the Eliminating Races provide some degree of seeding in the overcrowded events. Were the Eliminating Races to become the First Round of a five-day Regatta, the better crews would lose

even this degree of protection. If they must row six races instead
of five, it is much better for the potential winners and finalists—
and their interests must, of course, be considered first—to row
the additional race on the Saturday before the Regatta. In so far as
anything can be certain in boat racing, they have little fear of
losing, and it is not altogether fanciful to say that, in effect, they
are merely rowing their final practice courses under Regatta conditions. Such an arrangement may be, for them, a positive advantage. But to race on five consecutive days, with two races on one
of those days, might put an undue emphasis on physical strength,
and would certainly greatly increase the 'luck of the draw'.
Therefore, the verdict must be against a five-day Regatta.

To step up the actual number of races, and even rounds, within the time limit of the present four-day Regatta, presents other
difficulties. With the provision of more umpires, there is little
doubt that more races could be rowed. But the additional launches, and the loss of the quarter-hour intervals which separate
each batch of races, might well create a serious problem of rough
water. And, even more than with a five-day Regatta, the rowing
of more races each day would increase the element of luck. It
might adversely affect the entries for the small-boat events, too,
which would probably be a consideration with the Committee,
though it might not be an unrelieved disaster, since it would also
be a discouragement to multiple entries.

Lastly, there is the possibility of rowing three crews abreast.
This is the most attractive of the three alternatives, because it
caters for more crews in less races, and adds the interest and
excitement of a struggle for second place.

To make a straight course, wide enough for three crews over
the full Henley distance, it would be necessary to cut off a considerable slice of Temple Island, and of the Berkshire bank of the
river near the start. The cost would be heavy, but no doubt the
Committee could find a way of meeting it. But the real objection
is that it is problematical whether a fair course would result. It
seems probable that the centre station would generally be at a
disadvantage. Certainly this was the impression gained during

the 1948 Olympic Regatta, when a three-abreast course was laid out over 2,000 metres. The day may come when this objection can be met. But at present, the doubtful fairness of the course, coupled with the fact that it would aggravate the overcrowding of the river even more than the other alternatives, makes the wide course look an impracticable proposition.

The relative importance of these considerations may be a matter of opinion. But in the aggregate they must lead us to the conclusion that Eliminating Races will continue. We must therefore consider how they work out in practice.

We may tire of the cliché that the Law, to be acceptable, must not only be fair, but must also be seen to be fair. Here perhaps we have an example of a law—or a system—which may well be fair, but which often seems to be quite the reverse. In recent years it has aroused considerable ill feeling and adverse comment, much of it avoidable.

It is not within the bounds of reason to assume that the Committee of Management select crews for the Eliminating Races by sticking pins into a list of the competitors. On the contrary, from the circumstantial evidence of the trouble they take over everything else connected with the running of the Regatta, it is obvious that they must go to considerable pains to choose the weakest crews.

How, in practice, can this be done?

The Committee have, quite recently, taken to announcing the draw for the Eliminating Races after, instead of before, Marlow Regatta. It is more than mere reasonable inference that this is done in order to enable them to study the Marlow results. So much has actually been said, though there has never been an official announcement to this effect. It can also be assumed that the Committee study the results of earlier Regattas, and of the racing in Eights Week at Oxford, and in the May Races at Cambridge. This should provide a fair indication of the relative form of most crews.

In the case of crews on which there is no reliable indication of current form, it would be reasonable to take account of the showing in previous years, as an indication of the sort of crew a particular club is likely to send to Henley. One hopes that this, too, is done; if it were known to be done, it might provide one of the strongest deterrents to sub-standard entries.

If all these factors are indeed taken into consideration, the selection of crews for the Eliminating Races may be much fairer than it sometimes appears to be. But form, of course, will often be deceptive. College crews from Cambridge, and even more from Oxford, are often reconstituted for Henley; club crews may start the season well, and fail utterly at Henley, or they may deliberately aim their training at Henley, and make little effort to win races earlier in the season. For these reasons, the selections can never be infallible. Generally speaking, this will not matter much. But occasionally two good crews will meet in an Eliminating Race, as happened in the Ladies' Plate in 1949, when the unfortunate Trinity College Dublin were dismissed by only a quarter of a length by Lady Margaret, who went on to win the whole event quite easily. Such a 'mistake' naturally catches the eye.

It also sometimes happens that a club enters a bad eight, and, from amongst the same men, a bad four also. As yet the Committee have seldom required the same men to row in Eliminating Races in two events. And so we find a crew, which has escaped the Eliminating Races for a particular event, and yet is obviously slower than some of the crews which are taking part. Here, we may say, is a club which enters not one, but two sub-standard crews, and deserves scant sympathy. But consider that if the Committee were to place both these crews in Eliminating Races, many people would say, with some reason, that the unhappy club had been given no chance of proving its worth in either event.

Those who study the problem carefully may often find a perfectly sound reason for apparent mistakes in the selection of crews for the eliminators. But their deductions can only be speculative, and they will rarely convince the casual observer, let alone members of the clubs which feel that they have had an unfair deal.

So far as the selection of crews for the Eliminating Races is concerned, the conclusion must be that it is as fair as anyone could make it. At the same time, it may well be that the Committee of Management are over-confident, not so much in their ability to choose the right crews, as in their assumption that everyone else will have unquestioning faith in their choice. It is an occupational hazard of Committees to assume that 'Silence is Golden', and that their decisions should be made and accepted without explanation. Certainly it would be a mistake for the Henley Management to tie themselves down to rigid rules for selection. But some public explanation of the general principles upon which they work would undoubtedly go far to remove a largely avoidable source of ill feeling.

In the past there have been two other, now happily removed, sources of complaint about the Eliminating Races, both of which tended to aggravate the situation. They were, that the Eliminating Races were intentionally held at a time which was inconvenient to the participants, and that the results were omitted from the Regatta Programme.

The first of these complaints was very real between 1949 and 1953, when the Eliminating Races were held on the evening of the Friday before the Regatta. Nearly all the club oarsmen competing at Henley must sacrifice part, if not the whole of their annual holiday, in order to spend a week or ten days at Henley. To require them to be present on the preceding Friday evening, thus breaking into another working week, was altogether unreasonable.

This grievance was righted in 1954, when the Eliminating Races were removed to the Saturday morning. Although still inconvenient to those who wish to spend only a week at Henley, the present arrangement is entirely reasonable; there are, as we have seen, other objections, far outweighing mere convenience, to rowing races on the Monday or Tuesday of Regatta week. Furthermore, there are obvious advantages, from the point of view of the Management, in holding the Eliminating Races before the Draw, which traditionally takes place in the Town Hall on the

Saturday afternoon. Not the least of these advantages is that it eases the overcrowding of the boat tents and the river during the final stages of practice.

The other complaint, in itself apparently a small matter, was the omission of the results of the Eliminating Races from the Regatta programme. It is worthy of consideration only because it was symptomatic of an unreasonable attitude towards the problem of Eliminating Races. Until 1949 the names of the eliminated crews were included in the programme, and their omission in 1950 and subsequent years was clearly intended to emphasize the fact that the Eliminating Races were not part of the Regatta proper, and that eliminated crews had not even the right to say that they had competed at Henley.

Now there are, at times, some quite shameful entries at Henley. If it were true that Eliminating Races were confined to such substandard crews, few would have quarrelled with the decision to expunge them from the records. But, in fact, these crews form a small minority, and it is quite impossible to confine them to the Eliminating Races. For one thing, one must ask whether it is any more shameful to enter a crew for the Thames Cup, when it is not good enough to appear at Henley at all, than it is to enter a crew for the Grand Challenge Cup, which would be lucky to win a couple of heats in the Thames Cup. Whatever one may think of this particular problem, it is a fact that participation in the Eliminating Races is largely a matter of the chance of fluctuating demand for the limited number of places in each event. Scullers are amongst the worst offenders in the matter of sub-standard entries. Yet a man who is incapable of winning a senior sculling event can, at present, enter for the Double Sculls at Henley without any fear, and for the Diamonds with very little fear of suffering the indignity of defeat in an Eliminating Race.[1]

In the final analysis, of course, it is public opinion which holds

[1] But in recent years the Stewards have attached to home entry forms a note to the effect that entries for the individual events will not normally be accepted, unless signed by a responsible officer of the club or clubs represented. This is to discourage 'unattached' entries, and to make clubs accept responsibility for such of their members as enter for the individual events.

the key to sub-standard entries. The Committee's endeavours to stigmatize the Eliminating Races as such always appeared somewhat unrealistic, and quite fortuitously aggravated a number of faithful and worthy supporters. In 1956 this source of irritation was removed, with the inclusion of the results of the Eliminating Races in the programme, under the heading of Results of the Previous Day's Racing.

Before leaving the subject of Eliminating Races there are, perhaps, two other points worth mentioning. The complaint has been made that it is unjust to accept a club's entrance fee, to eliminate its crew before the Regatta begins, expunge its name from the records, perhaps even request the removal of its boat, and then to retain its entrance fee. This is the sort of complaint, so plausible at first sight, which could be silenced at once by the most elementary public relations system. For every crew which enters at Henley receives Enclosure badges and car park tickets, which, at their face value, far exceed the amount of their entrance fee. No doubt if an eliminated crew chose to surrender its badges, and to request a refund, it would receive it.

It is also sometimes said that it is unfair that foreign competitors should be exempt from taking part in Eliminating Races. But, of course, foreign entries are sponsored by the governing bodies of their country of origin. Their acceptance is, in a sense, an invitation to travel to England, and they could not possibly be eliminated before the Regatta begins. It is conceivable, however, that if foreign entries were continually to rise, the day might come when Henley would find it necessary to ask the foreign Associations to limit their entries in certain events.

COXED FOURS

Until 1873 all the four-oared events at Henley were contested in coxed boats. Perhaps it was a pity that one event was not retained for this class of boat. But the first wave of enthusiasm for coxswainless rowing swept all before it. In a few years coxed-four rowing ceased to be first-class rowing.

The demand for the reintroduction of a race for coxed fours at

Henley has arisen from the growing interest in international rowing. On the Continent coxed fours are ranked at least as highly as the coxswainless variety. Experience in the Olympic Games, and the European Championships, since the war, has shown how far English crews have fallen behind in this branch of the sport. The cry, backed by an upsurge of rowing in the provinces, where coxed fours are widely popular, has therefore been for the raising of the standard of coxed-four rowing.

Provincial clubs cannot do without coxed fours, because, for the most part, they row on narrow and winding rivers. The leading Thames clubs, and the Universities, on the other hand, can, and have done so. There is, of course, no compulsion on English crews to enter for international coxed-four events. But it seems that they want to do so. And if this is the case, then everything possible must be done to ensure that they attain the requisite standard.

Thus the Stewards of Henley Regatta find themselves in a difficult situation, which is not of their own making, unless they are to be held responsible for acceding to popular demand, eighty years ago. For it is not they, but the Amateur Rowing Association, who decide that English crews shall enter for coxed-four events abroad; but it is they, and not the Amateur Rowing Association, who hold the remedy for the present sorry state of coxed-four rowing.

This statement may be disputed as an over-simplification of the facts. Yet fundamentally it is true. The A.R.A. can arrange Coxed-Four Trials, and even sponsor a Coxed-Four Championship. But coxed-four rowing will never be espoused wholeheartedly by the leading clubs until there is an event for them to enter at Henley—a fact which is, of course, a compliment to Henley.

Why, then, do the Stewards not add a Coxed-Four Race to the Henley programme, or convert the Wyfold Cup to this purpose?

The answer seems to be that they are inhibited by their own quite laudable desire to maintain the standard of the Regatta. They might welcome a coxed-four event of a standard comparable to that of the Stewards' Cup; but they see a very real danger, amounting to something like a certainty, that they would get, instead, an event of a standard comparable to, or even lower than, that of the Wyfold Cup, since that is approximately the standard of the best of the British coxed fours.

The word 'British' is here relevant, for, as things now stand, such an event, if 'open to the world', would be a virtual gift to the Continental crews. That may seem a faint-hearted objection, but it is a very proper one to the organizers of Britain's leading Regatta. And if the event were not open to the world, it might not achieve the prestige necessary to attract entries from the leading British clubs.

For all its complications, the coxed-four problem is one which must be solved. And since it is unlikely that English crews will now drop out of international coxed-four competition, there must, in the long run, be a race for coxed fours at Henley Regatta. There are precedents for the introduction of special races; it was done, for instance, when coxswainless fours were tried out in 1869 and 1872. So it might be appropriate to follow a similar course now that the process needs to be reversed. Whilst it is evident that a closed event could not normally rank as first class, yet such a 'special event', introduced for a year or two, on the understanding that its continuation, and opening to foreign crews, shall be dependent on the support received and the standard achieved, might be a practical proposition.

THE DATE OF HENLEY

Henley Regatta takes place in the first week in July—that is, just after the end of the university terms at Oxford and Cambridge, and some three weeks before the end of the school term-time. There is a case, which is sometimes put forward, for postponing this date.

It has been argued that the Oxford colleges, in particular, would benefit from such a postponement, chiefly because their examinations at present extend right up to, and even into, Regatta week. We have considered elsewhere the sorry state of Oxford rowing, and there is no doubt that a postponement of a fortnight, or even of a week, would help. A stronger Oxford challenge would add interest to the Regatta, and on that score alone a postponement deserves consideration.

But there is a stronger, because more general, case for review. At present the Thames regatta season begins in June, and finishes with the first week-end in August. August and September, offering the best rowing weather, are virtually unused. But the position is even worse than these dates suggest, because Henley Royal Regatta, which is the peak of the season, and after which nearly all the best crews disband, or are reconstituted, falls comparatively early in the season. Instead of working up to a fitting climax, the English rowing season relapses into anticlimax when it is but half-matured.

At one end of the scale, this arrangement upsets the rank-and-file crews, because many men drop out after Henley, and club crews are largely reshuffled. At the other, our potential international crews have to produce their top form far too early in the summer, and are then faced with a gap of nearly two months before the European Championships. Undoubtedly this is a major factor in the failure of English crews in these Championships. It may be that the new A.R.A. Championships, instituted in 1956, will help to bridge this gap. But at best that is problematical.

This argument would seem to point to a Henley at the end of July, or even in early August. But, whilst that might be ideal in theory, it could not work in practice. Because of their term-time, neither university, college, nor school crews would be able to take part, in any numbers, at a date much later than at present. And a glance at the Henley entries would show that the Stewards could not contemplate an arrangement which would deprive them of this support. But this does not mean that a postponement of a week or two would not be worth while, and practicable. No doubt there would be opposition to such a scheme. But the case is a strong one.

THE QUALIFICATIONS

A glance at the Table of Winners reveals that, in fifteen Regattas between 1936 and 1956, the Thames Cup was won no less than thirteen times by crews from the United States. Once there was no foreign entry at all, and on three occasions the Americans provided the runners-up as well as the winners. It is evident, therefore, that the qualification for this event needs careful review, and perhaps amendment. This implies no prejudice against the Americans, but merely that the existing qualification rules seem to have forced them into an event for which their standard is too high.

The popular solution to this problem has been to admit the American crews, which are either school crews, or lightweight university crews, to the Ladies' Plate, which traditionally, and generally in practice, too, has a slightly higher standard than the Thames Cup.

In 1951 and 1952 there was a widespread belief that the Stewards might actually carry out this reform. But then, in 1952, Christ's College Cambridge produced the fastest crew in the Thames Cup, and lost only because they caught a crab in the final; and in 1953 the Royal Air Force won the event outright. These, admittedly welcome, English successes, apparently put the Thames Cup problem back on the shelf.

But there are those who consider that the Ladies' Plate itself is even more in need of reform than the Thames Cup, if it is to retain its position as the second senior eight-oared event at Henley. Traditionally the Ladies' Plate is the event in which the Oxford and Cambridge college crews, except for the very few which aspire to the Grand, clash with each other, and with the best of the school crews. But the poor state of Oxford rowing, which has persisted for thirty years, has largely removed the interest of inter-University rivalry, whilst the introduction of the Princess Elizabeth Cup has encouraged schools to hunt smaller game.

Since the war the Ladies' Plate entry has fallen considerably, partly because of the disaffection of the schools, and partly because, with a limit of sixteen starters, against thirty-two in the Thames Cup, many of the colleges feel that they have a better chance of avoiding, and certainly a better chance of surviving, the Eliminating Races in the latter event. Some, too, feel that, except for the one or two colleges which are hoping to win the Ladies' Plate, there is not much interest in racing against crews with which they have already been racing, on their home waters, for the past two months, whereas, in the Thames Cup, there is a wide range of new and challenging adversaries. There are even indications that the standard of the Thames Cup crews, which has often trodden closely on the heels of that of the winning Ladies' Plate crews, may now be in the process of overhauling it.

To admit American crews to the Ladies' Plate, whilst it might shock some traditionalists, would undoubtedly bring new life and prestige to the event. It would also solve the Thames Cup problem, leaving it to the crews for whom it was originally intended. But it must be remembered that the Ladies' Plate entry already tends to exceed its quota of sixteen. Any substantial increase in the entry would, therefore, lead to other complications and, perhaps, discourage any school crews at all from entering. Since these schools, though few in number, include past winners and finalists, amongst them Eton, who have won the Ladies' more often than any other club, there is a strong case against freezing them out of the event.

To this problem there is another possible solution, which has many advantages. But it involves changes so sweeping that it must be viewed with extreme caution. It is no less than the removal of all the existing restrictive qualifications from both the Ladies' Plate and the Thames Cup. In effect there would then be three eight-oared events—the Grand, Ladies', and Thames Cup—in that order of seniority, open to clubs, schools, and colleges, foreign and domestic alike. The Princess Elizabeth Cup would remain as a closed event for English schools.

There seems to be no reason why these crews should not soon find their proper level. But it might be necessary to have some sort of qualifying rule, if public opinion proved to be an insufficient deterrent to what is generally described as 'pot hunting'.

The implications of such a change would, of course, be far-reaching, and the best interests of all, and particularly, perhaps, of the schools, would need careful consideration. But, on the whole, it is a reform which seems practicable, and more in keeping with modern requirements than the mere transferring of the American crews from the Thames Cup to the Ladies' Plate. It also seems capable of solving more of the outstanding problems.

DUAL ENTRIES

Quite apart from, but in a sense parallel to, this problem of which crew should be admitted to which event, there is the problem of crews, or rather men, who wish to enter for more than one event.

From time to time there is a cry from the Enclosures, and even more often from the Press, that English oarsmen are handicapping themselves by entering for too many races. Criticism is by no means unanimous on this point. Dual entries are an old Henley tradition, and so long as Henley remained primarily a domestic Regatta, it added to the general interest if the star performers chose to handicap themselves in this way. And from the club point of view, entering for two events provides a second string to their bows, and creates at least an illusion of getting better value for their money. From the Regatta point of view, the four-oar and small-boat entries depend to a considerable extent on men who are also rowing in eights.

The criticism begins when Henley is regarded as an international regatta. And with the foreign challenge as it is today, and in the fierce glare of publicity, it is difficult not so to regard it. It then ceases to be a simple question of which club can do best, and becomes a question of which club 'can meet the foreign challenge'. This attitude may be deplored, but it can hardly be ignored. And if it is once accepted that there is a duty towards British rowing, it becomes obvious that this may conflict with the immediate interests of the clubs, and perhaps with the individual's enjoyment of the Regatta.

This conflict is seen every year at Henley, and most often, perhaps, between entries for the Grand Challenge Cup, and the Stewards' and Goblets. There are seldom more than one, or at the most two, English crews which have any real chance of winning the Grand. But the glamour of the 'Grand crew' is such that some clubs feel they cannot afford to forgo it. Yet it may often be that they have men who, if they were permitted to concentrate on a four, or a pair, might well win the Stewards' or Goblets. There is much force in the argument that they ought to try to do so.

In 1932 the Stewards altered the qualification rules, to prevent oarsmen from competing for the Grand and the Wyfold Challenge Cups, or for the Thames and Stewards' Challenge Cups, at the same Regatta. In 1954 this ruling was reversed, partly, no doubt, with the object of improving the standard in the Thames and Wyfold Cups. It must be questionable whether this was a wise decision, for, of course, it was an added invitation to clubs to dissipate their strength.

There is, in fact, only one method which the Stewards could adopt, which would put an end to this waste of effort, and that is to forbid dual entries in the open events. That would be an unpopular move, and contrary to the traditions of the Henley Management, which has always been to allow crews the greatest possible freedom of choice. It is also worth reflecting that, whilst the Stewards of Henley Regatta naturally have the interests of English rowing at heart, and may regret that English crews spoil their chances by injudicious entries, it is in no sense their business to direct what they shall or shall not do in this particular respect. Rather it is to be hoped that the clubs themselves will come to see that, in the long run, they best serve their own interests, as well as those of English rowing, by entering crews which can win. If there really is a pair which can win the Goblets, their club gains no credit by making them row in an indifferent Grand eight.

SUBSTITUTIONS

It was well over a hundred years ago that another controversial problem first arose at Henley, which, whilst it comes to the fore only occasionally, and is seldom of more than temporary general interest, is nevertheless long overdue for review. This is the problem of substitutes.

The original substitution rule was made in 1843, as a result of a dispute about the drafting of men who had already been beaten in a heat of the Grand Challenge Cup into another crew, which was rowing in the final. The rule debarred any substitution in a crew after it had rowed, and prevented any man rowing in two different crews for the same event.

The question of physical disability did not enter into the original rule, though those who framed it must have realized that this problem would arise. And, indeed, in the very first year of the rule's operation, it was invoked in a case of disability.

It is well to make this differentiation at the outset. Clearly there are two possible reasons for making a substitution in any sort of team. One is to strengthen it by bringing in a better man, and the other is to replace an unfit man. In the early days of the Regatta, when crews, even in the Grand Challenge Cup, were sometimes almost scratch affairs, the first of these motives was a reality. Today it is still a reality in many sports, for a fresh man may turn the scales in the later stages of a game, even though he is less skilled than the player whom he replaces. But in rowing this has long ceased to be the case, partly because there can never be any question of making a replacement in the middle of a race, but chiefly because rowing is the complete 'team sport'. Nobody to-day seriously considers the possibility that a coach might seek to make a substitution, during the Regatta, of one fit man for another. Perhaps such circumstances could arise, but there would be no difficulty in providing an adequate safeguard against a practice which no one would condone.

We are, therefore, concerned only with substitutions for unfit men.

The original Henley rule, forbidding substitutions for any reason whatsoever, remained in force until 1921, when the present rule was drafted. This rule permits the Committee to authorize substitutions if they are satisfied that the original competitor has been prevented from rowing, 'by circumstances which are outside his own control, and not attributable to his having taken part in the Regatta'.

It will be seen at once that this rule is an improvement, in that it removes the extreme penalty previously paid for sheer bad luck.

If an oarsman is knocked down by a bus, or develops chicken-pox, the crew are no longer automatically prevented from rowing.

What, then, is wrong with the present rule?

It is a bad rule for two reasons. In the first place, it leaves to the Committee a differentiation which it must often be almost impossible to make fairly. And in the second, it encourages unfit men to row in the Regatta, which can be an extremely dangerous practice. Let us deal first with the first allegation.

In 1929 a member of the University College Oxford crew had a poisoned hand, and in 1935 a member of the Eton eight had a strained back. In the first instance a substitution was allowed; in the second it was not. The rights and wrongs of these particular cases are no longer relevant. On the evidence, both decisions may have been justified. But in principle, how can one be sure whether a poisoned hand, which might be caused by using a dirty oar handle, or a strained back, which might be caused by lifting a bucket of coal, is directly due to, merely aggravated by, or coincidental to 'taking part in the Regatta'? Sometimes, of course, there will be a clear-cut case, as of an accident or an infectious disease, but in nearly every case in which a man has been able to go on rowing after his initial misfortune, it is a certainty that doing so will have aggravated his condition.

In favour of the rule it is argued that this is perfectly right, that fitness to stand up to four days' racing is one of the require-ments of a winning crew, and that if a man falls by the wayside, then the crew, of which he was an integral part, has failed to be fit to win.

With the proviso—which is a big one, as we have seen—that one must be able to differentiate between falling by the wayside through unfitness, and falling through sheer bad luck, that con-tention is reasonable. But not only the working of a rule, but also its cost, must be considered. And this brings us to the second and infinitely more serious count against the present substitution rule.

It is evident that, in most cases, if a man has actually started rowing in the Regatta, the odds are heavily against a substitute being allowed. To produce a potential winning Henley crew involves great effort, enthusiasm, and expense. If a man becomes unfit during the Regatta, the temptation to hope for the best is far too strong. In defence of the present rule the Stewards would doubtless point out that they never make an unfit man race, and that they do not approve of his doing so. It is the responsibility of the coach and captain of the crew. But that contention is not an adequate defence. Certainly, coaches ought not to row an unfit man. But the fact is that unfit men do row, and will continue to row, because the inflexibility of the rule makes it a virtual certainty that if they drop out their crew will be forced to scratch.

The Committee of Management, as organizers of the Regatta, and, incidentally, as a body of the leading oarsmen in the country, cannot divest themselves of their responsibility for injuries resulting from the enforcement of the rules they make.

Perhaps, at this stage, I should make an admission of personal prejudice; for it was I who rowed with a strained back in the Eton crew in 1935. And for doing so I have suffered ever since. It seems to me that this lays upon me a duty to fight for the revision of the rule.

One must not criticize a weakness in the Rules without suggesting the proper remedy. But in this case the remedy offers itself. A translation of Article 35 of the International Rules for Regattas states that:

No substitutes may be made after a crew has rowed in a heat, except in the event of serious illness, and with the approval of the Race Committee.

The Race Committee, of course, may call for a medical report. It is difficult to see any valid objection to the introduction of this rule at Henley. Indeed, it is the sort of rule which ought to commend itself to any 'Race Committee', because it leaves them every latitude in deciding whether or not a substitution is justified, and places the ultimate decision as to whether or not a man is fit to row, where it should rest, on the shoulders of a qualified medical officer.

CHAPTER NINE

Ambition and Success

THERE is a fascination in the limitless ambition of an oarsman to win races. Often it will result in his losing when he might well have won. Often it is a nuisance to the organizers of the Regatta, because it complicates the drawing up of the programme. Nevertheless, one cannot but admire the man who has confidence in his own strength.

The last man to win three events at Henley was H. R. A. Edwards, who, in 1931, won the Grand, Stewards', and Silver Goblets. That, of course, is not a record; but it is unlikely to be repeated, because of the ever-increasing strength of the competition. Since 1920, three events have been attempted about thirty-five times, including five times by Edwards himself. And only two other men have succeeded in bringing off the triple. They were E. C. Hamilton-Russell and R. E. Morrison, who won the Stewards', Visitors', and Goblets in 1925. Since the war no one has attempted three events in the same year.

Before the First War, multiple entries of this sort were quite common. And when three crews rowed abreast, and the holders were not required to row in the challenge rounds, they were also much easier. Indeed, there have been some eighty occasions on which a man has attempted four, and even five, events at the same Regatta.

For sheer ambition in this respect the palm must surely go to W. B. Woodgate. In 1863 he entered for the Grand, Ladies', Stewards', Visitors', Goblets, and Diamonds. But he won only two events, and both were uncontested. As a matter of fact, Woodgate's performance in the previous year, when he limited himself to four events, was the more remarkable. Then, on the first day, he won heats of the Stewards', Goblets, and Diamonds, the last of which, at least, was a hard race. Next day he won hard races in the Stewards' and Visitors', and then sculled a dead heat in the final of the Diamond Sculls against E. D. Brickwood. He got cramp in his arm, and lost the re-row. But his busy day was still not complete, for, in partnership with W. Champneys, he still had to win the Goblets final against the Cambridge Blues, J. C. Hawkshaw and J. G. Chambers. Thus in two days Woodgate had rowed eight times over the course, and lost only the re-row of the dead heat. That, I believe, is an achievement which has never been equalled.

There are something like 12,000 names in the published Henley records, up to 1938, so that my research in this direction cannot claim to be exhaustive. But I believe Woodgate to be the only man who ever attempted six events. Some nine men have attempted five events; but only two have won five finals.

Four or more events have been attempted at least eighty times, and fifteen men have actually won four finals in the same year. The last men to attempt four events were B. C. Johnstone and R. V. Powell, who, in 1906, entered for the Grand, Stewards', Visitors', and Goblets. They won the Visitors' and Goblets, racing eight times in three days. In the following year Powell tried again, substituting the Diamonds for the Visitors'. But his only success was in the Goblets, in which he was again partnered by B. C. Johnstone.

Table I shows how the most ambitious Henley oarsmen and scullers have fared.

Although no one has won three events at the same Regatta since 1931, it used to be quite common to do so. But although it was always a great achievement, it is only fair to point out that circumstances have changed in the past fifty years, and out of all recognition in the past seventy-five years. The size and quality of the Henley entry has progressively squeezed the multiple-entry man out of business.

Today this process has reached the stage where many people even consider it wrong to attempt more than one event.

TABLE I

INDIVIDUAL ENTRIES AND WINS

G—Grand; L—Ladies' Plate; T—Thames Cup; S—Stewards'; V—Visitors'; W—Wyfold Cup; X—presentation Coxswainless Fours of 1869 and 1872; P—Goblets; D—Diamond Sculls.

Heavy Type denotes a win.

6 events, 2 wins. 1863 W. B. Woodgate	G,L,S,V,**P**,**D**.	Two-day Regatta. 8 races, of which 2 were not contested.
5 events, 5 wins. 1848 W. H. Milman M. Haggard	**G,L,S,V,P.**	Two-day Regatta. 5 races, of which 2 were not contested, and 1 was won on a foul.
5 events, 4 wins. 1860 D. Inglis N. Royds	**G,L,S,V**,P.	Two-day Regatta. 5 races, of which 2 were not contested.

5 events, 3 wins.
1865 F. R. B. Walton
         (Coxswain)
         J. R. Selwyn
	G,**L**,**S**,V,W.
	
	G,**L**,**S**,V,P.
		Two-day Regatta. 7 races, of which 1 was not contested.

4 events, 4 wins. 1848 E. C. Buxton	**G,L,S,V.**	Same crew as Milman and Haggard.

1860 S. Heathcote
         J. T. Morland
         G. Cox
	G,L,S,V.	Same crew as Inglis and Royds.

1861 B. P. Gregson
         H. S. Wright
         G. H. Richards
         W. C. Smyly
         J. C. Carter
	G,L,S,V.	Two-day Regatta. 4 races.

1872 A. de L. Long F. S. Gulston	**G,S,X,P.**	Two-day Regatta. 4 races, of which 1 was not contested.

There is a great temptation for the individual oarsman, or sculler, and for clubs, to enter for two events. Every club wants to put on an eight if it can possibly do so. Yet only a few can produce eights with any real chance of carrying off a Henley trophy. By comparison, they are more likely to muster four good men, and there is a traditional belief that the four-oared events are easier to win. In the past that has probably been true, largely because of this duplication of entries, of which we are talking. And the same applies, or has applied, to the individual events. The sculler, or two men in pair-oar or double, may practise for months for one of these events. But they are needed for a club eight, and they answer the call.

We may ask, 'Why not?' Certainly it adds to the fun and enjoyment of the Regatta to see what 'So-and-so' can manage. The answer comes from those who are concerned at the international aspect of Henley racing. The foreign challenge is strong, and specialized. A Pomeranian four comes to Henley and wins the Stewards', perhaps by a narrow margin. And its English opponents are also rowing in the Grand, or perhaps the Visitors'. The point needs no elaboration.

The question of ambition at Henley leads naturally to that of success. Probably there is no certain answer to the question, 'Who has been the most successful Henley oarsman?' For one thing, the qualification for this distinction is not so straightforward as it might at first appear. Is the most successful man he who has won the most Henley medals, or the man who has won the Grand Challenge Cup most often? Or should it be the man who has won the most races, which is not the same as winning the highest number of medals? It might even be the man who has the highest percentage of wins.

Furthermore, we must still take into account the changed conditions, as we did in considering ambition. The modern oarsman has no prospect of winning as many Henley events as his grandfather. But he need not, on that account alone, be considered a less skilled, or even a less successful, performer.

Personal statistics have a certain fascination, and since no two rowing men will ever entirely agree on a list of the most successful oarsmen, perhaps the best thing to do is to provide the information on which young and old can argue the merits of their respective generations to their hearts' content.

Table II shows the most regular Henley winners. There are, of course, many more, of the older generations, who have exceeded the scores of what we may call the post-war generation. But in view of the information shown later, in Table III, I think it fair to say that the list is reasonable in its relative requirements for the two eras.

The total number of Henley competitors is now in the region of 20,000, so that it is prudent to say that Table II, like Table I, cannot claim infallibility. However, the list is thought to be complete down to V. Weston—that is to say, complete so far as those who have won eight or more races are concerned. There are then a number of other oarsmen, chiefly of the older vintages, who are not shown on Table II, but who did win six or seven Henley medals. Notable amongst them are J. A. Ford (1890–7) and R. S. C. Lucas (1920–5), each with 7 wins, including 5 Grands; G. S. MacLagan (coxswain, 1899–1907) with 6 wins, all in the Grand; E. D. Horsfall (1911–22) and C. W. Kent (1888–95) with 7 wins, including 4 Grands; F. Willan (1863–9), with 6 wins, including 4 Grands; and E. A. Safford, who coxed for no less than twenty-eight years (1874–1902) to win 5 Henley medals, 4 of them for the Grand.

Of the post-war oarsmen, in addition to the nine shown in Table II, seven others have won 3 Henley medals. They are H. H. Almond, A. S. F. Butcher, P. M. O. Massey, C. F. Porter, R. D. Burnell, P. A. de Giles, and J. F. K. Hinde (coxswain); the last three have each won the Grand twice.

From the point of view of family successes, the Nickalls are quite unchallenged, with 43 wins to their credit. Of those rowing since the war, N. J. Bradley, adding the Grand and the Stewards to 2 previous Stewards' wins (1933 and 1934), and P. Bradley, with 2 Grands, 1 Stewards', and 1 Double Sculls win, have been the most successful.

Quite clearly the statistics in Table II bear out the conclusion already drawn from Table I, that it has become increasingly difficult to win Henley trophies. The question which springs to mind is: 'How much more difficult?'

TABLE II

THE MOST FREQUENT HENLEY WINNERS

Name	Henley Seasons	Grand	Ladies'	Thames	Stewards'	Visitors'	Wysfold	Fours 1869 & 1872	Goblets	Diamonds	Double Sculls	Total
Guy Nickalls	1885–1907	4	1		7				6	5		23
F. S. Gulston	1868–80	5			10			1	5			21
A. de L. Long	1867–77	5			8			1	4			18
A. A. Casamajor	1855–61	3			3		1		4	5		16
S. Le B. Smith	1865–78	4			7				1			12
H. H. Playford	1852–61	2			3	2	1		1	2		11
W. B. Woodgate	1861–8	1			1	2	1		5	1		
W. F. Sheard (cox)	1877–97	5		6								
C. W. H. Taylor	1898–1904	2	2	1	3	1			2			
J. Hastie	1872–85	2		2	2		1		3			10
V. Nickalls	1888–96	1			3				5	1		
G. O. Nickalls	1920–8	7			1				2			
J. Beresford, jun.	1920–39	2			1				2	4	1	
W. H. Eyre	1870–82	2		1	1		2		3			9
F. L. Playford	1873–88	3			5					1		
C. D. Burnell	1894–1902	4	1		3							8
F. J. Escombe	1898–1907	3		2	1		2					
H. G. Gold	1893–9	3	3		2							
F. S. Kelly	1899–1906	3	1		1					3		
J. Lowndes	1878–84				2				2	4		
R. E. Morrison	1921–5		1		4	2			1			
J. Paine	1852–9	2			3	2	1					
J. C. Tinne	1865–70	2	1		2	3						
F. W. Warre	1896–1903	2	2		1	2			1			
V. Weston (cox)	1868–75	5		1	2							
J. H. T. Wilson	1932–48	1	1		3				2			7
D. D. Macklin	1949–	3	1		1	1						6
T. H. Christie	1946–52	1			1		1		2			5
H. W. Rushmere	1935–51	1			3		1					
P. Bradley	1946–51	2			1						1	4
C. G. V. Davidge	1948–	1	1		2							
P. C. Kirkpatrick	1934–52	1			3							
C. B. M. Lloyd	1949–52	2	1						1			
W. A. D. Windham	1949–53	3			1							

Table III attempts to answer this question. In it are shown the performances of seven outstanding Henley oarsmen and scullers whose careers, roughly speaking, cover the past hundred years. Column iv, which shows the percentage of wins to races contested, indicates that all these men were performers of a comparably high standard. The significant figures are then in Column vii, and are calculated by dividing Column iii by Column vi. The result shows how many races each man had to win in order to carry home a Henley medal. It will be seen that in the days of Casamajor and Gulston, a man was distinctly unlucky if one win did not earn him a prize. Today a man is lucky to get a medal after winning three races.

TABLE III

THE INCREASING DIFFICULTY OF WINNING HENLEY MEDALS

	i	ii	iii	iv	v	vi	vii
Name	Racing years	Total No. of races rowed	Races won	% of races won	Events con- tested	Events won	No. of races for each event won
A. A. Casamajor 1855–61	7	24	19	79·17	21	16	1·19
F. S. Gulston 1868–80	13	51	39	76·47	33	21	1·67
Guy Nickalls 1885–1907	16	75	64	85·33	34	23	2·26
D. Mackinnon 1907–11	5	21	18	85·71	9	6	2·67
G. O. Nickalls 1920–8	9	47	35	74·47	21	10	2·8
J. H. T. Wilson 1932–48	7	33	26	78·79	14	7	3·14
D. D. Macklin 1949–55	6	25	21	84·0	10	6	3·0

In considering these figures it should be remarked that the seven men concerned were all stars, and that almost without exception they were contesting the senior open events. And it is, of course, in the other events, and particularly in the Thames and Wyfold Cups, that the standard, and certainly the entries, have risen most markedly. Almost certainly, therefore, Table III tends to minimize rather than to exaggerate the increasing difficulty of winning at Henley.

Turning from individual to club successes at Henley, it is more than ever impossible to determine an order of merit. Table IV, shows, in alphabetical order, those clubs which have won most consistently in the main events. But a study of the figures will reveal how different have been the circumstances for the different clubs. Eton, for instance, have been outstandingly successful in the Ladies' Plate, and qualify for the list with 23 victories, all gained in that one event. Similarly, Leander have won the Grand more often than their two closest rivals put together, yet fall short of the totals of both these clubs, chiefly because they have never entered for the Thames and Wyfold Challenge Cups.

It may be thought that the colleges of the Universities of Oxford and Cambridge have an advantage over the clubs, in that they are eligible for the Ladies' Plate and Visitors' Challenge Cup, which are both restricted events (though considered to be senior in status to the Thames and Wyfold Cups). And this seems to be confirmed by the statistics. Yet it must be remembered that, as a rule, the college oarsman is available only for three or four years, whilst a club may sometimes have the nucleus of the same crew for a number of years, which encourages runs of success in particular events. An example of this was the success of the London fours during the 'seventies.

One fact which does emerge from Table IV is the importance of the part played by the two Universities. Ten wins, in any of nine events, and spread over a period of some hundred years, might not be thought very difficult to achieve. Yet only four clubs have managed it, against ten colleges—reckoning the Trinity Cambridge clubs as a single unit—one University Boat Club, and one school.

TABLE IV
THE CHIEF WINNERS

Showing those Clubs which have achieved ten or more wins in the main events at Henley Regatta

	Grand Challenge Cup	Ladies' Challenge Plate	Thames Challenge Cup	Stewards' Challenge Cup	Visitors' Challenge Cup	Wyfold Challenge Cup	Silver Goblets	Diamond Challenge Sculls	Double Sculls	Total
Balliol College Oxford		4			2	1	4**	1		12
Brasenose College Oxford		3		2	6	1	4	5		21
Christ Church Oxford	1	4	1	2	8		7			23
Eton College (i)		23								23
Jesus College Cambridge	3	12	1	1	5	2	2			26
Kingston R.C.	2		1	2		15	5	1		26
Lady Margaret B.C. Cambridge	1	7	1		5	1	1*	3 (ii)		19
Leander Club	27			10			9	7	1	54
London R.C.	16		10	17		16	13	9		81
Magdalen College Oxford	4	1		6	5	1	2	11		30
Oxford University B.C.	7			6			5*			18
Pembroke College Cambridge	1	3		2	3	2	2*	1		14
Thames R.C.	8		10	17		16	10	5	(iii)	66
First Trinity B.C. Cambridge (iv)	4	14	5	3	11	2	1	3		43
Second Trinity B.C.					1					1
Third Trinity B.C.	1	1		9	14			10	3	38
First and Third Trin. B.C.		2			2					4
Trinity Hall Cambridge	3	4	3	3	10	5	3	1		32
University College Oxford	1 (v)	4		3	8			1		17 (vi)

* Denotes that one of these wins was in partnership with an oarsman representing another club.

(i) Eton have also once won the Princess Elizabeth Cup, which is not included in this Table.

(ii) Three Diamond wins by A. C. Dicker, entered by 'St. John's College Cambridge'.

(iii) Thames R.C. also won the Centenary Double Sculls in 1939.

(iv) Various entries from 'Trinity College Cambridge' are included in the figures for First Trinity B.C.

(v) The Oxford Etonian Club won the Grand six times, but does not qualify for this list, having a total of less than ten wins in all.

(vi) Clubs just failing to qualify for this list are: The Oxford Etonian Club (9 wins), and Royal Chester R.C., Pembroke College Oxford, and Trinity College Oxford (8 wins each).

CHAPTER TEN

Foreign Entries

TODAY, Henley is generally regarded as being an international regatta. Theoretically this view is not strictly accurate, for Henley neither enforces, nor even adheres to, the International Rules, drawn up by the Fédération Internationale des Sociétés d'Aviron. It is certainly not regarded by its organizers as primarily an international regatta, and several of its events are not open to foreign crews. Yet it would be quite unrealistic to pretend that it is not international. Almost every page of this history, at least from the mid-seventies, proclaims that it is so.

But fifty years ago this issue hung precariously in the balance. In 1901, Dr. Warre submitted to the Stewards a motion 'that the good nature of the Stewards of Henley Regatta, in permitting the rowing trophies intrusted to them to be contended for by all the world, will endanger the best interests of amateur rowing, for the encouragement of which they were originally presented'. Warre's hypothesis was, of course, quite untrue, for the original Henley trophies were presented with the object of attracting crews, and therefore the general public, to come to Henley town, in the interests of the townspeople. But it was probably fair enough to say that, from the time when rowing men had secured control of the Regatta, the loftier motive (from their point of view) had been paramount. And, amongst others, Warre was supported by W. H. Grenfell (later Lord Desborough), Sir John Edwards-Moss, and R. C. Lehmann, 'a more powerful "four" than whom', as Theodore Cook pointed out, 'it would be difficult to find'.

The immediate object of Warre's motion was the holding of a referendum, for the purpose of ascertaining the wishes of the Universities and larger clubs. The referendum showed that opinion was strongly against the motion, though a number of clubs asked for additional safeguards against professional entries. Nevertheless, Dr. Warre pressed his motion, which was later defeated at a full Stewards' Meeting by a majority of four to one. But there is no doubt that there was, at that time, strong feeling against foreign competitors.

It is not necessary to enquire in any great detail, here, into the causes of this prejudice. To some extent they will have become apparent from the historical chapters. It might, perhaps, be summed up thus; English amateur rowing, at the turn of the century, was fiercely amateur, in a typically illogical English way. The definition was still based on the notion of the 'gentleman amateur'. The amateur could spend any amount of his own time and money on the sport. But the letter of the amateur definition was inviolable.

Probably the majority of the foreign competitors at Henley, in those days, honestly considered themselves to be amateurs. And most of them, in their own countries, were regarded as amateurs. But the proper interpretation of the Henley definition was not universally understood. And at the same time, there were undoubtedly a minority of competitors who had no claim to be considered amateurs in any country.

Thus there was an ever-present source of friction; and it was a two-way friction. Allegations were made that a particular sculler, or crew, were not amateurs. To the Englishman it seemed outrageous that a 'professional' should pass himself off as an 'amateur'. To the foreigner, and particularly to the Americans, who were most often involved, it seemed, on the contrary, that the English were simply bad sportsmen, and averse to being beaten. Such an accusation—and it was an age in which squabbles of this kind were invariably aired in the Press—was, of course, far worse than the original offence. Thus serious discord soon grew from small beginnings.

The referendum, and the Stewards' decision, in 1901, appeared, at least, to have reprieved foreign crews at Henley. A new ruling, in 1902, against the use of professional coaches, except for scullers, removed one serious source of objection. Yet it was little more than an uneasy truce. In 1903 the Stewards refused the entries of two American scullers. And in 1904 there was an attack in the Press, frivolous perhaps, yet indicative of the climate, on the Canadian sculler, L. F. Scholes.[1]

In 1905 matters finally came to a head, with the famous Vesper B.C. episode, which is described elsewhere.[2] Although the feelings then aroused were, if possible, stronger than ever before, putting the whole question of foreign entries back into the melting-pot, the Philadelphians may, in the long run, have rendered a service to Henley. For they caused the Stewards to alter their rule governing foreign entries.

As far back as 1893 the Stewards had signed their first foreign 'Agreement', with the French Union. Other similar Agreements had followed, including one with the National Association of American Oarsmen, sponsors of the Vesper entry. But these early Agreements, in effect, only required the governing bodies concerned to certify that entries from their countries were amateurs under their own rules. Nor were entries barred from countries which had signed no Agreement at all; in such cases entries had merely to be in by 31 March, instead of 1 June, thus, in theory, giving the Stewards time to make their own inquiries.

What was new, in 1906, was the decision to accept entries only from those countries which had signed an Agreement, and the inclusion in the Agreement of the Henley amateur definition.[3]

The immediate effect of this rule was that the only foreign entries still eligible were those from Belgium, Germany, Holland, and Canada. The N.A.A.O. were among the first to request an Agreement, but at that time they had only a few affiliated clubs, and no effective control of American rowing. Not until 1914 were the Americans able to sign an Agreement with Henley, just in time for Harvard University to enter for, and win, the Grand Challenge Cup. Similarly, the original French Agreement was cancelled, because the clubs affiliated to the Union were in revolt, and the proposed new governing body would not accept the

---

[1] See pp. 125–6.   [2] See pp. 127–8.   [3] See Appendix A, pp. 276–7.

Henley definition of an amateur. In the next few years many foreign entries were turned down. But gradually more and more foreign Associations signed the necessary Agreements. That the new system was successful is proved by the fact that it is still in force, unchanged, to this day.

Looking back over fifty years, it may be difficult to believe that there was ever a serious danger that foreign crews would be banned from Henley. Yet it was certainly a possibility to contemporary minds. Whether, if it had become an accomplished fact, such a state of affairs could have remained long in force, is another question altogether. The evidence is that the clock can sometimes be stopped, but very rarely put back. In all probability it became inevitable, from the acceptance of the first foreign competitor in 1872,[1] that sooner or later Henley would become an international regatta. If so, then probability became certainty in 1878, when Columbia College won the Visitors' Cup.

Among all those who have come, from all parts of the world, to teach British oarsmen a more or less salutary lesson, pride of place must go to the Belgians. Not only did they achieve the honour of being the first to wrest the coveted Grand Challenge Cup from these shores, but they did it no fewer than three times in a space of four years, at a time when English rowing was regarded as supreme. In the intervening year they held all England breathless, whilst they challenged us, unsuccessfully as it turned out, at the 1908 Olympic Games.

The shock administered by the Belgians was incalculable, and has no parallel in Henley history. Consider that the Grand Challenge Cup has been taken from these shores only twelve times, though more than seventy foreign crews have made the attempt. The Belgians tried seven times in all, and won three times. Their successes are outnumbered only by those of the Americans, who have won four times in seventeen attempts. In all, fourteen countries have tried for the Grand, and not one, apart from the Belgians and the Americans, has succeeded more than once.

[1] E. Smith, of New York, beaten in the second round of the Diamond Sculls by W. Chillingworth.

Very rightly did the Club Nautique and the Sport Nautique become respectively the Royal Club Nautique and the Royal Sport Nautique de Gand, after the two Belgian victories in 1906 and 1907. The names are written indelibly in the Henley annals, together with those of M. M. R. Poma and Oscar de Somville, who rowed stroke and seven in all these Belgian crews, and of Victor de Bisschop and M. E. Wauters, their coaches.[1]

The Americans stand in a somewhat different category, for they are a great rowing country, and unbeaten in the Olympic Eights since 1920. But though they have sent many crews to Henley, it is one club, the Harvard University B.C., which claims a place in the halls of Henley fame. They, like Ghent, have won the Grand Challenge Cup three times. Only half a dozen English clubs have done more.

Apart from this, the Americans have made their mark at Henley in a less exalted sphere. For they have sent more than forty crews, the majority from schools, but some the lightweight crews from their universities, to contend for the Thames Cup. And it is no exaggeration to say that they have dominated this event for the past twenty years, winning it fifteen times.

It is quite true, of course, that this has been due in a large measure to the framing of the Henley qualification rules, which prevent these crews, which otherwise might well have found themselves a place in the Ladies' Plate, from competing for that event. But this in no way detracts from the force of the American impact at Henley. Indeed, they have set the Committee of Management a thorny problem, and one which is still unsolved.

· If the name of any other foreign club rivals that of the Ghent clubs, and of Harvard, it is the Ruder Club Zurich, of Switzerland.[2] Zurich won the Stewards' Cup and the Diamond Sculls in 1935, achieved the 'treble', with the Grand, Stewards', and

[1] The three winning Belgian crews were all manned jointly by the two Ghent clubs.

[2] This club was originally a section of the Football Club, Zurich. In 1935 and 1936 they entered as the F. C. Zurich Ruder Club; by 1939 they had changed the name to Ruder Club Zurich.

Diamonds in 1936, and took the Stewards' again in 1939. A series of finer crews has never been seen at Henley.

So far as the events in the Henley programme are concerned, only the Diamond Sculls have known a foreign domination comparable to that in the Thames Cup. Only one Englishman, T. G. Askwith, won the Diamonds between 1928 and 1949. But this was not the domination of any one country, though the United States scored four, and Canada three victories during this period. Nor, perhaps, is it altogether fair to start such a survey in 1928, which happened to follow five consecutive English successes. Also, it must be remembered that the Diamond Sculls is the most representative of all the Henley events. For obvious reasons, many great crews have been unable to come to Henley. But it is probably true to say that there have been very few individuals who really fancied their chances of carrying off the Diamonds who have not been able to make at least one attempt.

Table V shows how the foreign countries have fared at Henley. Those which can claim a closer relationship with Great Britain will forgive the generic use of the term 'foreign', to describe all those countries whose entries are, in the phraseology of the Henley Rules, 'out of the United Kingdom'. From this list only the Irish crews are omitted, a fact which denotes no imperialistic tendencies on the part of the author, but only a lethargy which fights shy of the task of separating the Guelphs from the Ghibellines. From Ireland, only Trinity College Dublin have been successful, and they have won the Visitors' three times, and the Ladies' Plate, Thames Cup, and Wyfold Cup once each.

Table V shows that 418 foreign crews and scullers have competed at Henley, and eighty have taken home a prize of one sort or another. Even allowing for the fact that foreign crews, unlike domestic crews, come to Henley only when their chances of success seem bright, a winning ratio a little better than 1:5 is high, and indicative of the standard of the foreign challenge at Henley.

In applying this ratio to Table V, it will be seen that most of the surplus wins have gone to countries which have competed only occasionally. Austria, for instance, has sent but one contestant,

TABLE V

ENTRIES AND SUCCESSES OF FOREIGN COUNTRIES AT HENLEY

	Grand Challenge Cup	Thames Challenge Cup	Stewards' Challenge Cup	Wyfold Challenge Cup	Silver Goblets	Diamond Sculls	Double Sculls	Total Wins	Total Entries
Argentina		0/1		0/1		0/1	1/1	1	4
Australia	1/3				0/1	2/7	0/1	3	12
Austria						1/1		1	1
Belgium	3/7	0/1	0/1	0/1	3/8	0/15	1/5	7	38
Brazil						0/6		0	6
Canada	0/10	0/1	1/8	0/1		4/28	0/1	5	49
Czecho-slovakia			0/1			0/4	0/1	0	6
Denmark	0/1		1/2		0/2	0/1	2/2	3	8
Egypt						0/2		0	2
France	1/6	1/3	0/1		0/3	1/14		3	27
Germany	1/5	0/2	0/10		2/2	2/19	0/1	5	39
Holland	0/8	1/2	1/4		0/4	3/10	0/1	5	29
Hungary						0/1		0	1
Italy	0/1	0/1	0/2		0/1	1/1	1/1	2	7
Japan	0/1							0	1
New Zealand		0/1						0	1
Norway	0/3	1/2		0/1		0/4		1	10
Poland					0/1	2/5		2	6
Russia	1/2		2/3		2/2	0/4	1/2	6	13
Saar					0/2	0/2		0	4
Singapore				0/1				0	1
South Africa		0/1	0/1	1/1		0/4		1	7
Spain	0/1					0/2		0	3
Sweden	0/1				0/1			0	2
Switzerland	1/5		3/7		0/2	2/7	2/3	8	24
Tasmania						1/3		1	3
Uruguay				0/1		0/2	0/2	0	5
U.S.A.[1]	4/17	15/42	0/5	0/4		6/39		25	107
Yugoslavia			0/1			1/1		1	2
Totals	12/71	18/57	8/46	1/11	7/29	26/183	8/21	80	418

[1] U.S.A. also entered for and won the Visitors' Challenge Cup in 1878, before this event was closed to foreign entries.

and that a winning sculler for the Diamonds. Among the countries which have made a number of, but not necessarily frequent, entries at Henley, two have achieved results far above this average ratio. They are Switzerland and Russia. The Russian figures, as shown in Table V, include two unsuccessful attempts in the Diamonds, in 1912 and 1913. The U.S.S.R. have made only eleven entries, all in 1954 and 1955, and have won six trophies.

The arrival of the Soviet crews on the Henley scene naturally aroused great interest, and gave rise to many more or less ill-founded speculations. In 1954 their visit went off without any friction, save such as could be stirred up, presumably with malicious intent, by some sections of the Press. In fact, such minor misunderstandings as did arise were no more nor less than what this phrase implies—misunderstandings due to differences in language and custom. In 1955, however, a dock strike, leading to the withdrawal and subsequent readmission of the Russian entries,[1] amounted to something more, and led to a good deal of adverse comment.

To put matters in their proper perspective, it is perhaps worth quoting a remark, which was made after the 1954 Regatta, to the effect that 'the difficulties caused by the arrival of the Russians were nothing compared to the difficulties when the Americans first came to Henley'.

This remark must not be taken out of its context, though I have no doubt that, sooner or later, someone will try to do so. The point is that, as we have seen, the friction caused by the first impact of American rowing on Henley, some sixty years ago, was, at the time, so acute that it led to a serious attempt to bar foreign entries altogether. Yet today we can see that the trouble was caused, primarily, by misunderstanding, and by differences in the conditions in the two countries. There is an infinitely greater difference today between the conditions obtaining in the Soviet Union and Great Britain, and the possibilities of misunderstanding are aggravated by the fact that we do not speak the same language. Is it not reasonable to hope, therefore, that in a few

[1] See pp. 204–6.

years' time we shall look back on the 'Russian difficulties' as no more than temporary, and caused by lack of understanding?

Nevertheless, the problems are real enough today, and it may serve a useful purpose to consider what they are. This can be done under two headings.

The first, and more immediately alarming, though perhaps in the long run less important, is the heading of politics. The Russian decision, in 1955, to scratch their crews during the Regatta, must be regarded as a political decision. From the purely rowing point of view it must have been obvious to them, as it was to everyone else, that they had everything to gain, and very little to lose, by rowing, in the face of adversity, in their borrowed boats. Since this is a book about rowing, and not about politics, it is not the place to discuss this aspect in any detail; indeed, the poor rowing scribe could hardly be expected to fathom the tortuous reasoning of the politician. It must suffice, therefore, to give a rowing man's opinion that the Stewards of Henley Regatta have been very wise to refuse to make concessions to political expediency.

The other problem raised by the Russian entries is that they represented the first impact of a 'national team' on what is otherwise, essentially, a 'club regatta'. The Russian entries were, of course, from individual clubs. But grouped together they undoubtedly constituted a fully fledged 'national team', such as we might wish to send to the Olympic Games. From Henley's point of view it would be a pity if the Russians were to continue to regard the Regatta as an international meeting, comparable with the European Championships or the Olympic Games. It would be an even greater pity, because it would tend to perpetuate this approach, if other countries were to follow suit.

It was suggested, in 1956, that the Stewards themselves were encouraging just such a development, in that they relaxed the qualification rules, just as they had previously done in 1948 and 1952, to permit the entry of composite crews, drawn from more than one club. The object of this relaxation was to encourage British oarsmen, in an Olympic year, to put aside club rivalries, in order to produce potential Olympic crews, early in the season.

But the problem here is not so much one of 'national teams', as of what properly constitutes a 'club'. The Royal Air Force, for instance, drafts rowing men to a station which offers rowing facilities. In a sense they form a 'composite crew'; yet they all become members of an established club. The Swedish Roddklubben Three Towns was actually formed for the purpose of enabling men, drawn from different parts, to row, at Henley or elsewhere, as a representative Swedish crew, and yet still to qualify as a club crew. Hypothetically, the A.R.A. might found an 'All-England Rowing Club'—rather as the A.R.A.'s own ancestor, the Metropolitan Rowing Association[1] was founded— to sponsor national crews which would nevertheless satisfy the Henley qualifications. There may here be a headache for the future, but it is not as yet such an immediate problem as the national team.

So far as the Russian entries are concerned, the answer, perhaps, is that so long as nobody else attempts to meet their challenge with a rival national team, they ought, quite soon, to appreciate what Henley is, and to conclude that there is little prestige to be gained by pitting a full national team against a chance collection of individual clubs.

There is one other aspect of this problem which should be mentioned, because it is a potential source of friction. There are those who say that the Russians are not amateurs, and that they should never have been admitted to Henley at all. As to the latter contention, it is difficult to see how the Henley Stewards could have done otherwise than admit them, since they have been accepted as members of the International Federation. As to the former, there is no reason at all to doubt that the Soviet oarsmen fulfil the requirements of the Henley Agreement, which they signed in 1954. It is, of course, arguable that under a totalitarian régime, where all are directly or indirectly employed by the State, the terms amateur and professional cease to have any meaning. It would be more honest to admit that they have little meaning in

[1] See p. 44.

most countries, and that the fact that rowing has remained mainly 'amateur' is due more to the fact that it offers little financial reward, than to any intrinsic 'amateurism' amongst oarsmen. The accusation that the Russians are not amateurs is unsubstantiated, and unworthy. If they achieve more than their share of success it will be because they are numerically strong, and take their sport more seriously than other nations, not because they infringe the Rules. It would be fair enough, though perhaps a little out of keeping with the times, to say that rowing ought to be a week-end recreation, and that English regattas should be confined to those who approach it in this manner. It is quite unfair so suggest that all those foreigners who win must be infringing the Rules, and it is high time that this attitude was rooted out.

Four

RECORDS AND APPENDICES

Record Times

THE first race for the Grand Challenge Cup, in 1839, was won by Trinity College Cambridge in 8 min. 30 sec. The published histories of Henley show the times, not of all, but of most of the races from that day to this. But they are certainly not all accurate, nor comparable.

We know from the evidence of John Cooper, who was Secretary of the Regatta for thirty-seven years, that before about 1855 the timekeeping was a very chancy business. Woodgate considered it to be less than chancy, and accused Towsey, who was Cooper's predecessor, of indulging a strong prejudice in favour of the *status quo*, so far as fast times were concerned. He had a habit, it seems, of adding a whole minute if an old-established 'record' was threatened. It is worth remembering, too, that until 1906 there were no official timekeepers; the job was done by the Umpire,[1] if he was not too much engrossed in the race. Nevertheless, Cooper considered that most of the times from the 'eighties onwards were reasonably accurate.

Apart from the reliability of the timekeepers, there was no flag at Fawley until 1906, and none at the Barrier until 1929, and there are also the alterations to the course to be considered. For although the length of the course has always been nominally the same, the actual distance covered by the crews, in the days when they had a wide course, and corners to cut off, may have varied quite a lot. It is interesting to compare the old with the new records, but since no one can accurately assess the difference made by the changes in the course, it is not a very profitable pastime to look back beyond 1924, when the new Straight Course was adopted, with any hope of comparing the pace of the crews.

[1] Until 1868 the Umpire had also to steer the watermen's eight from which he officiated.

Since 1924 the times have been comparable; but even now we must face the complication of varying conditions, which means that times are not necessarily a reliable guide to merit.

At Henley there are two factors, beyond the control of the oarsmen, which have to be considered. They are the stream, and the strength and direction of the wind. No one who has seen the astonishing difference in times, between apparently equal crews, rowing within an hour or so of each other, can doubt the importance of these factors.

The Thames Conservancy maintain daily records of the water-levels, above and below every lock. But these give no indication of the speed at which the water is flowing. As a matter of fact, the Thames Conservancy do more than this. For they endeavour to control the water in the upstream reaches, so as to maintain the water-level, at Henley, at a convenient height for the boat stages, and also to close down the weirs at Marsh and Hambleden whilst racing is in progress. But in spite of all they can do, the rate of flow varies very considerably.

The wind is just as elusive, and perhaps more so. Its strength and direction are recorded by the Air Ministry, at stations all over the country. But the nearest with comprehensive records in a readily accessible form is at Kew, which is thirty-odd miles from Henley. From these records only the most general picture may be expected of what the wind is doing in the Thames Valley at Henley, and none at all of what is happening during any particular race.

And so we are forced to the conclusion that there are no statistics from which, in conjunction with the times recorded in their races, we might accurately compare the performances of different crews in different, or even in the same, years. Unless the Regatta Committee consider it worth while to install wind and water gauges, at several points on the course, this will always be so. Perhaps it is as well, for if all the answers were known it would remove an evergreen topic of conversation from rowing circles.

The following Table shows how the records have moved since the adoption of the present Straight Course, in 1924. For com-

parison, in so far as this is possible, the fastest times recorded
before 1924 are shown in italics.

TABLE OF FASTEST TIMES

Times in italics are the fastest recorded before the adoption of the
Straight Course in 1924.
Equal fastest times are not shown.

		Fawley	*Finish*
GRAND CHALLENGE CUP			
1891	*Leander Club*		*6·51*
1913	*Leander Club*	*3·19*	
1925	Leander Cup	3·17	
1934	London R.C.	3·15	
	Leander Club		6·44
1952	Leander Club	3·11	6·38
LADIES' CHALLENGE PLATE			
1911	*Eton College*	*3·19*	
1921	*Pembroke College Cambridge*		*6·55*
1934	Trinity College Dublin	3·18	
	Jesus College Cambridge		6·48
1949	Lady Margaret B.C. Cambridge	3·13	6·43
THAMES CHALLENGE CUP			
1921	*Corpus Christi College Cambridge*	*3·25*	*7·6*
1926	Kingston R.C.	3·24	
1934	Westminster Bank R.C.	3·22	
	London R.C.		6·58
1949	Lady Margaret B.C. Cambridge	3·19	6·51
1953	Princeton University, U.S.A.	3·18	6·45
PRINCESS ELIZABETH CUP			
1952	Radley College	3·21	6·57
STEWARDS' CHALLENGE CUP			
1908	*Magdalen College Oxford*	*3·36*	*7·28*
1925	Third Trinity B.C. Cambridge		7·27
1930	London R.C.	3·35	
1934	Pembroke College Cambridge	3·33	7·24
1935	F.C. Zurich R.C., Switzerland	3·28	7·14
1949	Trinity College Oxford		7·13

	Fawley	*Finish*
VISITORS' CHALLENGE CUP		
1908 Magdalen College Oxford	*3·41*	*7·30*
1911 Third Trinity B.C. Cambridge	*3·39*	
1925 Third Trinity B.C. Cambridge	3·37	
1938 Oriel College Oxford	3·31	7·18
1952 Trinity College Oxford	3·30	
Pembroke College Cambridge		7·15
WYFOLD CHALLENGE CUP		
1921 Jesus College Cambridge	*3·39*	*7·35*
1934 Reading R.C.	3·38	
1949 Lensbury R.C.		7·24
1952 Corpus Christi College Cambridge	3·36	
1953 Royal Air Force R.C.	3·31	7·20
SILVER GOBLETS		
1906 B. C. Johnstone and R. V. Powell	*3·51*	
1911 J. Beresford and A. H. Cloutte and B. Logan		
and C. G. Rought (Dead Heat)		*8·8*
1952 H. C. I. Bywater and T. H. Christie		8·5
1953 R. Baetens and M. Knuysen	3·46	7·51
DIAMOND SCULLS		
1905 F. S. Kelly		*8·10*
1911 W. D. Kinnear	*3·55*	
1934 H. Buhtz	3·50	
1938 J. W. Burk		8·2
1953 R. George		8·0
DOUBLE SCULLS		
1953 E. Schreiver and P. Stebler	3·52	7·21

Undoubtedly the spate of records in recent years has been made possible by the exceptionally favourable conditions in 1949, 1952, and 1953. But it must also be remembered that it takes more than fast conditions to make a record-breaking crew. Indeed, as a rule, it takes more than one potential record-breaking crew to make sure of a new record time. The keenness of the competition has a great deal to do with it. And there is a further, intangible, and perhaps psychological factor, which we might call 'example'. It is to be seen in all branches of athletics. A new record, once established, becomes a magnet—a target for the 'normal' performance. It is sometimes said that the athlete must be nearing the limits of his capabilities. That is doubtful; but so far as the oarsman is concerned, I am sure that it is untrue. With the competition which exists today, a few more favourable years will surely see the course record for eights below the six-and-a-half-minute mark, and the times for the other events dropping in proportion.

Course Records

	Barrier	*Fawley*	*Finish*
Eights	1.53 Leander 1952 and 1953	3.11 Leander 1952	6.38 Leander 1952
Fours	2.4 F. C. Zurich R.C. 1935 Trinity College Oxford 1952, and Leander 1953	3.28 F.C. Zurich R.C. 1935	7.13 Trinity College Oxford 1949
Double Sculls	2.4	3.32 All by E. Schreiver and P. Stebler 1953	7.21
Pair-Oar	2.14	3.46 All by R. Baetens and M. Knuysen 1953	7.51
Single Sculls	2.15 H. Buhtz 1934	3.50 H. Buhtz 1934	8.0 R. George 1953

Table of Winners

THE GRAND CHALLENGE CUP

1839	First Trinity B.C. Cam.	8.30	1872	London R.C.	8.27
1840	Leander Club	9.15	1873	London R.C.	7.52
1841	Cambridge Subscription Rooms	—	1874	London R.C.	7.41
			1875	Leander Club	7.19
1842	Cambridge Subscription Rooms	8.30	1876	Thames R.C.	7.26
			1877	London R.C.	8.2½
1843	Oxford University B.C.	9.0	1878	Thames R.C.	7.42
1844	Etonian Club, Oxf.	8.25	1879	Jesus College Cam.	8.39
1845	Cambridge University B.C.	8.30	1880	Leander Club	7.3
			1881	London R.C.	7.23
1846	Thames Club, London	8.15	1882	Exeter College Oxf.	8.11
1847	Oxford University B.C.	8.0	1883	London R.C.	7.51
1848	Oxford University B.C.	9.11	1884	London R.C.	7.27
1849	Wadham College Oxf.	—	1885	Jesus College Cam.	7.22
1850	Oxford University B.C.	R.O.	1886	Trinity Hall Cam.	6.53½
1851	Oxford University B.C.	7.45	1887	Trinity Hall Cam.	6.56
1852	Oxford University B.C.	—	1888	Thames R.C.	7.1
1853	Oxford University B.C.	8.3	1889	Thames R.C.	7.4
1854	First Trinity B.C. Cam.	8.15	1890	London R.C.	7.4½
1855	Cambridge University B.C.	8.32	1891	Leander Club	6.51
			1892	Leander Club	7.48½
1856	Royal Chester R.C.	—	1893	Leander Club	7.12
1857	London R.C.	7.55	1894	Leander Club	7.22
1858	Cambridge University B.C.	7.26	1895	Trinity Hall Cam.	7.30
			1896	Leander Club	7.43
1859	London R.C.	7.45	1897	New College Oxf.	6.51
1860	First Trinity B.C. Cam.	8.45	1898	Leander Club	7.13
1861	First Trinity B.C. Cam.	8.10	1899	Leander Club	7.12
1862	London R.C.	8.5	1900	Leander Club	7.6
1863	University College Oxf.	7.42	1901	Leander Club	7.4⅖
1864	Kingston R.C.	7.43	1902	Third Trinity B.C. Cam.	7.17
1865	Kingston R.C.	7.25	1903	Leander Club	7.9
1866	Etonian Club, Oxf.	8.29	1904	Leander Club	7.20
1867	Etonian Club, Oxf.	7.54	1905	Leander Club	6.58
1868	London R.C.	7.20	1906	Club Nautique de Gand, Belgium	7.9
1869	Etonian Club, Oxf.	7.28			
1870	Etonian Club, Oxf.	7.18	1907	Sport Nautique de Gand, Belgium	7.31
1871	Etonian Club, Oxf.	8.5			

1908	Christ Church Oxf.	7.10
1909	Royal Club Nautique de Gand, Belgium	7.8
1910	Magdalen College Oxf.	7.19
1911	Magdalen College Oxf.	7.2
1912	Sydney R.C., Australia	7.6
1913	Leander Club	7.11
1914	Harvard Athletic Assoc. B.C., U.S.A.	7.20
1920	Magdalen College Oxf.	7.24
1921	Magdalen College Oxf.	6.54
1922	Leander Club	7.36
1923	Thames R.C.	6.45
1924	Leander Club	8.3
1925	Leander Club	6.53
1926	Leander Club	6.56
1927	Thames R.C.	7.16
1928	Thames R.C.	6.56
1929	Leander Club	7.0
1930	London R.C.	6.59
1931	London R.C.	7.33
1932	Leander Club	7.19
1933	London R.C.	7.36
1934	Leander Club	6.45
1935	Pembroke College Cam.	6.52
1936	F.C. Zurich Ruder Club, Switzerland	7.25
1937	R. Wiking, Germany	7.33
1938	London R.C.	6.58
1939	Harvard University, U.S.A.	7.40
1946	Leander Club	7.1
1947	Jesus College Cam.	7.14
1948	Thames R.C.	7.2
1949	Leander Club	6.54
1950	Harvard University, U.S.A.	7.23
1951	Lady Margaret B.C. Cam.	7.16
1952	Leander Club	6.38
1953	Leander Club	6.49
1954	Club Krylia Sovetov, U.S.S.R.	7.16
1955	University of Pennsylvania, U.S.A.	6.56
1956	Centre Sportif des Forces de l'Armée Française	7.6

THE LADIES' CHALLENGE PLATE

1845	St. George's Club, London	8.25
1846	First Trinity B.C. Cam.	—
1847	Brasenose College Oxf.	9.0
1848	Christ Church Oxf.	—
1849	Wadham College Oxf.	—
1850	Lincoln College Oxf.	R.O.
1851	Brasenose College Oxf.	8.10
1852	Pembroke College Oxf.	R.O.
1853	First Trinity B.C. Cam.	8.15
1854	First Trinity B.C. Cam.	7.55
1855	Balliol College Oxf.	7.58
1856	Royal Chester R.C.	—
1857	Exeter College Oxf.	7.57
1858	Balliol College Oxf.	7.51
1859	First Trinity B.C. Cam.	7.55
1860	First Trinity B.C. Cam.	R.O.
1861	First Trinity B.C. Cam.	8.10
1862	University College Oxf.	8.17
1863	University College Oxf.	7.23
1864	Eton College	R.O.
1865	Third Trinity B.C. Cam.	—
1866	Eton College	8.16
1867	Eton College	7.55
1868	Eton College	7.25
1869	Eton College	7.58
1870	Eton College	7.46
1871	Pembroke College Ox .	7.59
1872	Jesus College Cam.	8.35
1873	Jesus College Cam.	7.53
1874	First Trinity B.C. Cam.	8.6
1875	Trinity Coll. Dublin	7.30
1876	Jesus College Cam.	7.31
1877	Jesus College Cam.	8.23
1878	Jesus College Cam.	8.52
1879	Lady Margaret B.C. Cam.	8.52
1880	Trinity Hall Cam.	7.26
1881	First Trinity B.C. Cam.	7.51
1882	Eton College	8.37
1883	Christ Church Oxf.	7.51
1884	Eton College	7.37
1885	Eton College	7.21
1886	Pembroke College Cam.	7.17
1887	Trinity Hall Cam.	7.10
1888	Lady Margaret B.C. Cam.	7.18
1889	Christ Church Oxford	7.22
1890	Balliol College Oxf.	7.16

1891 Balliol College Oxf. 7.20
1892 First Trinity B.C. Cam. 7.43½
1893 Eton College 7.32
1894 Eton College 7.36
1895 Eton College 7.25
1896 Eton College 8.6
1897 Eton College 7.1
1898 Eton College 7.3
1899 Eton College 7.20
1900 New College Oxf. 7.18
1901 University College Oxf. 7.28
1902 University College Oxf. 7.16
1903 Magdalen College Oxf. 7.33
1904 Eton College 7.20
1905 Eton College 7.12
1906 First Trinity B.C. Cam. 7.23
1907 Trinity Hall Cam. 7.44
1908 Jesus College Cam. 7.5
1909 St. John's College Oxf. 7.9
1910 Eton College 7.16
1911 Eton College 6.56
1912 Eton College 7.4
1913 First Trinity B.C. Cam. 7.24
1914 Pembroke College Cam. 7.24
1920 Christ Church Oxf. 7.30
1921 Eton College 7.9
1922 Brasenose College Oxf. 7.47
1923 Trinity College Oxf. 6.55
1924 Shrewsbury School 8.4

1925 Lady Margaret B.C. Cam. 7.7
1926 Jesus College Cam. 7.5
1927 First Trinity B.C. Cam. 7.29
1928 Jesus College Cam. 7.6
1929 First Trinity B.C. Cam. 7.16
1930 Lady Margaret B.C. Cam. 7.10
1931 Jesus College Cam. 8.7
1932 Shrewsbury School 7.40
1933 Lady Margaret B.C. Cam. 7.38
1934 Jesus College Cam. 6.48
1935 Trinity Hall Cam. 7.7
1936 First Trinity B.C. Cam. 7.48
1937 Clare College Cam. 7.38
1938 Radley College 6.56
1939 Clare College Cam. 8.13
1946 Jesus College Cam. 7.8
1947 First and Third Trinity
       B.C. Cam. 7.21
1948 Eton College 7.15
1949 Lady Margaret B.C. Cam. 6.50
1950 New College Oxf. 7.25
1951 Pembroke College Cam. 7.25
1952 Lady Margaret B.C. Cam. 6.50
1953 Jesus College Cam. 7.0
1954 First and Third Trinity
       B.C. Cam. 7.33
1955 Queens' College Cam. 7.26
1956 Peterhouse Cam. 7.41

THE THAMES CHALLENGE CUP

1868 Pembroke College Oxf. 7.46
1869 Oscillators Club, Surbiton R.O.
1870 Oscillators Club, Surbiton 7.53
1871 Ino R.C. 8.36
1872 Thames R.C. 8.42
1873 Thames R.C. 8.2
1874 Thames R.C. 8.19
1875 London R.C. 7.33
1876 West London R.C. 7.36
1877 London R.C. 8.29
1878 London R.C. 7.55
1879 Twickenham R.C. 8.55
1880 London R.C. 7.24
1881 Twickenham R.C. 7.50
1882 Royal Chester R.C. —
1883 London R.C. 8.5

1884 Twickenham R.C. 7.48
1885 London R.C. 7.36
1886 London R.C. 7.8½
1887 Trinity Hall Cam. 7.20
1888 Lady Margaret B.C. Cam. 7.19
1889 Christ Church Oxf. 7.16
1890 Thames R.C. 7.21½
1891 Molesey B.C. 7.18
1892 Jesus College Cam. 8.10
1893 Thames R.C. 7.49
1894 Trinity College Oxf. 7.58
1895 Nereus B.C., Amsterdam,
       Holland 7.29
1896 Emmanuel College Cam. 8.7
1897 Kingston R.C. 7.9
1898 Trinity College Oxf. 7.19

1899	First Trinity B.C. Cam.	7.25	1930	Vesta R.C.	7.23
1900	Trinity College Cam.	7.24	1931	London R.C.	7.43
1901	Trinity Hall Cam.	7.23	1932	London R.C.	7.41
1902	Trinity Hall Cam.	7.34	1933	Kent School, U.S.A.	7.30
1903	Trinity College Dublin	7.37	1934	Thames R.C.	7.4
1904	Caius College Cam.	7.30	1935	London R.C.	7.5
1905	Thames R.C.	7.28	1936	Tabor Academy, U.S.A.	7.44
1906	Christ's College Cam.	7.23	1937	Tabor Academy, U.S.A.	7.31
1907	Christ's College Cam.	7.45	1938	Kent School, U.S.A.	7.3
1908	Wadham College Oxf.	7.15	1939	Tabor Academy, U.S.A.	7.53
1909	Wadham College Oxf.	7.21	1946	Imperial College B.C.	7.11
1910	Anglian B.C.	7.36	1947	Kent School, U.S.A.	7.22
1911	First Trinity B.C. Cam.	7.13	1948	Princeton University,	
1912	R.C. de Paris, France	7.33		U.S.A.	7.20
1913	Oriel College Oxf.	7.30	1949	Princeton University,	
1914	Caius College Cam.	7.27		U.S.A.	6.58
1920	Thames R.C.	7.43	1950	Kent School, U.S.A.	7.34
1921	Christiania Roklub, Nor-		1951	University of Pennsyl-	
	way	7.12		vania, U.S.A.	7.19
1922	Worcester College Oxf.	7.56	1952	University of Pennsyl-	
1923	First Trinity B.C. Cam.	7.12		vania U.S.A.	7.3
1924	Maidenhead R.C.	8.29	1953	Royal Air Force	6.59
1925	First Trinity B.C. Cam.	7.16	1954	Massachusetts Institute of	
1926	Selwyn College Cam.	7.9		Technology, U.S.A.	7.24
1927	Thames R.C.	7.34	1955	Massachusetts Institute of	
1928	Thames R.C.	7.23		Technology, U.S.A.	7.21
1929	Browne and Nichols		1956	Princeton University,	
	School, U.S.A.	7.28		U.S.A.	7.10

THE PRINCESS ELIZABETH CHALLENGE CUP

1946	Bedford School	4.54[1]	1952	Radley College	7.0
1947	Bedford School	7.25	1953	St. Paul's School	7.6
1948	Bedford School	7.20	1954	Winchester College	7.59
1949	Winchester College	7.11	1955	Shrewsbury School	7.24
1950	St. Paul's School	7.44	1956	Eton College	7.25
1951	Bedford School	7.27			

THE STEWARDS' CHALLENGE CUP

1841	Oxford Club, London		1844	Oxford University B.C.	9.16
	(The Midge)	—	1845	Oxford University B.C.	8.25
1842	Oxford Club, London		1846	Oxford University B.C.	—
	(The Midge)	9.16	1847	Christ Church Oxf.	R.O.
1843	St. George's Club,		1848	Christ Church Oxf.	R.O.
	London	10.15	1849	Leander Club	—

[1] Shortened course from Remenham Barrier.

1850	Oxford University B.C.	R.O.	1897	Leander Club	7.30
1851	Cambridge University		1898	Leander Club	7.42
	qualification	8.54	1899	Magdalen College Oxf.	7.51
1852	Oxford University B.C.	—	1900	Leander Club	7.55
1853	Oxford University B.C.	8.57	1901	Third Trinity B.C. Cam.	7.54
1854	Pembroke College Oxf.	9.38	1902	Third Trinity B.C. Cam.	7.45
1855	Royal Chester R.C.	—	1903	Third Trinity B.C. Cam.	8.5
1856	Argonaut Club, London	—	1904	Third Trinity B.C. Cam.	7.30
1857	London R.C.	8.25	1905	Leander Club	R.O.
1858	London R.C.	R.O.	1906	Leander Club	7.36
1859	Third Trinity B.C. Cam.	8.25	1907	Magdalen College Oxf.	8.42
1860	First Trinity B.C. Cam.	9.26	1908	Magdalen College Oxf.	7.40
1861	First Trinity B.C. Cam.	9.35	1909	Thames R.C.	7.38
1862	Brasenose College Oxf.	8.40	1910	Winnipeg R.C., Canada	7.52
1863	University College Oxf.	8.24	1911	Thames R.C.	7.35
1864	London R.C.	8.45	1912	New College Oxf.	7.36
1865	Third Trinity B.C. Cam.	8.13	1913	New College Oxf.	—
1866	University College Oxf.	9.28	1914	Leander Club	7.52
1867	University College Oxf.	8.45	1920	Magdalen College Oxf.	8.3
1868	London R.C.	8.22	1921	Magdalen College Oxf.	7.32
1869	London R.C.	8.36	1922	Eton Vikings Club	8.25
1870	Etonian Club, Oxf.	8.5	1923	Third Trinity B.C. Cam.	7.30
1871	London R.C.	9.9	1924	Third Trinity B.C. Cam.	8.37
1872	London R.C.	9.21	1925	Third Trinity B.C. Cam.	7.27
1873	London R.C.	8.23	1926	Thames R.C.	7.34
1874	London R.C.	9.0	1927	Thames R.C.	8.1
1875	London R.C.	7.56	1928	Thames R.C.	7.43
1876	London R.C.	8.27	1929	First Trinity B.C. Cam.	7.32
1877	London R.C.	9.7	1930	London R.C.	7.34
1878	London R.C.	8.37	1931	London R.C.	8.45
1879	Jesus College Cam.	9.37	1932	Thames R.C.	8.9
1880	Thames R.C.	7.58	1933	Pembroke College Cam.	8.16
1881	Hertford College Oxf.	8.15	1934	Pembroke College Cam.	7.24
1882	Hertford College Oxf.	—	1935	F.C. Zurich Ruder Club,	
1883	Thames R.C.	—		Switzerland	7.14
1884	Kingston R.C.	—	1936	F.C. Zurich Ruder Club,	
1885	Trinity Hall Cam.	7.53		Switzerland	7.50
1886	Thames R.C.	7.39	1937	Leander Club	8.32
1887	Trinity Hall Cam.	7.53	1938	Leander Club	7.33
1888	Trinity Hall Cam.	8.25	1939	R.C. Zurich, Switzerland	8.9
1889	Thames R.C.	7.53	1946	Leander Club	7.48
1890	Brasenose College Oxf.	7.37	1947	Thames R.C.	8.4
1891	Thames R.C.	7.45	1948	Thames R.C.	7.48
1892	Royal Chester R.C.	8.38	1949	Trinity College Oxf.	7.13
1893	Magdalen College Oxf.	7.45	1950	Hellerup Roklub, Den-	
1894	Thames R.C.	8.20		mark	8.3
1895	London R.C.	7.43	1951	Thames R.C.	7.53
1896	London R.C.	8.42	1952	Thames R.C.	7.24

1953 Leander Club	7.25	1955 Club Krylia Sovetov,	
1954 Club Krylia Sovetov,		U.S.S.R.	7.40
U.S.S.R.	8.26	1956 Thames R.C.	8.6

THE VISITORS' CHALLENGE CUP

1847 Christ Church Oxf.	9.0	1888 Brasenose College Oxf.	7.59
1848 Christ Church Oxf.	R.O.	1889 Third Trinity B.C. Cam.	8.6
1849 Second Trinity B.C. Cam.	R.O.	1890 Brasenose College Oxf.	7.42
1850 Christ Church Oxf.	—	1891 Trinity Hall Cam.	7.45
1851 Christ Church Oxf.	9.0	1892 Third Trinity B.C. Cam.	8.23
1852 Argonaut Club, London	—	1893 Third Trinity B.C. Cam.	8.21
1853 Argonaut Club, London	9.2	1894 New College Oxf.	R.O.
1854 Lady Margaret B.C. Cam.	8.48	1895 Trinity College Oxf.	8.17
1855 Lady Margaret B.C. Cam.	—	1896 Caius College Cam.	8.29
1856 Lady Margaret B.C. Cam.	—	1897 Trinity College Oxf.	7.53
1857 Pembroke College Oxf.	8.40	1898 New College Oxf.	7.37
1858 First Trinity B.C. Cam.	—	1899 Balliol College Oxf.	8.1
1859 Third Trinity B.C. Cam.	R.O.	1900 Trinity College Cam.	7.53
1860 First Trinity B.C. Cam.	R.O.	1901 Balliol College Oxf.	8.27
1861 First Trinity B.C. Cam.	8.57	1902 Jesus College Cam.	7.59
1862 Brasenose College Oxf.	9.40	1903 University College Oxf.	8.25
1863 Brasenose College Oxf.	R.O.	1904 Third Trinity B.C. Cam.	7.46
1864 University College Oxf.	R.O.	1905 Trinity Hall Cam.	7.53
1865 Third Trinity B.C. Cam.	R.O.	1906 Third Trinity B.C. Cam.	7.49
1866 University College Oxf.	8.49	1907 Magdalen College Oxf.	8.7
1867 University College Oxf.	R.O.	1908 Magdalen College Oxf.	7.30
1868 University College Oxf.	8.15	1909 Christ Church Oxf.	7.53
1869 University College Oxf.	9.5	1910 Trinity Hall Cam.	7.56
1870 Trinity College Dublin	8.36	1911 Third Trinity B.C. Cam.	7.37
1871 First Trinity B.C. Cam.	9.8	1912 Christ Church Oxf.	8.19
1872 Pembroke College Oxf.	9.28	1913 Pembroke College Cam.	8.13
1873 Trinity College Dublin	R.O.	1914 Lady Margaret B.C. Cam.	8.26
1874 Trinity College Dublin	8.47	1920 Merton College Oxf.	8.26
1875 University College Oxf.	8.20	1921 Lincoln College Oxf.	7.44
1876 University College Oxf.	8.5	1922 Third Trinity B.C. Cam.	8.28
1877 Jesus College Cam.	9.7	1923 Magdalen College Oxf.	7.44
1878 Columbia College, New		1924 Third Trinity B.C. Cam.	9.14
York, U.S.A.	8.42	1925 Third Trinity B.C. Cam.	7.45
1879 Lady Margaret B.C. Cam.	9.22	1926 Christ Church Oxf.	8.15
1880 Third Trinity B.C. Cam.	8.16	1927 Christ's College Cam.	8.16
1881 First Trinity B.C. Cam.	8.22	1928 First Trinity B.C. Cam.	7.54
1882 Brasenose College Oxf.	9.23	1929 Third Trinity B.C. Cam.	7.46
1883 Christ Church Oxf.	—	1930 Brasenose College Oxf.	8.6
1884 Third Trinity B.C. Cam.	8.39	1931 Pembroke College Cam.	8.45
1885 Trinity Hall Cam.	7.41	1932 Jesus College Cam.	8.21
1886 First Trinity B.C. Cam.	8.20½	1933 Christ's College Cam.	8.16
1887 Trinity Hall Cam.	8.8	1934 First Trinity B.C. Cam.	7.38

1935 Jesus College Cam.	7.40	1949 Clare College Cam.	7.31
1936 Jesus College Cam.	8.34	1950 Lady Margaret B.C. Cam.	8.8
1937 Trinity Hall Cam.	8.16	1951 Trinity Hall Cam.	8.9
1938 Oriel College Oxf.	7.18	1952 Pembroke College Cam.	7.15
1939 Trinity Hall Cam.	8.9	1953 Magdalen College Oxf.	7.29
1946 First and Third Trinity B.C. Cam.	7.59	1954 First and Third Trinity B.C. Cam.	7.57
1947 Trinity Hall Cam.	8.0	1955 Trinity Hall Cam.	7.58
1948 Magdalen College Oxf.	7.51	1956 Merton College Oxf.	7.47

THE WYFOLD CHALLENGE CUP

1855[1] Royal Chester R.C.	—	1881 Dublin University B.C.	8.8
1856 Argonaut Club, London	—	1882 Jesus College Cam.	8.58
1857 Pembroke College Oxf.	8.30	1883 Kingston R.C.	8.51
1858 First Trinity B.C. Cam.	R.O.	1884 Thames R.C.	8.58
1859 First Trinity B.C. Cam.	8.21	1885 Kingston R.C.	—
1860 London R.C.	10.8	1886 Thames R.C.	8.4
1861 Brasenose College Oxf.	9.43	1887 Pembroke College Cam.	7.50
1862 London R.C.	9.20	1888 Thames R.C.	7.59
1863 Kingston R.C.	8.50	1889 London R.C.	7.58
1864 Kingston R.C.	R.O.	1890 Kingston R.C.	7.46
1865 Kingston R.C.	8.23	1891 Royal Chester R.C.	7.50
1866 Kingston R.C.	—	1892 Molesey B.C.	8.42
1867 Kingston R.C.	—	1893 Molesey B.C.	8.28
1868 Kingston R.C.	8.32	1894 Thames R.C.	8.16
1869 Oscillators Club, Surbiton	—	1895 London R.C.	8.16
1870 Thames R.C.	8.34	1896 Trinity College Oxf.	8.41
1871 Thames R.C.	9.6	1897 Kingston R.C.	8.0
1872 Thames R.C.	8.42	1898 Kingston R.C.	8.28
1873 Kingstown Harbour R.C.	8.37	1899 Trinity Hall Cam.	7.57
1874 Newcastle R.C.	9.0	1900 Trinity Hall Cam.	8.14
1875 Thames R.C.	8.10	1901 Trinity Hall Cam.	8.9
1876 West London R.C.	8.24	1902 Burton-on-Trent R.C.	7.43
1877 Kingston R.C.	R.O.	1903 Kingston R.C.	8.23
1878 Kingston R.C.	8.44	1904 Birmingham R.C.	—
1879 London R.C.	9.56	1905 London R.C.	7.59
1880 London R.C.	8.4	1906 London R.C.	7.58

[1] See page 56. From 1847 to 1854 the Wyfold Challenge Cup was awarded to the winners of the challenge heat for the Grand. If only one crew challenged, they automatically took the Wyfold Cup, and if they also won the Grand they took both cups. In this way the Wyfold Cup was won by:

1847 Oxford University B.C.*	1851 Cambridge University B.C.
1848 Thames Club, London	1852 Oxford Aquatic Club
1849 Wadham College Oxf.*	1853 Cambridge University B.C.
1850 Oxford University B.C.*	1854 First Trinity B.C. Cam.*

* These crews also won the Grand.

1907 Magdalen College Oxf.	8.49	1933 London R.C.	8.28
1908 Thames R.C.	7.55	1934 Reading R.C.	7.36
1909 Balliol College Oxf.	7.44	1935 Reading R.C.	7.39
1910 Trinity Hall Cam.	8.9	1936 London R.C.	8.26
1911 Pembroke College Cam.	7.40	1937 London R.C.	8.20
1912 Queens' College Cam.	8.3	1938 London R.C.	7.41
1913 Lady Margaret B.C. Cam.	8.1	1939 Maidenhead R.C.	9.10
1914 London R.C.	8.35	1946 King's College London	7.57
1920 Thames R.C.	8.10	1947 Quintin B.C.	8.19
1921 Jesus College Cam.	7.46	1948 Victoria Lake R.C., South	
1922 Thames R.C.	9.6	Africa	7.55
1923 Imperial College B.C.	7.50	1949 Lensbury R.C.	7.41
1924 Royal Chester R.C.	9.16	1950 Royal Engineers	8.13
1925 Thames R.C.	7.35	1951 Caius College Cam.	7.55
1926 London R.C.	7.59	1952 Corpus Christi College	
1927 Thames R.C.	8.23	Cam.	7.28
1928 Trinity Hall Cam.	7.47	1953 Royal Air Force	7.38
1929 Thames R.C.	7.44	1954 Royal Engineers	8.6
1930 London R.C.	7.52	1955 Thames R.C.	7.51
1931 Thames R.C.	9.13	1956 Royal Engineers	7.56
1932 London R.C.	8.29		

THE SILVER GOBLETS AND NICKALLS CHALLENGE CUP

1845	G. Mann and F. M. Arnold (Caius College Cambridge)	—
1846	M. Haggard and W. H. Milman (Christ Church Oxford)	—
1847	W. S. Falls and W. Coulthard (St. George's Club, London)	—
1848	M. Haggard and W. H. Milman (Christ Church Oxford)	—
1849	E. G. Peacock and F. Playford (Thames Club, London)	—
1850	J. J. Hornby (Brasenose College Oxford) and J. W. Chitty (Balliol College Oxford)	—
1851	J. Aitken (Exeter College Oxford) and J. W. Chitty (Balliol College Oxford)	—
1852	H. R. Barker and P. H. Nind (Christ Church Oxford)	R.O.
1853	R. Gordon and J. B. Barlee (Christ's College Cambridge)	10.0
1854	W. F. Short (New College Oxford) and E. Cadogan (Christ Church Oxford)	9.36
1855	A. A. Casamajor and J. Nottidge (Wandle Club)	—
1856	A. A. Casamajor and J. Nottidge (Argonaut Club, London)	—
1857	E. Warre and A. P. Lonsdale (Balliol College Oxford)	9.22
1858	H. H. Playford and A. A. Casamajor (London R.C.)	—
1859	E. Warre (Balliol College Oxford) and J. Arkell (Pembroke College Oxford)	9.0
1860	A. A. Casamajor and W. Woodbridge (London R.C.)	11.50
1861	W. Champneys and W. B. Woodgate (Brasenose College Oxford)	—
1862	W. Champneys and W. B. Woodgate (Brasenose College Oxford)	9.45
1863	R. Shepherd and W. B. Woodgate (Brasenose College Oxford)	R.O.
1864	J. R. Selwyn and R. A. Kinglake (Third Trinity B.C. Cambridge)	9.29

1865	J. C. F. May and F. Fenner (London R.C.)	9.7
1866	E. L. Corrie and W. B. Woodgate (Kingston R.C.)	9.23
1867	E. L. Corrie and M. M. Brown (Kingston R.C.)	9.49
1868	W. C. Crofts and W. B. Woodgate (Brasenose College Oxford)	—
1869	A. de L. Long and W. Stout (London R.C.)	9.20
1870	E. L. Corrie and E. Hall (Kingston R.C.)	—
1871	A. de L. Long and F. S. Gulston (London R.C.)	10.17
1872	A. de L. Long and F. S. Gulston (London R.C.)	—
1873	C. C. Knollys and A. Trower (Kingston R.C.)	9.22
1874	A. de L. Long and F. S. Gulston (London R.C.)	10.3
1875	W. Chillingworth and C. Herbert (Ino R.C.)	—
1876	S. Le B. Smith and F. S. Gulston (London R.C.)	8.55
1877	W. H. Eyre and J. Hastie (Thames R.C.)	—
1878	T. C. Edwards-Moss and W. A. Ellison (Etonian Club, Oxford)	9.14
1879	R. H. Labat and F. S. Gulston (London R.C.)	11.16
1880	W. H. Eyre and J. Hastie (Thames R.C.)	8.45
1881	W. H. Eyre and J. Hastie (Thames R.C.)	9.4
1882	D. E. Brown and J. Lowndes (Hertford College Oxford)	—
1883	G. Q. Roberts and D. E. Brown (Twickenham R.C.)	9.22
1884	J. Lowndes and D. E. Brown (Twickenham R.C.)	9.1
1885	H. McLean and D. H. McLean (Etonian Club, Oxford)	—
1886	F. E. Churchill and S. D. Muttlebury (Third Trinity B.C. Cambridge)	8.40
1887	C. T. Barclay and S. D. Muttlebury (Third Trinity B.C. Cambridge)	8.15
1888	N. P. Symonds (Cambridge University B.C.) and E. Buck (Oxford University B.C.)	—
1889	J. C. Gardner and S. D. Muttlebury (Cambridge University B.C.)	8.25
1890	Lord Ampthill and G. Nickalls (Oxford University B.C.)	8.38
1891	Lord Ampthill and G. Nickalls (Leander Club)	8.36
1892	V. Nickalls and W. A. L. Fletcher (Oxford University B.C.)	9.7
1893	V. Nickalls and W. A. L. Fletcher (Oxford University B.C.)	8.44
1894	V. Nickalls and G. Nickalls (Formosa B.C.)	9.35
1895	V. Nickalls and G. Nickalls (London R.C.)	9.11
1896	V. Nickalls and G. Nickalls (London R.C.)	9.10
1897	E. R. Balfour and G. Nickalls (Leander Club)	8.59
1898	A. Bogle and W. J. Fernie (Thames R.C.)	8.41
1899	C. K. Philips and H. W. M. Willis (Leander Club)	8.49
1900	C. J. D. Goldie and G. M. Maitland (Trinity College Cambridge)	8.33
1901	H. J. Hale and F. W. Warre (Balliol College Oxford)	8.50
1902	W. Dudley Ward and C. W. H. Taylor (Third Trinity B.C. Cambridge)	8.36
1903	L. Klaus and A. Ehrenberg (Victoria R.C., Berlin, Germany)	8.45
1904	C. J. D. Goldie and C. W. H. Taylor (Third Trinity B.C. Cambridge)	8.33
1905	R. H. Nelson and P. H. Thomas (Third Trinity B.C. Cambridge)	8.40
1906	B. C. Johnstone and R. V. Powell (Third Trinity B.C. Cambridge)	9.15
1907	B. C. Johnstone and R. V. Powell (Leander Club)	8.52
1908	H. R. Barker and A. C. Gladstone (Christ Church Oxford)	8.26

1909	B. C. Johnstone and E. G. Williams (Leander Club)	8.30
1910	J. S. Burn and G. L. Thomson (Leander Club)	8.45
1911	J. Beresford and A. H. Cloutte (Thames R.C.)	8.15
1912	B. Logan and C. G. Rought (Thames R.C.)	8.36
1913	A. A. Swann and S. E. Swann (Trinity Hall Cambridge)	8.39
1914	A. A. Swann and S. E. Swann (Trinity Hall Cambridge)	9.2
1920	G. O. Nickalls and R. S. C. Lucas (Magdalen College Oxford)	8.53
1921	J. A. Campbell and H. B. Playford (Jesus College Cambridge)	8.52
1922	G. O. Nickalls and R. S. C. Lucas (Magdalen College Oxford)	9.19
1923	W. F. Godden and R. E. Eason (Trinity College Oxford)	8.12
1924	C. R. M. Ely and J. A. Macnabb (Third Trinity B.C. Cambridge)	10.6
1925	R. E. Morrison and E. C. Hamilton-Russell (Third Trinity B C. Cambridge)	8.17
1926	H. R. Carver and E. C. Hamilton-Russell (Third Trinity B.C. Cambridge)	8.36
1927	R. A. Nisbet and T. N. O'Brien (London R.C.)	9.23
1928	G. C. Killick and J. Beresford, jun. (Thames R.C.)	9.57
1929	G. C. Killick and J. Beresford, jun. (Thames R.C.)	8.32
1930	W. A. Prideaux and H. R. N. Rickett (Third Trinity B.C. Cambridge)	8.42
1931	H. R. A. Edwards and L. Clive (Christ Church Oxford)	9.57
1932	H. R. A. Edwards and L. Clive (Christ Church Oxford)	9.5
1933	J. H. C. Powell and J. E. Gilmour (Eton Vikings Club)	9.17
1934	H. Braun and H. G. Moller (R. Wiking, Germany)	8.9
1935	T. S. Cree and D. W. Burnford (Jesus College Cambridge)	8.20
1936	R. E. Offer and J. S. Offer (Kingston R.C.)	9.17
1937	E. W. Wingate and W. D. Baddeley (Vesta R.C.)	9.43
1938	W. G. R. M. Laurie and J. H. T. Wilson (Leander Club)	8.8
1939	C. B. Sanford and H. Parker (Trinity Hall Cambridge)	9.5
1946	J. F. Burgess and C. G. Burgess (Leander Club)	8.47
1947	J. H. Pinches and E. M. Sturges (London R.C.)	8.46
1948	W. G. R. M. Laurie and J. H. T. Wilson (Leander Club)	8.30
1949	A. S. F. Butcher and T. H. Christie (Thames R.C.)	8.20
1950	J. Rosa and C. van Antwerpen (Société Royale Nautique Anversoise, Belgium)	9.10
1951	J. G. P. Crowden (Pembroke College Cambridge) and C. B. M. Lloyd (Lady Margaret B.C. Cambridge)	8.52
1952	H. C. I. Bywater and T. H. Christie (Westminster Hospital B.C.)	8.6
1953	R. Baetens and M. Knuysen (Antwerp S.C., Belgium)	8.10
1954	I. Buldakov and V. Ivanov (Club Khimik, U.S.S.R.)	8.44
1955	I. Buldakov and V. Ivanov (Club Khimik, U.S.S.R.)	8.30
1956	R. J. Thompson and G. M. Wolfson (Pembroke College Cambridge	8.45

THE DIAMOND CHALLENGE SCULLS

1844	T. B. Bumpsted (London Amateur Scullers Club)	10.32
1845	S. Wallace (Leander Club)	—
1846	E. G. Moon (Magdalen College Oxford)	—

1847	W. Maule (First Trinity B.C. Cambridge)	10.45
1848	W. L. Bagshawe (Third Trinity B.C. Cambridge)	—
1849	T. R. Bone (London)[1]	—
1850	T. R. Bone (Meteor Club)	—
1851	E. G. Peacock (Thames Club)	—
1852	E. Macnaghten (First Trinity B.C. Cambridge)	—
1853	S. R. Rippingall (Peterhouse Cambridge)	10.2
1854	H. H. Playford (Wandle Club)	—
1855	A. A. Casamajor (Argonaut Club, London)	9.27
1856	A. A. Casamajor (Argonaut Club, London)	—
1857	A. A. Casamajor (London R.C.)	—
1858	A. A. Casamajor (London R.C.)	R.O.
1859	E. D. Brickwood (Richmond)[1]	10.0
1860	H. H. Playford (London R.C.)	12.8
1861	A. A. Casamajor (London R.C.)	10.4
1862	E. D. Brickwood (London R.C.)[2]	9.40
1863	C. B. Lawes (Third Trinity B.C. Cambridge)	9.43
1864	W. B. Woodgate (Brasenose College Oxford)	10.10
1865	E. B. Michell (Magdalen College Oxford)	9.11
1866	E. B. Michell (Magdalen College Oxford)	9.55
1867	W. C. Crofts (Brasenose College Oxford)	10.2
1868	W. Stout (London R.C.)	9.6
1869	W. C. Crofts (Brasenose College Oxford)	9.56
1870	John B. Close (First Trinity B.C. Cambridge)	9.43
1871	W. Fawcus (Tynemouth R.C.)	10.9
1872	C. C. Knollys (Magdalen College Oxford)	10.48
1873	A. C. Dicker (Lady Margaret B.C. Cambridge)	9.50
1874	A. C. Dicker (Lady Margaret B.C. Cambridge)	10.50
1875	A. C. Dicker (Lady Margaret B.C. Cambridge)	9.15
1876	F. L. Playford (London R.C.)	9.28
1877	T. C. Edwards-Moss (Brasenose College Oxford)	10.20
1878	T. C. Edwards-Moss (Brasenose College Oxford)	9.37
1879	J. Lowndes (Hertford College Oxford)	12.30
1880	J. Lowndes (Derby)[1]	9.10
1881	J. Lowndes (Derby)[1]	9.28
1882	J. Lowndes (Derby)[1]	11.43
1883	J. Lowndes (Twickenham R.C.)	10.2
1884	W. S. Unwin (Magdalen College Oxford)	9.44
1885	W. S. Unwin (Magdalen College Oxford)	9.22
1886	F. I. Pitman (Third Trinity B.C. Cambridge)	9.5
1887	J. C. Gardner (Emmanuel College Cambridge)	8.51
1888	G. Nickalls (Magdalen College Oxford)	8.36
1889	G. Nickalls (Magdalen College Oxford)	8.56
1890	G. Nickalls (Magdalen College Oxford)	8.57$\frac{1}{2}$
1891	V. Nickalls (Magdalen College Oxford)	R.O.

[1] These scullers would today be described as 'unattached'. Reference is to town of origin, not to a club.

[2] After a dead heat with W. B. Woodgate, in 9 min. 22 sec.

1892	J. J. K. Ooms (Neptunus R.C., Amsterdam, Holland)	10.9
1893	G. Nickalls (Magdalen College Oxford)	9.12
1894	G. Nickalls (Formosa B.C.)	9.32
1895	Hon. R. Guinness (Leander Club)	9.11
1896	Hon. R. Guinness (Leander Club)	9.35
1897	E. H. Ten Eyck (Wachusett B.C., Worcester, U.S.A.)	8.35
1898	B. H. Howell (Trinity Hall Cambridge)	8.29
1899	B. H. Howell (Thames R.C.)	8.38
1900	E. G. Hemmerde (University College Oxford)	8.42
1901	C. V. Fox (Guards Brigade R.C.)	8.52
1902	F. S. Kelly (Balliol College Oxford)	8.59
1903	F. S. Kelly (Leander Club)	8.41
1904	L. F. Scholes (Toronto R.C., Canada)	8.23
1905	F. S. Kelly (Leander Club)	8.10
1906	H. T. Blackstaffe (Vesta R.C)	8.35
1907	Captain W. H. Darell (Household Brigade B.C.)	9.24
1908	A. McCulloch (Leander Club)	8.25
1909	A. A. Stuart (Kingston R.C.)	8.30
1910	W. D. Kinnear (Kensington R.C.)	8.51
1911	W. D. Kinnear (Kensington R.C.)	8.14
1912	E. W. Powell (Eton Vikings Club)	8.49
1913	C. McVilly (Derwent R.C., Tasmania)	8.49
1914	S. Sinigaglia (Lario Club, Como, Italy)	9.0
1920	J. Beresford, jun. (Thames R.C.)	8.57
1921	F. E. Eyken (Delft University B.C., Laga, Holland)	8.26
1922	W. M. Hoover (Duluth B.C., Minnesota, U.S.A.)	9.32
1923	M. K. Morris (London R.C.)	8.23
1924	J. Beresford, jun. (Thames R.C.)	10.32
1925	J. Beresford, jun. (Thames R.C.)	8.28
1926	J. Beresford, jun. (Thames R.C.)	8.45
1927	R. T. Lee (Worcester College Oxford)	9.6
1928	J. Wright (Argonaut R.C., Canada)	8.24
1929	L. H. F. Gunther (Roei-Zeilvereening de Amstel, Holland)	8.42
1930	J. S. Guest (Don R.C., Canada)	8.29
1931	R. Pearce (Leander B.C., Hamilton, Canada)	10.3
1932	H. Buhtz (Berliner R.C., Germany)	9.15
1933	T. G. Askwith (Peterhouse Cambridge)	9.7
1934	H. Buhtz (Berliner R.C., Germany)	8.10
1935	E. Rufli (F.C. Zurich Ruder Club, Switzerland)	8.15
1936	E. Rufli (F.C. Zurich Ruder Club, Switzerland)	9.22
1937	J. Hasenohrl (Ruderverein Ellida, Austria)	9.12
1938	J. W. Burk (Penn Athletic Club, U.S.A.)	8.2
1939	J. W. Burk (Penn Athletic Club, U.S.A.)	9.13
1946	J. Séphériadés (Société Nautique de la Basse Seine, France)	8.21
1947	J. B. Kelly (University of Pennsylvania, U.S.A.)	8.49
1948	M. T. Wood (New South Wales Police R.C., Australia)	8.24
1949	J. B. Kelly (University of Pennsylvania, U.S.A.)	8.12
1950	A. D. Rowe (Leander Club)	9.11

1951	T. A. Fox (Pembroke College Cambridge)	8.59
1952	M. T. Wood (Sydney R.C., Australia)	8.12
1953	T. A. Fox (London R.C.)	8.12
1954	P. Vlašic (Mornar Club, Yugoslavia)	8.42
1955	T. Kocerka (A.Z.S. Bydgoszcz, Poland)	8.33
1956	T. Kocerka (A.Z.S. Bydgoszcz, Poland)	8.37

THE DOUBLE SCULLS CHALLENGE CUP

1939[1]	J. Beresford, jun., and L. F. Southwood (Thames R.C.) and G. Scherli and E. Broschi (Societa Canottieri di Trieste, Italy), dead heat	8.35
1946	R. E. Panelo and E. D. Chafuen (Buenos Aires R.C., Argentina)	8.8
1947	W. E. C. Horwood and D. C. H. Garrod (Quintin B.C.)	8.23
1948	B. Piessens (Antwerp S.C.) and W. A. Collet (Société Royale Sport Nautique de Bruxelles) (Belgium)	8.2
1949	E. W. Parsner and A. E. Larsen (D.F.D.S. Roklub, Denmark)	7.39
1950	E. W. Parsner and A. E. Larsen (D.F.D.S. Roklub, Denmark)	8.21
1951	P. Bradley and R. D. Burnell (Leander Club)	8.41
1952	R. George (Union Nautique de Leige) and J. van Stichel (Antwerp S.C.) (Belgium)	7.37
1953	E. Schriever and P. Stebler (Seeclub, Zurich, Switzerland)	7.37
1954	E. Schriever and P. Stebler (Seeclub, Zurich, Switzerland)	8.46
1955	G. Zhilin and I. Emchuk (Club Burevestnik, U.S.S.R.)	7.55
1956	S. C. Rand and W. H. Rand (Royal Air Force R.C.)	7.47

The following events are no longer included in the Henley programme:

Presentation Cup for Four without Coxswains

| 1869 Oxford Radleian Club | 8.40 | 1872 London R.C. | R.O. |

The Public Schools' Challenge Cup

1879 Cheltenham College	11.6	1882 Magdalen College School	—
1880 Bedford Grammar School	8.42	1883 Hereford School	—
1881 Bedford Grammar School	9.22	1884 Derby School	—

The Town Challenge Cup for Fours

1839 'The Wave', Henley	—	1845 Henley Aquatic Club	R.O.
1840 'The Dreadnought', Henley	10.15	1846 The Dreadnought Club, Henley	R.O.
1841 The Dreadnought Club, Henley	R.O.	1847 The Dreadnought Club, Henley	R.O.
1842 The Dreadnought Club, Henley	R.O.	1848 The Dreadnought Club, Henley	—
1843 The Albion Club, Henley	10.45	1849 The Albion Club, Henley	R.O.
1844 Henley Aquatic Club	10.5	1850 First Albion, Henley	—

[1] Instituted in 1939 as the Centenary Double Sculling Race, for presentation prizes. Became a challenge event in 1946.

1851	No entry	
1852	No entry	
1853	No entry	
1854	Defiance B.C., Wargrave	9.5
1855	Henley B.C.	—
1856	Henley B.C.	—
1857	Henley B.C.	R.O.
1858	Henley B.C.	R.O.
1859	Henley B.C.	R.O.
1860	The Dreadnought Club, Henley	11.0
1861	Henley B.C.	R.O.
1862	Oxford Staff R.C.	9.56
1863	Henley B.C.	9.15
1864	Henley B.C.	10.32
1865	Henley B.C.	9.7
1866	Eton Excelsior R.C.	9.28
1867	Eton Excelsior R.C.	—
1868	Henley R.C.	R.O.
1869	Eton Excelsior R.C.	—
1870	Eton Excelsior R.C.	—
1871	Reading R.C.	—
1872	Marlow R.C.	—
1873	Henley R.C.	—
1874	Marlow R.C.	9.34
1875	Marlow R.C.	R.O.
1876	Marlow R.C.	—
1877	Marlow R.C.	10.16
1878	Henley R.C.	—
1879	Greenwood Lodge B.C., Wargrave	—
1880	Reading R.C.	8.32
1881	Reading R.C.	8.45
1882	Reading R.C.	—
1883	Marlow R.C.	

The District Challenge Cup for Fours

1840	The Dreadnought Club, Henley	—
1841	The Dreadnought Club, Henley	R.O.
1842	Windsor and Eton Club	—
1843	The Albion Club, Henley	R.O.
1844	Windsor and Eton Club	—
1845	Henley Aquatic Club	10.12
1846	No entry	
1847	No entry	

The District Goblets for Pair Oars

1858	L. F. Chapman and W. Pyle (Staines)	—
1859	E. J. Giles and H. Sergeant (Henley)	—
1860	J. Dolley and T. Dolley (Oxford)	—
1861	J. O Hopkins and G. Norsworthy	11.0
1862 and 1863	No entry	
1864	H. Hunt and F. W. Pescud (Henley)	10.30
1865	L. W. Carter and H. L. Cripps (Eton and Parmoor)	
1866	G. H. Morrell and F. Willan (Oxford)	10.11
1867	F. Prickett and J. Plowman (Oxford City Club)	R.O.

Local Amateur Scullers' Race

1846	H. Sergeant	—	1852	T. Piper	—
1847	H. Sergeant	—	1853	W. Popjoy	—
1848	H. Sergeant	—	1854	T. Piper	—
1849	E. J. Giles	—	1855	E. J. Giles	—
1850	F. Williams	—	1856	E. J. Giles	—
1851	A. Ive	—	1857	E. J. Giles	—

Appendix A

The Henley Agreement, which must be signed by the Governing Bodies of rowing in all countries, before their entries are accepted for Henley Regatta.

HENLEY ROYAL REGATTA

This Agreement made the   day of   19   , between the (i)   of the one part AND THE COMMITTEE OF MANAGEMENT OF HENLEY ROYAL REGATTA of the other part:—

The (i)   undertakes not to authorize or make the entry of any competitor for HENLEY ROYAL REGATTA who is not an Amateur according to the Henley Royal Regatta definition and duly qualified to compete under the Rules of the Regatta; and in particular the (i)   undertakes not to make or authorize the entry of any competitor:—

(*a*) Who has ever rowed or steered in any race for a stake money or entrance fee.

(*b*) Who has ever knowingly rowed or steered with or against a professional for any prize.

(*c*) Who has ever taught, pursued or assisted in the practice of athletic exercise of any kind for profit.

(*d*) Who is disqualified as an amateur in any other branch of sport.

(*e*) Who has received or intends to receive any contribution towards his expenses in competing at the Regatta except from the Club he represents. (NOTE.—It is open to any *bona-fide* member of such Club to contribute to the Club funds for the above purpose.)

(*f*) Who has not been a member for two months of the Club which he represents, such Club having been duly established at least one year previous to the date of entry.

The Committee of Management of Henley Royal Regatta undertakes that it will receive and consider any entry from (ii) which is accompanied by a declaration made in compliance with the above undertaking by the Secretary or other responsible official of (i)

Signed on behalf of the (i)

.....................President

.....................Secretary

NOTE (i) Insert here the name of the Union or Federation.
(ii) Insert here the name of the Country, Dominion, or Colony.

Appendix B

LEANDER, LONDON, AND THAMES

APART from the University and college clubs and a few school boat clubs, the Leander Club is the oldest rowing club in England. Yet the year of its foundation has never been exactly established.

The arms of Leander bear a star and an arrow, and it has long been averred that the club 'arose from the ashes' of two other clubs, known respectively as *The Star* and *The Arrow*. In the early years of the nineteenth century there were no big clubs, and no clubhouses, such as we know today. Rather there were small bands of enthusiasts, who bought or hired a boat, and rented a changing room at one of the boatyards. Often they called themselves by the name of their boat, or after an emblem painted on the door of their clubroom. *The Star* and *The Arrow* are therefore by no means surprising names for rowing clubs.

It has been suggested that the *Star* and *Arrow* clubs were invented to explain the Leander arms. But this is certainly untrue, for *The Arrow* was mentioned in contemporary press reports. There is no reason to doubt that both clubs existed at the beginning of the nineteenth century. Mr. Guy Nickalls, writing in *Fry's Magazine* in June 1913, stated that he had seen a cutting from an 1818 newspaper, which mentioned a six-oar cutter named *Leander*, but so far as I know it has never been directly claimed that this boat gave its name to the club. He also quoted a report of a match between *The Arrow* and the Guards Amateurs, for £1000, between Vauxhall Bridge and Kew Bridge, a distance of about ten miles. *The Arrow* won, the *Leander* was in attendance, and all but one of the *Arrow* crew were stated to be members of Leander.

Mr. H. T. Steward, the compiler of the first volume of *Henley*

Records, and for many years president of Leander Club, went to great pains to establish the date of the foundation of the club, but could not localize it more exactly than as having taken place between 1815 and 1820, and probably in 1818 or 1819. For this the evidence is as follows. Several members of *The Shark Club*, which was prominent in the early years of the century, and which ceased to exist about 1815, declared to Mr. Steward that Leander Club was not in being in their day. And another friend, an old Cambridge man who had been an active member of the *Funny Club*[1] in 1820, stated that Leander was 'very strong then'.

Certainly there is evidence that it was 'very strong' a few years later, and *Bell's Life*, reporting the 1837 wager race between Leander and Cambridge, remarked that Leander had been in existence for 'eighteen or nineteen years', which confirms the foundation date as being in or about 1818.

My own researches, unfortunately, have served only to add confusion to, rather than to confirm, Mr. Steward's conclusions. For in *Bell's Life* for 6 June 1830 there is a notice that 'A match, under the patronage of the Arrow and Leander Clubs, will take place at Hammersmith . . . between some of the most celebrated Thames watermen. . . .' Since both clubs are thus mentioned together, this quotation seems to be at variance with the theory that Leander absorbed *The Arrow Club*. But it is possible that the members of *The Arrow Club*, perhaps being weak in numbers, or in purse, joined forces with the Leander men, and yet continued, for some years, to look upon it as merely an alliance.

As already mentioned, the early rowing clubs were very different from the clubs we know today. Probably Leander was fairly typical, though pre-eminent, and, incidentally, the only one to survive into the modern era. The membership of Leander was first limited to sixteen, but by 1856 it had risen to twenty-five, who used to meet at Westminster once or twice a week, and either make up crews, or, sometimes, man a fleet of various small craft, to row up to Putney or down to Greenwich, where they would partake of dinner together. One of their members was a sub-

[1] The 'Funny' was a type of sculling boat.

stantial shipowner, and sometimes the club members used to row down to the Albert Docks, there to dine aboard one of his sloops.

In 1856 the membership of Leander was increased to thirty-five and, in 1862, to compete with the newly formed London Rowing Club, it was put, according to W. B. Woodgate, 'on a more modern footing', with no limit to its membership. At the same time the club's headquarters were moved to Putney, where a tent was provided for boats. Putney was then a riverside village in the open country. In 1864 the tent site was bought by London Rowing Club for their new boathouse. Leander then leased the adjoining ground, and built on it in 1866.

At this period Leander was still regarded as essentially a Metropolitan club. But during the 'eighties it built up a strong University connection, which to some extent filled the gap left by the closing down of the old Oxford and Cambridge Subscription Rooms. Although Leander remained a London club, the University connection was an accomplished fact by 1890, and had largely altered the nature of the club; it also greatly strengthened it, both financially and on the river.

About this time Leander began to rent a clubroom for the period of Henley Regatta, in the old Royal Hotel, near the station, and opened an enclosure on Temple Island. Guests and members drove by carriage down Remenham Lane, and along the towing-path from the Barrier, being ferried over to the Island. The course was then on the Buckinghamshire side of Temple Island.

Building of the present clubhouse was commenced in 1895. Had the decision to build been delayed a few years, it is possible that the Henley scene would be different today. For, shortly after the completion of the clubhouse, Leander had the opportunity of buying Phyllis Court. This was impossible in the circumstances, but Leander later moved their enclosure to the meadow below the White House, next to what is now the Remenham Club. When the Stewards' Enclosure was opened in 1919, Leander gave up their private enclosure, not wishing to compete with the Regatta. But if they had owned Phyllis Court it is questionable whether the Stewards' Enclosure could have been successfully launched.

There are probably more misconceptions about Leander than about any other rowing club in the world. It is not, as popularly believed, an exclusively University club. Nor is it by intention a club for the rowing *élite*, though the fact that there is a strict rowing qualification, for those elected whilst they are undergraduates at Oxford and Cambridge, makes membership particularly desirable to the University oarsmen, and therefore tends to raise Leander's rowing prestige. But for those who join after leaving the University, and for non-University members, the only qualifications are 'good fellowship and proficiency in oarsmanship'. 'Proficiency' is intentionally a very loose word. The truth is that Leander is not really a rowing club at all, but rather a social club for rowing men.

This statement may need some amplification.

Leander does not exist today—though it did eighty years ago —to provide facilities for rowing. No one is taught to row at Leander, and only very rarely is a man elected to the club for the specific purpose of rowing for it. Leander crews are recruited by invitation, mainly from ex-University oarsmen and from undergraduates who, for one reason or another, are not rowing in college crews at Henley. And if the system is sometimes criticized as haphazard, it nevertheless has two strong recommendations. It caters for just those men who cannot, or do not want to, row throughout the year, and are therefore of least value to other clubs; and it is successful.

But we must look back a hundred years, to the foundation of the second of the three great clubs.

It was in 1856 that Mr. Josias Nottidge convened a meeting by circular, at the Craven Hotel in the Strand. It took place on 9 April, and Mr. Nottidge then proposed the formation of a club, 'whose members should meet periodically in town to discuss the interests of rowing'. But most of those who attended the meeting were more actively inclined, and before the evening was through they had formed themselves into the London Rowing Club.

The first published report of the London Rowing Club, which appeared some two years later, described the state of affairs which had led to the demand for a new club.

> Some ten or twelve years ago [it read] the river between Westminster and Putney was enlivened and animated by the cutters of twenty different clubs, among which may be enumerated the splendid crews from the respective Subscription Rooms of Oxford and Cambridge, the invincible *Leander*, the *St. George's Club*, the *Thames*, and the *Argonauts*. Within the last few years, most of these clubs have become extinct, or, if in existence, are but mere shadows of their former greatness.

The London Rowing Club had a great and immediate success. Within three weeks of Mr. Nottidge's meeting there were 106 members. In May, boats were purchased, and rooms hired at the Star and Garter Hotel at Putney. On 22 May 1856 a London crew 'made its debut on the bosom of old Father Thames'.

The promoters of the London Rowing Club at once announced the principle on which the club was to be run, and which reveals the secret of its success. It was to enrol 'a large number of members at a small annual subscription . . . perfect freedom to its members from all fines . . . a well-assured immunity from any calls beyond their annual subscription; and an extensive fleet of boats, so that racing crews may be formed, when necessary, without interfering with the usual pleasure-rowing of the rest of the members'. This was a great attraction, for earlier clubs had been strictly limited in membership, with relatively high subscriptions; at the end of the season the members frequently had to dip into their pockets to balance the club accounts.

London Rowing Club swallowed up a number of small clubs, the foremost amongst them being the *Argonauts*. In 1856 some members of the new club actually contended for, and won, the Stewards' Challenge Cup, under *Argonaut* colours. This they did because the London Rowing Club had not been formed long enough to qualify for a Henley entry. London prospered exceedingly in its early days, and was soon the acknowledged champion of Metropolitan rowing. In 1866, when London members took a leading part in establishing the Metropolitan Regatta, the club had 340 members, the next largest clubs being the Thames Rowing Club, with 150 members, and the Ino Rowing Club, with 100 members. London Rowing Club provided most of the funds for launching the Metropolitan Regatta, and in 1869 accepted full responsibility for its organization.

It would be hard to exaggerate the effect which the foundation of London had upon rowing in general, and on Henley Regatta in particular. London provided the pattern for the modern rowing club. And the growth and flowering of clubs throughout the country, and especially on the Thames, provided a healthy counterweight to the Universities, and vastly increased the interest—and prosperity—of regattas everywhere.

The Thames Rowing Club, the last of the 'big three', had its origins in the City of London, and was formed chiefly for the clerks and salesman in the 'rag trade'— the drapery warehouses of Fore Street and St. Paul's Churchyard. In fact, it started life as the City of London Rowing Club, in 1860, rather with the object of providing 'organized pleasure' and exercise, than of producing racing crews. An early notice announced that 'the rowing train will leave Waterloo at 6.34 p.m., and crews be formed at 7.0 p.m.'.

Very soon the members turned their attention to racing and, certainly by 1862, they changed the name of the club to the Thames Rowing Club, having asked leave of Frank Playford, the only known survivor of the old *Thames Club*, which was famous in the 'forties. Thames were soon firmly established, boating from Simmons' boatyard, on the site now occupied by Messrs. Ayling & Sons, the Putney oar makers. The clubroom was at the Red Lion Hotel[1] by Putney Bridge.

By 1863 the club had 152 members, but was still something of the poor relation to London Rowing Club, which attracted most of the top-class oarsmen. Not until 1870 did Thames enter at Henley, and then it was a crew which was got together privately by W. H. (Piggy) Eyre, and practically disowned by the officers of the club. It trained from the Feathers at Wandsworth, and won

[1] There were then both a Red and White Lion at Putney, in adjoining premises.

the Wyfold Cup at the first attempt. Thereupon, it need hardly be said, the exiles were welcomed back to the club with open arms.

After 1870 Thames grew rapidly in stature, until it was the rival of London on the tideway waters. With varying fortunes these two clubs have continued ever since, as keen rivals, and jointly as the acknowledged leaders of Metropolitan rowing. London first entered for, and won, the Grand Challenge Cup in 1857. Thames first entered in 1874, and first won in 1876.

Appendix C

COMPARISON OF ENTRIES AND RESULTS OF THE
1908 AND 1948 OLYMPIC REGATTAS AT HENLEY

* Denotes an entry. In 1908 each country was permitted to enter two crews for each event.

(i) (ii) (iii) The roman numerals indicate the finishing order in the finals.

OLYMPIC REGATTA 1908

		Eights	Coxswainless Fours	Coxed Fours	Coxswainless Pairs	Coxed Pairs	Double Sculls	Single Sculls	Total Entry
1	Belgium	* (ii)						*	2
2	Canada	*	*		*			**	5
3	Germany				*			*	2
4	Great Britain	**(i)	** (i) and (ii)		** (i) and (ii)			** (i) and (ii)	8
5	Holland		*						1
6	Hungary	*						**	3
7	Italy							*	1
8	Norway	*							1
		6	4		4			9	23

Olympic Regatta 1948

		Eights	*Coxswainless Fours*	*Coxed Fours*	*Coxswainless Pairs*	*Coxed Pairs*	*Double Sculls*	*Single Sculls*	*Total Entry*
1	Argentina	*	*	*	*	*	*	*	7
2	Australia			*	*			* (i)	3
3	Austria			*	*				2
4	Belgium				*		*		2
5	Brazil				*	*			2
6	Canada	*					*		2
7	Cuba			*					1
8	Czechoslovakia		*						1
9	Denmark	*	* (ii)	* (iii)	*	* (i)	* (ii)		6
10	Egypt							*	1
11	Finland			*					1
12	France	*		*	*	*	*	*	6
13	Great Britain	* (ii)	*	*	* (i)	*	* (i)	*	7
14	Greece			*		*		*	3
15	Holland		*				*		2
16	Hungary		*	*		* (iii)	*		4
17	Ireland	*							1
18	Italy	*	* (i)	*	* (iii)	* (ii)	*	* (iii)	7
19	Norway	* (iii)		*					2
20	Portugal	*		*					2
21	South Africa		*					*	2
22	Spain							*	1
23	Sweden					*		*	2
24	Switzerland	*		* (ii)	* (ii)		*	*	5
25	United States	* (i)	* (iii)	* (i)	*	*	*	*	7
26	Uruguay						* (iii)	* (ii)	2
27	Yugoslavia	*	*	*		*		*	5
		12	10	16	12	10	12	14	86

Bibliography

(A) ROWING

Annals of Public School Rowing, Ed. L. Cecil Smith (Blackwell, 1919).
Aquatic Notes, by a Member of the C.U.B.C. (Cambridge: J. Deighton; London: G. Bell, 1852).
Aquatics, by a Rower of Thirty Matches (Whittaker, 1851).
The Aquatic Oracle, by An Amateur (Simpkin Marshall, 1852).
Boating, by W. B. Woodgate (Badminton Library, 1888).
The Complete Oarsman, by R. C. Lehmann (Methuen, 1908).
Henley Royal Regatta, 1839–1902, by H. T. Steward (Grant Richards, 1903).
Henley Races, 1903–1914, by Sir Theodore Cook (Oxford University Press, 1919).
Henley Records, 1919–1938, by C. T. Steward (Hamish Hamilton, 1939).
Journal of the Thames Rowing Club.
Records of the London Rowing Club.
Reminiscences of an Old Sportsman, by W. B. Woodgate (Eveleigh Nash, 1909).
Rowing, by R. C. Lehmann (Isthmian Library, 1896).
Rowing at Henley, by Sir Theodore Cook (Oxford University Press, 1919).
Newspapers and periodicals: *Bell's Life and Sporting Chronicle, The Field, Fry's Magazine, Henley Standard, Lock-to-Lock Times, Rowing, Rowing Almanack, The Times.*

(B) HENLEY AND DISTRICT

The Green Roads of England, by R. Hippisley Cox (Methuen, 1923).
A Guide to Henley-on-Thames, by Emily J. Climenson (S. H. Higgins, 1896).
Hell-Fire Francis, by Ronald Fuller (Chatto & Windus, 1939).
A History of Henley-on-Thames, by John Southerdon Burn (Longmans, 1861).

The History of Shiplake, Oxon, by Emily J. Climenson (Eyre & Spottiswoode, 1894).

Stonor, by R. J. Stonor (R. H. Johns, 1951).

A History of the Town of Reading, by Michael Hinton (Harrap, 1954).

The Manor and Parish Records of Medmenham, by A. H. Plaisted (Longmans, 1925).

The Myth of the Pent Cuckoo, by John E. Field (Elliot Stock, 1913).

Natural History of Oxfordshire, by Dr. Plot (Oxford, 1677).

Park Place, Ed. by Percy Noble, for private circulation (E. Calder Turner, 1905).

In Thames Land, by H. W. Wack (Putman, 1906).

The Thames and Its Story, Anon. (Cassell, 1906).

Time on the Thames, by Eric de Maré (Architectural Press, 1952).

River Thames, by F. V. Morley (Methuen, 1926).

The Upper Thames Valley, by Lord Wyfold (George Allen & Unwin, 1923).

Index

PRINTED AND BOUND IN ENGLAND BY
HAZELL WATSON AND VINEY LTD
AYLESBURY AND LONDON